W. Edwards Deming

Quality, Productivity, and Competitive Position

Massachusetts Institute of Technology
Center for Advanced Engineering Study

Published by the Massachusetts Institute of Technology, Center for Advanced Engineering Study, Cambridge, MA 02139.

Printed in the United States of America.

Library of Congress Catalog Card Number: 82-61320

International Standard Book Number: 0-911379-00-2

About the Author

W. Edwards Deming is the internationally renowned consultant whose work led Japanese industry into new principles of management and revolutionized their quality and productivity. The adoption of Dr. Deming's 14 points for management is spreading rapidly in industry in the United States.

Dr. Deming's projects have resulted in a worldwide practice in the use of statistical techniques in complex apparatus, physical depreciation of plant, investigations in chemical and physical tests, psychiatric care, care of the aged, transportation and traffic, and accounting. His clients include manufacturing companies, carriers of motor freight, railways, government agencies, research organizations, hospitals, and legal firms.

Dr. Deming is best known for his work in Japan. In recognition of his contribution to the economy of Japan, the Union of Japanese Science and Engineering instituted the Annual Deming Prize, to be awarded for advancement of precision and dependability of product. Dr. Deming received in 1956 the Shewhart Medal from the American Society for Quality Control. He was awarded by the Emperor of Japan in 1960 the Second Order Medal of the Sacred Treasure.

The Metropolitan Section of the American Society for Quality Control established in 1980 the Annual Deming Medal to be awarded for achievement in theory or application of statistical techniques for improvement of quality and productivity.

The W. Edwards Deming Institute for Quality and Productivity was formed by the University of Miami with the aim to help industry in the United States regain its position.

Preface

The aim of this book is to try to explain to top management of America what their job is to improve competitive position. One need not be an economist to understand from the papers that many American products are not competitive at home or abroad, lost to foreign invasion, causing unemployment at home. Failure of management to plan for the future and to foresee problems has nurtured waste of manpower, of materials, and of machine-time, all of which raise the manufacturer's cost and the price that the purchaser must pay. The consumer is not always willing to subsidize this waste. Loss of market begets unemployment. Emphasis has been on short-term profit, to the undernourishment of plans that might generate new product and service that would keep the company alive and provide jobs and more jobs. It is no longer socially acceptable performance to lose market and to dump hourly workers on to the heap of unemployed.

The basic cause of sickness in American industry and resulting unemployment is failure of top management to manage. Loss of market, and resulting unemployment, are not foreordained. They are not inevitable. They are not acceptable. The day is past when people in management need not know anything about management--by which I mean to include problems of production, supervision, training.

What must management do? Management obviously has a new job. Where can they learn what it is? The fact is that management can not learn by experience on the job what they must do to improve quality and productivity and the competitive position of the company. Nor can they learn in school. In fact, anyone could pass with high marks all the regular courses offered in colleges and universities in business, statistics, and engineering, yet come off with not the faintest idea about how to improve quality, productivity, and competitive position. Seminars for adult education under autonomous auspices, totally independent of regular departments in universities, are nevertheless providing help to top management. In fact, this book forms a text for such seminars.

Everyone doing his best is not the answer. It is necessary that people know what to do. Drastic changes are required. The responsibility for change rests on management. The first step is to learn how to change.

Long-term commitment to new learning and new philosophy is required of any management that seeks to improve quality and productivity. The timid and the faint-hearted, and people that expect quick results, are doomed to disappointment.

Performance of management is no longer measured by the quarterly dividend of today. It is instead measured by the aim to stay in business, to protect investment, to earn dividends, and to ensure jobs and more jobs through improvement of product and service for the future.

The day is over for a career in management. The job of management is inseparable from the welfare of the company. In and out, from the management of one company to the management of another is no longer something that American industry can afford.

Massive expansion of computers, gadgets, new machinery, robots, is not the answer to improvement in productivity and to better economic position of American industry. There is no substitute for knowledge.

There are conferences almost any day in this country on the subject of productivity, to talk about how to measure productivity. Measurements of productivity are important. Without them we should not have figures for comparison of productivity in the U.S., Japan, England, Germany. Unfortunately, measurements of productivity do nothing about productivity. As William E. Conway said, measurements of productivity are like accident statistics. They tell you that there is a problem, but they don't do anything about accidents. This book is an attempt to do something about productivity; to improve productivity, not just to measure it.

When we size up the job ahead, it is obvious that a long thorny road lies ahead.

Dependence on protection by tariffs and quotas to reduce imports is temporary, and only prolongs the life of inefficiency and incompetence.

This is not a book on techniques. It is a book on knowledge. Techniques come into play here only to illustrate the kind of education that is necessary in the new economic age. Some of the most important techniques (decision theory, theory of failure) are barely mentioned here. There are plenty of good textbooks and manuals on techniques. The great need at this time is not more writings on techniques, but better understanding of what has brought about the debacle that plagues American industry, and what to do about it.

It was Dr. Ernest J. Kurnow of the Graduate School of Business Administration of New York University who suggested to me years ago that a non-mathematical course teaching the 14 points, illustrating use of techniques, but with no pretense to teach the techniques themselves, could make an impa on students of management. His idea was sound. Students with no statistical background at all wrote some of the best papers in the course. Experience at the George Washington University and elsewhere is parallel.

I am thankful for unusual privileges to work as apprentice to a number of great men, such as Walter A. Shewhart, founder of the statistical control of quality, and with Harold F. Dodge, and with George Edwards, all of the Bell Telephone Laboratories, all now deceased. Equally valued is apprenticeship under other esteemed colleagues, such as Morris H. Hansen, Philip M. Hauser, Frederick Franklin Stephan, General Leslie E. Simon, Eugene L. Grant, Holbrook Working, Franz J. Kallman, P. C. Mahalanobis.

This book could never have seen print without the dedicated skill and perseverance of my secretary Cecelia S. Kilian. She has assisted me now 28 years in a lively statistical practice, and has constructed out of scribblings on scribblings written on my lap on aeroplanes one version after another of notes to use as text for my seminars, and finally this book as the reader finds it.

Help has come also from many kind friends that have read pages of text in earlier versions, with suggestions for clarity. Notes of thanks appear in the text for specific contributions.

Table of Contents

QUALITY, PRODUCTIVITY, AND COMPETITIVE POSITION

by

W. Edwards Deming

Table of Contents, continued

Table of Contents, continued

Chapter 1

WHY PRODUCTIVITY INCREASES WITH IMPROVEMENT OF QUALITY

Who is it that darkeneth counsel by
words without knowledge?--Job xxxvii, 2.

Aim of this chapter. The aim of this chapter is to illustrate with some
simple examples that productivity increases with improvement of quality. Low
quality means high cost and loss of competitive position.

Some folklore. Folklore has it in America that quality and production are
incompatible: that you can not have both. A plant manager will usually tell
you that it is either or. In his experience, if he pushes quality he falls
behind in production. If he pushes production, his quality suffers. This will
be his experience when he knows not what quality is nor how to achieve it.

A clear, concise answer came forth in a meeting with 22 production workers,
union representatives, in response to my question: "Why is it that productivity
increases as quality improves?"

Less rework.

There is no better answer. These people know how important quality is to
their jobs. They know that quality is achieved by improvement of the process.
Improvement of the process increases uniformity of output of product, reduces
rework and mistakes, reduces waste of manpower, machine-time, and materials and
thus increases output with less effort. Other benefits of improved quality are
lower costs, better competitive position, and happier people on the job, and
more jobs, through better competitive position of the company.

These are some of the lessons that management must learn and act on.

Reduction of waste transfers man hours and machine hours from the manufacture of defectives into the manufacture of additional good product. In effect, the capacity of a production line is increased. The benefits of better quality through improvement of the process are thus not just better quality, and the long-range improvement of market position that goes along with it, but greater productivity and much better profit as well. Improved morale of the work force is another gain: they now see that the management is making some effort themselves, and not blaming all faults on to the production workers.

A clear statement of the relationship between quality and productivity comes from my friend Dr. Yoshikasu Tsuda of Rikkyo University in Tokyo, who wrote to me as follows, dated 23 March 1980.

> I have just spent a year in the northern hemisphere, in 23 countries, in which I visited many industrial plants, and talked with many industrialists.

> In Europe and in America, people are now more interested in cost of quality and in systems of quality-audit. But in Japan, we are keeping very strong interest to improve quality by use of methods which you started ... when we improve quality we also improve productivity, just as you told us in 1950 would happen.

A simple example. Some figures taken from experience will illustrate what happens. A schoolboy can understand them. The superintendent in a plant knew that there were problems with a certain production line. His only explanation was that the work force (24 people) made a lot of mistakes.

The first step was to get data from inspection and plot the fraction defective day by day over the past six weeks (Fig. 1). This plot (a run chart) showed stable random variation above and below the average (in other words,

WHY PRODUCTIVITY INCREASES WITH IMPROVEMENT OF QUALITY

pretty good statistical control*). What does this mean? It means that any
substantial improvement must come from action on the system, the responsibility
of management.

The management had never used the figures from inspection. Hence the
superintendent was totally unaware that the proportion defective here had been
running along at 11 per cent.

Question: Ought the superintendent to have known that the proportion
defective had been running around 11 per cent? The answer to this question is
always, no hesitation, a thunderous yes. WRONG. What could he have done with
the figure had he known it? Nothing. He already knew that he had a problem.

The action to take would have been the same whether the proportion defective
had been 2 per cent, 11 per cent, or 17 per cent. The observation of statistical control (Fig. 1) and that any substantial improvement must come from action
on the system was the important observation, not the proportion 11 per cent.

Illustration of gain in productivity with improved quality

Item	Before improvement 11 per cent defective	After improvement 5 per cent defective
Total cost	100	100
Spent to make good units	89	95
Spent to make defective units	11	5

* The reader that is unfamiliar with the meaning of statistical control may
merely note, for a first reading of this chapter, that statistical control
denotes variation in a stable state of randomness, in which limits of variation
are predictable and will remain for practical purposes fixed until the system
is altered. Chapter 7 provides a quick view of statistical control.

The management had heretofore been unaware of any responsibility for quality. No one had ever used the figures from inspection.

What could the management do? The statisticians made the suggestion, based on experience, that possibly the people on the job, and the inspector also, did not understand well enough what kind of work is acceptable and what is not. The manager and two supervisors eventually accepted this possibility and went to work on the matter. With trial and error they came up in seven weeks with operational definitions, with examples posted for everyone to see. A new set of data showed the proportion defective to be 5 per cent. The results are in the accompanying table and in Fig. 1.

Gains

Quality up

Production of good product up 6 per cent

Capacity up 6 per cent

Cost per unit of good product is lower

Profit improved

Customer happier

Everybody happier

These gains were immediate (7 weeks); cost, zero: same work force, same burden, no investment in new machinery.

This is an example of gain in productivity accomplished by a change in the system, viz., improvement in definitions, effected by the management, to help people to work smarter, not harder.

Next step: wipe out the 5 per cent. How? Here are some suggestions:

-- Incoming materials difficult to work with.
-- Some machines not working properly.
-- There may still be some difficulty in the definitions of what is acceptable work, and what is not.

WHY PRODUCTIVITY INCREASES WITH IMPROVEMENT OF QUALITY

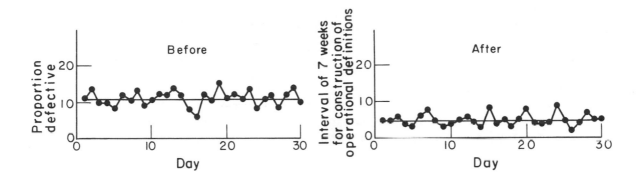

Fig. 1. Proportion defective day by day, before and
after attempt to construct operational definitions of what
is acceptable work and what is not. The proportion defective was 11 per cent before, 5 per cent after.

Keep a record in the form of a chart for fraction defective for each

operator. Perhaps one or two of them are making far more than their share of

defects. If so, make tests to learn whether further training could help them,

or whether they should be moved into other jobs. Look carefully at the incoming

materials. Are they uniform? Are they spotty?

A little history may be helpful here. The manager knew that there
was trouble on this line, and that was all that he knew. Ought he to
have known that the proportion defective was so high (11 per cent)?
We have already disposed of this question.

There were 24 people on the line. The inspector would take a case
of items as they went by her, inspect them, and record the results,
then intercept another case for inspection. "What do you do with the
tickets that you fill out?" Answer: "I put them on the pile here,
and when the pile gets too high, I discard the bottom half into the
trash."

"Could I have the top half?" I asked her. She was delighted.

We took the top half, which gave us the tickets for the preceding six weeks; did some simple calculations, and made the run chart shown for the proportion defective day by day.

Remark. It is important to note that meaningful observations do not occur in the absence of theory.* Theory may be only a hunch, but it must be there. In this case, the question is whether the proportion of defective items day by day shows statistical control. If yes (as is so here), then the problems of low quality and high cost are mostly in the system, the responsibility of the management to find and reduce or eliminate. If no, then special causes, which the operators can find and remove, will bring better quality and will reduce costs (Ch. 7).

In any case, management has the continuing responsibility to improve the system.

Another example. Reduction in cost.

Taken from a speech delivered in Rio de Janeiro, March 1981, by William E. Conway, President of the Nashua Corporation.

At Nashua, the first big success took place in March 1980, improvement of quality and reduction of cost in the manufacture of carbonless paper.

Water-based coating that contains various chemicals is applied to a moving web of paper. If the amount of coating is right, the customer will be pleased with a good consistent mark when he uses the paper some months later. The coating head applied approximately 3.6 pounds of dry coating to 3000 square feet of paper at a speed of approximately 1100 linear feet per minute on a web 6 or 8 feet wide. Technicians took samples of paper and made tests to determine the intensity of the mark. These tests were made on the sample both as it came off the coater and after it was aged in an oven to simulate use by the customer. When tests showed the intensity of the mark to be too low or too high, the operator made adjustments that would increase or decrease the amount of coating material. Frequent stops for new settings were a way of life. These stops were costly.

---

* C.I. Lewis, MIND AND THE WORLD-ORDER (Scribners, 1931), Chs. 6,7,8.

WHY PRODUCTIVITY INCREASES WITH IMPROVEMENT OF QUALITY

The engineers knew that the average weight of the coating material was too high, but did not know how to lower it without risk of putting on insufficient coating. A new coating head, to cost $700,000, was under consideration. There would be, besides the cost of $700,000, time lost for installation, and the risk that the new head might not achieve uniformity of coating much better than the equipment in use.

In August 1979, the plant manager decided to try statistical methods to study the operation. It was thereby found that the coating head, if left untouched, was actually in pretty good statistical control at an average level of 3.6 dry pounds of coating on the paper, plus or minus .4.

Elimination of various causes of variation, highlighted by points outside the control limits, reduced the amount of coating and still maintained good consistent quality.

The coater had by April 1980 settled down to an average of 2.8 pounds per 3000 square feet, varying from 2.4 to 3.2, thereby saving 0.8 pounds per 3000 square feet, or $800,000 per year at present volume and cost levels.

What the operator of the coating head had been doing, before statistical control was introduced and achieved, was to over-adjust his machine, to put on more coating, or less, reacting to tests of the paper. In doing his best, in accordance with the training and instructions given to him, he was actually doubling the variance of the coating. The control charts, aids to supervision, once in operation, helped him to do a much better job, with less effort. He is happy. His job is easier and more important.

<u>Innovation to improve the process</u>. The rest of Mr. Conway's story is still more interesting. Statistical control opened the way to engineering innovation. Without statistical control, the process was in unstable chaos, the noise of

which would mask the effect of any attempt to bring improvement. With statistical control achieved, engineers and chemists became innovative, creative. They modified the chemical content of the material used for the coating, and found how to use less and less. A long range effort is now underway which may ultimately enable them to reduce the amount of coating to a level of only 1.3 pounds per 3000 square feet of paper. Reduction of a tenth of a pound means an annual reduction of $100,000 in the cost of coating.

The reader can do his own arithmetic to compute the annual reduction in cost from the starting point (3.6 pounds).

The engineer also improved the coating head, to achieve greater and greater uniformity of coating. All the while, statistical control of the coating was maintained at ever decreasing levels.

Before statistical control was achieved, the engineers and chemists had not entertained thought of improvement of the coating head. How could they in a state of chaos? Once statistical control was achieved, it was easy for them to measure the effect of small changes in the chemistry of the coating and in the coating head, and they became innovative. The next step then became obvious-- try to improve the coating and the coating head, to use less and less coating, with greater and greater uniformity.

All this was accomplished without making the proposed capital investment of $700,000, which might or might not have improved the process and the quality of the coated paper.

Low quality means high costs. A plant was plagued with a huge amount of defective product. "How many people have you on this line for rework of defects made in previous operations?" I asked the manager. He went to the blackboard and put down three people here, four there, etc.--in total, 21 per cent of the work force on the line.

WHY PRODUCTIVITY INCREASES WITH IMPROVEMENT OF QUALITY

Defects are not free. Somebody makes them, and gets paid for making them. On the supposition that it costs as much to correct a defect as to make it in the first place, then 21 per cent of his payroll and burden was being spent on rework.

Once the manager saw the magnitude of the problem, and saw that he was paying out good money to make defects as well as to correct them, he found ways to help the people on the line to understand better how to do the job. The cost of rework went down from 21 per cent to 9 per cent in a space of two months.

Next step: reduce the proportion defective from 9 per cent to 0.

In some work that I did for a railway, study showed that mechanics in a huge repair shop spent three quarters of their time waiting in line to get parts.

From 15 per cent to 40 per cent of the manufacturer's costs of almost any American product that you buy today is for waste embedded in it--waste of human effort, waste of machine-time, loss of accompanying burden.* No wonder that many American products are hard to sell at home or abroad.

People sometimes ask me what level of defectives is acceptable. Would 2 per cent be acceptable? The answer is no: zero is the only acceptable level to aim at, but shouting zero defects accomplishes nothing. No improvement will take place without a road map.

New machinery and gadgets are not the answer. We have just seen an example in which important gains in quality and productivity were accomplished by learning to use effectively the machinery on hand.

---

* A.V. Feigenbaum, "Quality and Productivity," Quality Progress, November 1977.

Lag in American productivity has been attributed in editorials and in letters in the newspapers to failure to install new machinery, gadgets, and the latest types of automation. Such suggestions make interesting reading and still more interesting writing for people that do not understand problems of production.

Gadgets for automation and automatic recording in the office and in the factory are not the answer, either. Exhibits of such gadgets are attended by thousands of people seeking an easy way out of the lag in productivity, trusting hopefully to hardware. Some gadgets may increase productivity enough to pay their own expenses, but they are not the answer to the loss of market that plagues American industry today.

One should add to the purchase price of machinery the cost of learning to use it.

The only way out is education in the theory of management, the 14 points in Chapter 2.

The following paragraph received from a friend in a large manufacturing company will serve as illustration.

> This whole program (design and installation of new machines) has led to some unhappy experiences. All these wonderful machines performed their intended functions, on test, but when they were put into operation in our plants, with our people, they were out of business so much of the time for this and that kind of failure that our overall costs, instead of going down, went up. No one had evaluated the overall probable failure rates and maintenance. As a result, we were continually caught with stoppages and with not enough spare parts, or with none at all; and no provision for alternate production lines.

The reader's own estimate of the cost of common practices in the United States, such as awarding business to the lowest bidder, barriers that rob the hourly worker of his right to pride of workmanship, and dependence on inspection, may well lead to figures higher than 40 per cent waste.

WHY PRODUCTIVITY INCREASES WITH IMPROVEMENT OF QUALITY

If I were a banker, I would not lend money for new equipment unless the company that asked for the loan could demonstrate by statistical evidence that they are using their present equipment to reasonably full capacity.

Service industries. Eventually quality improvement will reach not only the production of goods and food (the birthplace of modern statistical theory was agriculture) but the service industries as well--hotels, restaurants, transportation of freight and passenger, wholesale and retail establishments, hospitals, medical service, care of the aged, perhaps even the U.S. mail.

Statistical technology is improving service and lowering costs in the banking business (Ch. 12). In fact, one of the most successful applications of statistical methods on a huge scale, including sample design and improvement of operations, is in our own Census, not only in the decennial Census, but in the regular monthly and quarterly surveys of people and of business, an example being the Monthly Report on the Labor Force. Statistical technology has for many years contributed to telecommunications, both in the manufacture of equipment and in service.

Buying, making, and delivery of electric power to customers is one of the most important services of the country. A large power company in the United States, under guidance from an excellent consultant, is improving service and cutting costs, with substantial profit, no one working harder, only smarter, from management to linemen and truck drivers.

Some service industries in Japan have been active in improvement of productivity from the start in 1950, e.g., the Japanese National Railways, Nippon Telegraph and Telephone Corporation, the Tobacco Monopoly of Japan, the Post Office. Takenaka Komuten (architecture and construction) won recognition in 1979 for thorough-going improvement of buildings of all types, and for decrease in cost, by studying the needs of the users (in offices, hospitals, factories, and hotels) and by reducing the costs of rework in drawings and in the actual construction.

Measures of productivity do not lead to improvement of productivity. There is in the U.S., any day, a conference on productivity, usually more than one. There is in fact a permanent conference on productivity, and there is now the President's Committee on Productivity. The aim of these conferences is to construct meaningful measures of productivity. It is important to have measures of productivity for meaningful comparisons of productivity in the U.S. year by year, and meaningful comparisons between countries. Unfortunately, however, figures on productivity in the U.S. do not help to improve productivity in the U.S. Measures of productivity are like statistics on accidents: they tell you all about the number of accidents in the home, on the road, and at the work place, but they do not tell you how to reduce the frequency of accidents.

It is unfortunately to be feared that quality assurance means in many places a deluge of figures that tell how many defective items of this type and that type were produced last month, with comparisons month to month and year to year. These figures tell the management how things are going, but they do not point the way to improvement.

WHY PRODUCTIVITY INCREASES WITH IMPROVEMENT OF QUALITY

Chapter 2

WHAT TOP MANAGEMENT MUST DO TO IMPROVE PRODUCTIVITY

How poor are they that have not patience.--Iago to
Roderigo, in Shakespeare's Othello, Act II, Scene III.

A. AIM AND PREAMBLE

Purpose of this chapter. The purpose of this chapter is to explain to top
management in America what their job is to recapture the competitive position
once held by American industry. The problem is to improve quality and productivity. No one in management need ask again, "What must we do?" This
chapter also provides criteria by which anyone in the company may measure the
performance of management. Everyone in the company, and the bank, will now
have a basis by which to answer the question: "How is our management doing?"

Top management can not learn by experience on the job what to do to improve
quality and productivity and competitive position. They must seek help from
outside.

Best efforts not sufficient.

By everyone doing his best.   (Wrong)

This is the answer that came forth in a meeting in response to my question,
"And how do you go about it to improve quality and productivity?"

Best efforts are essential. Unfortunately, best efforts alone will not
accomplish the purpose. Everyone is already doing his best. Best efforts, to
be effective, require guidance to move in the right direction. It is especially
important that top management know what their job is.

For example, ways of doing business with vendors and with customers that were good enough in the past must now be revised to meet new requirements of quality and productivity. Management must get involved with production and the hourly worker (Ch. 2, page 46). Drastic revision is required. It is not enough for everyone to do his best.

What happens when top management senses loss of competitive position and knows not what to do, is that they embark on a random walk, trying one idea after another, searching for something, they know not what.

A random walk dissipates energy and fails to reach a goal. The effect on middle management, and on everyone else in the company, when top management embarks on a random walk, is bewilderment, uncertainty, paralysis. No one in the organization can work effectively when the signals from top management are continually changing direction. Hysteria added to the random walk enhances the confusion, and the organization becomes a falling body.

> By top management, I mean the officers that can be held responsible for the 14 points to follow. If they require authority from someone else to carry out any of the 14 points, then they are not top management.

Theory of management now exists. There is now a theory of management for improvement of quality, productivity, and competitive position. No one can ever again claim that there is nothing in management to teach. Students in a school of business now have a yardstick by which to judge the curriculum that is open to them. Does it show some attempt to present a curriculum for today's problems, or does it show obsolescence? Obsolescence need not be planned: it can just move in.

Short-term profits are no index of ability. The short term outlook of men in top management is a drag on productivity in America. A new president comes in to raise the quarterly dividend, then moves along to destroy some other company.

WHAT TOP MANAGEMENT MUST DO TO IMPROVE PRODUCTIVITY

Short-term profits are not a reliable indicator of good management. Anybody can pay dividends by deferring maintenance, cutting out research, or by acquiring another company. A better indicator than short-term profit is the effect on production. Unfortunately, the president's right-hand man is in many companies his Minister of Finance.

Paper profits, the yardstick by which stockholders and Boards of Directors often measure performance of the president, make no contribution to material living for people anywhere, nor do they improve the competitive position of a company or of American industry. Paper profits do not make bread: improvement of quality and productivity do. They make a contribution to better material living for all people, here and everywhere.

People that depend on dividends to live on should be concerned, not merely on the size of dividends today, but also with the question of whether there will be dividends three years from now, five years from now, ten years from now, and how much. Management has the obligation to protect investment.

<u>Support of top management is not sufficient.</u> It is not enough that top management commit themselves for life to quality and productivity. They must know what it is that they are committed to--i.e., what they must do. These obligations can not be delegated.

"... and if you can't come, send nobody."

These are words in a letter that William E. Conway (President and Chief Executive Officer of the Nashua Corporation) wrote to a Vice President in response to the latter's request for an invitation to visit the Nashua Corporation.

In other words, Mr. Conway told him, if you don't have time to do your job, there is not much that I can do for you.

Chapter 2

B. CONDENSATION OF THE 14 POINTS FOR MANAGEMENT

Origin of the 14 points. It will not suffice merely to solve problems that walk in day by day. The important problems do not walk in: one has to find them. Adoption and action on the 14 points is a signal that the management intends to stay in business, and aims to protect investors and jobs. Such a system formed the basis for conferences with top management in Japan in 1950 and in subsequent years (cf. Ch. 6 and Fig. 9 on page 103).

The 14 points are obviously the responsibilities of top management. No one else can carry them out. Quality is everybody's job, but quality must be led by management.

The 14 points apply anywhere, to small organizations as well as to large ones. The management of a service industry has the same obligations and the same problems as management in manufacturing.

1. Create constancy of purpose toward improvement of product and service, with a plan to become competitive and to stay in business. Decide whom top management is responsible to.

2. Adopt the new philosophy. We are in a new economic age. We can no longer live with commonly accepted levels of delays, mistakes, defective materials, and defective workmanship.

3. Cease dependence on mass inspection. Require, instead, statistical evidence that quality is built in, to eliminate need for inspection on a mass basis. Purchasing managers have a new job, and must learn it.

4. End the practice of awarding business on the basis of price tag. Instead, depend on meaningful measures of quality, along with price. Eliminate suppliers that can not qualify with statistical evidence of quality.

WHAT TOP MANAGEMENT MUST DO TO IMPROVE PRODUCTIVITY

5. Find problems. It is management's job to work continually on the s
(design, incoming materials, composition of material, maintenance, improveme
of machine, training, supervision, retraining).

6. Institute modern methods of training on the job.

7. Institute modern methods of supervision of production workers (see
Ch. 10). The responsibility of foremen must be changed from sheer numbers to
quality. Improvement of quality will automatically improve productivity.
Management must prepare to take immediate action on reports from foremen
concerning barriers such as inherited defects, machines not maintained, poor
tools, fuzzy operational definitions.

8. Drive out fear, so that everyone may work effectively for the company.

9. Break down barriers between departments. People in research, design,
sales, and production must work as a team, to foresee problems of production
that may be encountered with various materials and specifications.

10. Eliminate numerical goals, posters, and slogans for the work force,
asking for new levels of productivity without providing methods.

11. Eliminate work standards that prescribe numerical quotas.

12. Remove barriers that stand between the hourly worker and his right to
pride of workmanship.

13. Institute a vigorous program of education and retraining.

14. Create a structure in top management that will push every day on the
above 13 points.

C. ELABORATION ON THE 14 POINTS

1. <u>Create constancy of purpose for improvement of product and service.</u>
There are two problems: (i) problems of today; (ii) problems of tomorrow, for

the company that hopes to stay in business. Problems of today encompass maintenance of quality of product put out today, regulation of output not to exceed too far immediate sales, budget, employment, profits, sales, service, public relations, forecasting, etc. It is easy to stay bound up in an inextricable knot in the problems of today, becoming ever more and more efficient in them, as by (e.g.) mechanized equipment for the office.

Problems of the future command first and foremost constancy of purpose and dedication to improvement of competitive position to keep the company alive, and to provide jobs for their employees. Whom does the Board of Directors and the President report to? To their own sacred cows, dedicated to quick profits, or to the institution of constancy of purpose? The next quarterly dividend is not as important as existence of the company 10, 20, or 30 years from now. Establishment of constancy of purpose means acceptance of obligations like the following.

a. Innovate. Allocate resources for long-term planning. Plans for the future call for consideration of:

-- New service and new product that may help people to live better materially, and which will have a market.

-- New materials that will be required; probable cost.

— Method of production; possible changes in equipment for production.

-- New skills required, and in what number?

— Training and retraining of personnel.

-- Training of supervisors.

— Cost of production.

-- Cost of marketing; plans for service; cost of service.

—— Performance in the hands of the user.

-- Satisfaction of the user.

One requirement for innovation is faith that there will be a future. Innovation, the foundation of the future, can not thrive unless the top management has declared unshakable policy of quality and productivity. Until this policy can be enthroned as an institution, middle management and everyone in the company will be skeptical about the effectiveness of their best efforts.

b. Put resources into:

—— Research

-- Education

c. Constantly improve design of product and service. This obligation never ceases. The consumer is the most important part of the production line.

It is a mistake to suppose that efficient production of product and service can with certainty keep an organization solvent and ahead of competition. It is possible and in fact fairly easy for an organization to go downhill and out of business making the wrong product or offering the wrong type of service, even though everyone in the organization performs with devotion, employing statistical methods and every other aid that can boost efficiency.

d. Put resources into maintenance of equipment, furniture, and fixtures, new aids to production in the office and in the plant.

2. <u>Adopt the new philosophy</u>. We are in a new economic age. We can no longer live with commonly accepted levels of mistakes, defects, material not suited to the job, people on the job that do not know what the job is and are afraid to ask, handling damage, failure of management to understand their job, antiquated methods of training on the job, inadequate and ineffective supervision.

Acceptance of defective materials, poor workmanship, and inattentive and sullen service as a way of life in America is a roadblock to better quality and productivity. We have learned to live in a world of mistakes and defective products as if they were necessary to life. It is time to adopt a new religion in America.

It is not unusual for a manufacturing concern to receive a part with no holes where holes there should be, wrong count, or even the wrong item, a carload of parts intended for a competitor. (This could be a disaster to both companies, if they are about to run short of the materials mishandled.)

Some companies have constructed systems by which to follow materials through production to learn about problems created by materials not suited to the job. Material in inventory has in many instances lost its identity. Some of it turns out to be defective. There is no history about the material, and nothing to do about it except to inspect it all, or to put it straight into production with no inspection. (Chapter 13 will tell us that it might be preferable not to inspect it, but in the absence of history of quality, the only safe course is 100 per cent inspection.) Some companies have a system by which to learn about equipment out of order, and to take action. Some do not.

Some suppliers are already qualified and are conforming to the recommendations made here. Some follow their product through the purchaser's production lines to learn what problems turn up, and to take action, so far as possible, to avoid problems in the future.

I have often wondered on board an aeroplane, finding that the seat would drift backward into the lap of the passenger behind, or would not budge at all, or finding a light burned out, whether the airline had any system for reporting need for this type of maintenance. Disembarking one day, after a trip in a seat that would not budge, I asked a flight attendant about the matter. She assured me that the mechanic makes a record of anything reported out of order, and that repair is made at the next layover; then added: "Oh, thank you for reminding me about that seat. I must tell the mechanic about it."

Would she have thought to tell him, had I not enquired about the system of maintenance? Did she? What is her job? To report seats out of order? She has duties that are more engaging than to report a seat out of order. The result is that small needs pile up.

The cost of living depends inversely on the goods and services that a given amount of money will buy. Dependability of service is an important quality-characteristic. Reliable service reduces costs. Delays and mistakes raise costs. Alternative plans in expectation of delays are costly. The economy of a single plan that will work is obvious. As an example, I may cite a proposed itinerary in Japan:

> 1725 h leave Taku City
>
> 1923 h arrive Hakata
>
> Change trains
>
> 1924 h leave Hakata (for Osaka,
> at 210 kms per hour)

Only one minute to change trains? You don't need a whole minute. You will have 30 seconds left over. No alternate plan was necessary.

On another day, a driver was to pick me up at 1702 at Ueno Station. The train would be due at 1658. The driver knew just how long it would take to leave the train, ride up the moving stairs, walk to a certain point, ride down the moving stairs to the spot where he would be. He could plan within 15 seconds when I would show up.

Think of the economic advantage that other countries enjoy in mail service that Americans have never known. A letter posted in the evening in London will be delivered on the first round next morning in Edinburgh, Glasgow, Hamburg, Frankfurt, Paris, Amsterdam, Copenhagen. Likewise for a letter posted in Tokyo, destined for (e.g.) Osaka.

Defects and defective items are not free. The total cost to produce and dispose of a defective item exceeds the cost to produce a good one. A manufacturer of beer that I talked to recently had no problem with cans, because

the suppliers of cans replace free any defective cans found. It had not occurred to him that he is paying for the defective cans, plus the cost of halting
production and replacing cans. It had not occurred to him that his customers
are footing the bill with higher prices which may well be a cause of loss of
market.

After passing through tight security at the offices and plant of one of
America's largest chemical companies, someone observed that (1) the name on the
pass that the guard gave me was wrong, and that (2) the date was wrong. Otherwise, the pass was in good order.

3. Cease dependence on mass inspection. Routine 100 per cent inspection is
the same thing as planning for defects, acknowledgement that the process can not
make the product correctly, or that the specifications made no sense in the
first place.

Inspection is too late, ineffective, costly. When a lot of product leaves
the door of a supplier, it is too late to do anything about the quality of the
lot. Scrap, downgrading, and rework are not corrective action on the process.
Quality comes not from inspection, but from improvement of the process. The
only permissible exception is critical or semi-critical parts, and critical
subassemblies and assemblies. Chapter 13 gives rules by which to minimize the
total cost under the circumstance where it is necessary to deal with defective
items.

In place of 100 per cent inspection should go improvement of the process
and elimination of inspection.

Plans by which lots are accepted or rejected or screened, depending
on tests of samples drawn from the lots are an advertisement that the
purchaser is in the market for defective material. He can always find
a vendor that is able and willing to meet this requirement. For
example, Military Standard 105D, prescribed by government contracts,
advertises the fact that the government expects defects and plans to
pay for them. More in Chapter 13.

WHAT TOP MANAGEMENT MUST DO TO IMPROVE PRODUCTIVITY

long-term partnership with vendor

4. <u>End the practice of awarding business on price tag alone.</u> We can no
longer leave quality, service, and price to the forces of competition for price
--not in today's requirements for uniformity and reliability.*

Price has no meaning without a measure of the quality being purchased.**
Without adequate measures of quality, business drifts to the lowest bidder, low
quality and high cost being the inevitable result. American industry and the
U.S. Government, civil and military, are being rooked by rules that award
business to the lowest bidder. A large portion of the problems of poor quality
and low productivity are poor quality of incoming materials, and low quality of
tools and machines. An economic mutation is needed.

A buyer's job today is to be on the alert for lower prices, to find a new
vendor that will offer a lower price. The other vendors of the same material
must meet it.

The buyer is not at fault. That is his job. Can you blame him for doing
his job? The management is at fault for terms of reference that are outmoded.

The policy of forever trying to drive down the price of anything purchased,
with no regard to quality and service, can drive good vendors and good service
out of business.

He that has a rule to give his business to the lowest bidder deserves to get
rooked.

Municipal transit authorities are an example of legitimate plunder, inviting
thievery by their policy of doing business with the lowest bidder. They are

----

* Stated in these words by James K. Bakken of the Ford Motor Company on the
27th of January 1981.

** Walter A. Shewhart, THE ECONOMIC CONTROL OF QUALITY OF MANUFACTURED
PRODUCT (Van Nostrand, 1931. Reprinted in 1981 by the American Society for
Quality Control).

forced into this policy, in the United States, by the Urban Transit Authority, which grants funds only to the lowest bidder.

A few bad experiences in mass transit because of erratic performance of equipment, purchased on the basis of the price tag alone, may have retarded by a generation mass expansion of mass transit in the United States.

It is my understanding that the government awards to the lowest bidder contracts for demographic, social, and scientific research and development. All that a company has to do to get a job is to bid low enough. Whether the company has had any experience in the line of work sought, or has in its employ anyone capable of directing it, is not a factor in the award. Investigation of qualifications would require knowledge and perseverance.

Examples

AWARD OF CONTRACT.

    a. The contract will be awarded to the responsible offeror whose offer conforming to the solicitation will be most advantageous to the Government, price and other factors considered.
      .
      .
      .

    f. The right is reserved to accept other than the lowest offer and to reject any or all offers.

This last clause is meaningless without a yardstick by which to measure quality. Who in the government has the necessary education to distinguish between two offerors, both of whom meet the specifications, one with demonstrable experience, the other without?

A flagrant example is a request for professional help, to be awarded to the lowest bidder. Example (actual, from a government agency):

    For delivery and evaluation of a course on management for quality control for supervisors... . An order will be issued on the basis of price.

WHAT TOP MANAGEMENT MUST DO TO IMPROVE PRODUCTIVITY

Purchasing managers have a new job. Economists teach the world that competition in the market-place gives everyone the best deal. This would be true if the purchaser could know what he is doing--i.e., if he could know the quality of what he is buying. This was true in days gone by, when the baker had his customers, the tailor his, the cheese-maker his, etc. In those days, it was fairly easy to make an intelligent purchase.

It is different today. The price tag is still easy to read, but understanding of quality requires education. Ability to judge quality requires education in statistical evidence of quality, supplemented by experience, which means trial and error and relearning. One of the first steps for managers of purchasing to take is to learn enough about the statistical control of quality to be able to assess the qualifications of a supplier, to be able to talk to him in statistical language. Don't expect him to carry on the conversation in French if you don't know French.

The purchasing department must understand the problems of use of materials purchased.

It is also necessary to learn that specifications of incoming materials do not tell the whole story. What problems does the material encounter in production? (Cf. the section, "The supposition that it is only necessary to meet specifications," page 77.)

Materials and components may all be excellent, each by itself, yet not work well together in production or in the finished product. It is thus necessary to follow a sample of materials through the whole production process into complex assemblies, and onward to the customer. There was nothing wrong with the glass in a large building in Boston, nor with the steel. Both met the specifications. Yet somehow they did not work well together in service. Glass windows fell from the steel frames to the ground below.

In one instance, the man in charge of procurement of materials, in attendance at seminars, declared that he has no problems with procurement, as he accepts only perfect materials. (Chuckled I to myself, "That's the way to do it.") Next day, in one of his plants, a superintendent showed to me two pieces of a certain item from two different suppliers, same item number, both beautifully made, both met the specifications, yet they were sufficiently different for one to be usable, the other usable only with costly rework, a heavy loss to the plant. The superintendent was charged with 20,000 of each one.

Both pieces satisfied the specifications. Both suppliers had fulfilled their contracts. The explanation lay in specifications that were incomplete and unsuited to the requirements of manufacture. The explanation was that one supplier understood what the blocks were to be used for, the other did not; he merely satisfied the specifications.

There was no provision for a report on material used in desperation. It seems that difficulties like this bring forth solace in one or both of the following remarks:

> This is the kind of problem that we see any day in this business.

> Or

> Our competitors are having the same kind of problem.

What would some people do without their competitors? Surely one responsibility of management in production is to provide help in such difficulties, and not leave a plant manager in a state of such utter hopelessness.

The manager of a plant that belongs to one of America's largest corporations lamented to me that he spends most of his time defending good vendors. A typical problem runs like this. A vendor has not for years sent to him a defective item, and his price is right. The corporate purchasing department awards the business to a new and untried vendor because he offers a better price. These parts go into repeaters. The telephone company might incur a cost of several thousand dollars to dig up the pavement and replace a defective repeater. The plant manager, trying to protect the company and the whole system, must spend many hours in argument to hold on to the vendor that knows his business.

He had adopted a new philosophy. It is not an easy road.

How does a supplier qualify? Almost every company has a manual of some kind or procedure by which to "qualify" vendors. Military Standard 9858 is an example. These manuals talk about quality, but do nothing about it. They relieve the vendor from responsibility. Once he satisfies the questions put to him, he has discharged his responsibility, and the purchaser accepts whatever he gets.

A better plan would be to discard these booklets and to give consideration to any vendor that can furnish evidence of active involvement of management with the 14 points, and evidence of sustained use of $\bar{x}$- and R-charts, and who will cooperate with us on tests and use of instruments and gauges.

The aim of any supplier should be to improve quality and to decrease costs to the point where he need not search for customers: instead, let quality and service be so good that customers plead for his product.

Purchase of bulk materials and yard goods is subject to the same principles. Records, especially if plotted on a run chart, or on a control chart, or in a display suggested by Figs. 48 and 49, may disclose pockets of trouble and problems with some vendors.

We are not talking here about hardware, nor salt, sugar, oil. The prices of commodities are posted daily on the Commodities Exchange. A bidder may justify purchase of sugar from the lowest bidder. But the purchase of critical and semi-critical parts and materials is another story.

<u>Necessity for mutual confidence and aid between purchaser and vendor</u>. The
following paragraphs may indicate that in Japan steady dependable source,
responsive to needs, on a long-term arrangement, is more important than price.

   A final point made by American firms is that the large markups
   generated by Japan's multilayered distribution system often eliminate
   whatever price advantages imports have at dockside.

   The Japanese respond that problems can be better understood as an
   extension of the long-standing customer-supplier relationship in Japan.
   Buyers expect suppliers to be a reliable source of merchandise, to
   understand their needs and respond quickly to them, and to offer
   reliable after-sales service. The relationship depends heavily on
   these factors, to the exclusion of such economic considerations as
   lowest cost in the quality range required. Thus, although a firm
   customer-supplier relationship is not intended to shut out competitive
   foreign firms, working within the system can be frustrating.

                     -- Japan Economic Institute, Washington, 1982:
                        JAPAN'S IMPORT BARRIERS: ANALYSIS OF DIVERGENT
                        BILATERAL VIEWS

The reader is referred at this point to Chapter 24, "Control of vendor
quality," by Dorian Shanin and L. A. Seder in Joseph M. Juran's QUALITY CONTROL
HANDBOOK (McGraw-Hill).

   <u>Some further remarks about suppliers</u>. A letter from a supplier in reply
to an enquiry about his quality control usually fits into a pattern like the
following paragraph:

   In reply to your enquiry about our methods of quality control, we
   are pleased to inform you that quality is our motto. We believe in
   quality. You will see from the enclosed pamphlet that nothing goes out
   of this plant until it has been thoroughly inspected. In fact, a large
   portion of our effort in production is spent on inspection, to be sure
   of our quality.

This paragraph is a true confession of ignorance of what quality is, and of
how to achieve it.

A client told me that it had been for years their practice to write to a
vendor, upon receipt of faulty material, as follows:

   The material that you sent to us turned out to be faulty. Please
   fill out the enclosed form to tell us what corrective action you plan
   to take.

WHAT TOP MANAGEMENT MUST DO TO IMPROVE PRODUCTIVITY

Not a single form ever came back.

Vendors sometimes furnish reams of figures, such as records of adjustment, input of materials (2 kg. chromium added at 1000 h). Figures like these are as worthless to the buyer as they are to the vendor.

Obviously, a more companionable relationship between vendor and purchaser is required.

Reduction in number of suppliers. The requirement of statistical evidence of process control in the purchase of critical parts will mean in most companies drastic reduction in the number of vendors that they deal with. A company will be lucky to find one vendor that can supply statistical evidence of quality. A second vendor, if he can not furnish statistical evidence of his quality, will have higher costs than the one that can furnish the evidence, or he will have to chisel on his quality, or go out of business. A man that does not know his costs nor whether he can repeat tomorrow today's distribution of quality, is not a good business partner.

Determination to reduce the number of vendors, and to require statistical evidence of quality, will of course require time, learning, cooperation, and patience. One company that I work with is in the act of reducing the number of vendors from 4000 to 800 over a period of five years.

Advantages of a single source and long-term relationship. Long-term relationship between purchaser and supplier is necessary for best economy. How can a supplier be innovative and develop economy in his production processes when he can only look forward to short-term business with a purchaser?

There are some operational advantages. Even though two suppliers send excellent materials, there will be differences, and a certain amount of time in production is lost in changing from one supplier to another. Moreover, one should not overlook the simplification in accounting and paper work.

The financial people in the company like to have several suppliers, pitting one against another for price. Ask anyone in operations: he prefers to have a single good supplier.

A company that adopts the recommendations made here will do more than improve its own lot. It will have wide influence. The suppliers that serve one company also serve other companies, and will deliver to them better quality at an economic level of cost. Everybody will come out ahead.

A second source, for protection, for every item purchased (other than hardware or regular commodities), is a costly practice.

> A company had been buying cans from three different suppliers, playing one vendor against another to try to get a lower bid. In 1975, the vice presidents of manufacturing, research and development, and purchasing, took it into their heads that it might be better to have one supplier of cans instead of three; that by having one supplier, they might share with him the benefits of mass production and they might work with him to improve quality. Moreover, although all three suppliers were delivering excellent cans, there were differences between the cans of the three different suppliers, and time was lost to change over from one supplier to another.

> It is now six years since this company adopted the plan of having a single supplier of cans. They are pleased with the results. Savings amount to $5,000,000 to date, and the supplier of cans now sends control charts every week along with the cans that he supplies.

Purchase of materials may in some cases be simplified, for both purchaser and vendor, by reduction in the number of different items carried in stock. It may be a fairly simple matter to replace two items, nearly alike, with either one, or with something that will serve the purpose of both. One company that I work with reduced from 27,000 to 12,000 the number of different items used in a group of factories.

5. <u>Constantly and forever improve the system of production and service.</u> This means continual reduction of waste and continual improvement of quality in every activity: procurement, transportation, engineering, methods, maintenance, locations of activities, instruments and measures, sales, methods of distribu-

tion, accounting, payroll, service to customers. Continual improvement of quality brings continual rise in productivity.

Only a small portion of this obligation can be achieved by the production workers, even when the management listens and acts on suggestions and recommendations made by them. The lion's share of improvement in any process or activity must come from action by management. One line of improvement lies in action on Point 12.

Management will improve a process by active participation with experts in subject matter, such as chemists, engineers, consumer research, sales, and with people that know the problems of production. Statistical leadership will be required in the design and analysis of tests, and to separate special causes from common causes (Ch. 7).

It is important to remember that study of the defects and faults produced by a process that is in statistical control will be ineffective. Study of a system that is in statistical control is not study of defects. Neither is it study only of the good product turned out. A process that is in a state of statistical control can be improved only by study of the process. We saw an example in Chapter 7, and shall see more.

6. <u>Institute modern methods of training on the job.</u> Training must be totally reconstructed. Poor training of hourly workers, or none at all, and dependence on unintelligible printed instructions, seem to be a way of life. Sweeping changes are necessary. Statistical methods must be used to learn when training is finished. If not finished, further training would be beneficial (Ch. 10).

A big problem in training and in supervision in the United States is a variable standard of what is acceptable work and what is not. The standard is too often dependent on whether the foreman is in difficulty to meet his daily

quota in terms of numbers, not quality.

DERAILMENT PROBE

by John Burgess and Kenneth Bredemeier

Metro's in-house investigation of the subway derailment that killed
three passengers last month has concluded that a wide range of Metro
employees committed a series of dangerous errors before and after the
accident, errors that it suggested were due to the transit system's
"inadequate" training program.

While the report released yesterday reaffirmed earlier findings
that put heavy blame on the train's operator and a supervisor who was
on the scene, it emphasized that other personnel in Metro's central
control room violated standard procedures at a number of points.

Despite calls to the room to keep power off at the accident site,
for example, controllers allowed the potentially deadly 750-volt
"third rail" to turn back on automatically 37 minutes after the crash,
the investigation found. Passengers apparently were still being
evacuated from the train at the time. "Our initial impression is that
training is erratic, inadequate and lacks direction and [Metro] cannot
escape responsibility," said the report, adding that, "...budgetary
restrictions have hindered the programs of retraining, testing, and
recertification."

-- Washington Post, 26 Feb. 1982, page A-1

7. Institute modern methods of supervision. Supervision belongs to the
system, and is the responsibility of management.

a. Remove barriers that make it impossible for the hourly worker to do his
job with pride of workmanship.

b. Foremen must be empowered and directed to inform upper management
concerning conditions that need correction (inherited defects, machines not
maintained, poor tools, fuzzy definitions of acceptable workmanship, emphasis
on numbers, not on quality). Management must take action on corrections so
indicated.

WHAT TOP MANAGEMENT MUST DO TO IMPROVE PRODUCTIVITY

c. Most acts of supervision in management and on the floor of the factory and of the department store, instead of providing help to people, accomplish just the opposite. The book abounds with examples.

8. Drive out fear.* a. Most people on a job, especially people in management positions, do not understand what the job is, nor what is right or wrong. Moreover, it is not clear to them how to find out. Many of them are afraid to ask questions or to take a position. The economic loss from fear is appalling. It is necessary, for better quality and productivity, that people feel secure. Se comes from Latin, meaning without, cure means fear or care. Secure means without fear, not afraid to express ideas, not afraid to ask questions, not afraid to ask for further instructions, nor afraid to report equipment out of order, nor material that is unsuited to the purpose, poor light, or other working conditions that impair quality and production.

b. People on the job are afraid to enquire more than three or four times into the job: what is the job; what is acceptable, and what is not. The foreman has no time to explain further to the man what the job is. Another enquiry may indicate that the man can not learn the job. So he pushes along, as best he can.

c. Another related aspect of fear is inability to serve the best interests of the company through necessity to satisfy specified rules, or the necessity to satisfy, at all costs, a quota of production, no matter if the materials be unsuitable or machines out of order.

d. An example appears in Chapter 10, where the foreman dared not to halt production for repairs. He knew what was best for the company, but he could

---

* I am indebted to Mr. William J. Latzko for pointing out to me long ago the prevalence of fear and the economic losses therefrom.

only push ahead on his quota of castings for the day, at the risk of breakdown. Sure enough, the bearing froze. He not only failed to put out his quota: the whole line went down for four days for repairs.

e. A further illustration may be helpful here, an example related to me by my friend David S. Chambers. A supervisor held out for examination and discussion the defective items that the seven people made during the day. She would spend the last half hour of the day with her seven people for examination and scrutiny, with great patience and compassion, of every defective item produced today. Her seven people thought that she was a great supervisor, and so did everyone else.

The fact is that what she was doing was to send her seven people this way and that way in attempt to change their methods, making things worse than they would have been had she left them alone, and she was guaranteeing the same problems forever.

What is wrong? Those seven people did not make the defects; the system did. They delivered defects from the system into the production line. Patience with the people did not improve the system.

f. One common result of fear is seen in inspection. An inspector records incorrectly the result of an inspection for fear of overdrawing the quota of allowable defectives of the work force (more in Ch. 10).

g. Fear is a symptom of failings in hiring, training, supervision, and bewilderment from aims of the company that are hard to follow. Fear will disappear as management improves, and as employees develop confidence in the management.

WHAT TOP MANAGEMENT MUST DO TO IMPROVE PRODUCTIVITY

U.S. WORKERS FEEL THAT REPORTING WASTE
DOESN'T DO ANY GOOD, SURVEY FINDS

by Philip Schandler

The board mailed a questionnaire to 13,000 randomly chosen
employees of 15 agencies. About 8,600 responded. Of these, nearly
45 per cent, about 4,000 said they had "personally observed or
obtained direct evidence of a wasteful or illegal activity within the
past year," the report says.

And one in 10 of those who claimed knowledge of an improper
activity said it involved more than $100,000.

However, only 30 per cent of the workers who claimed knowledge of
improper activity reported it to anyone else.

Fifty-three per cent of those who failed to report an impropriety
said it was because they "did not think anything would be done to
correct the activity." Another 20 per cent said they didn't think
anything could be done.

Twenty per cent said they didn't say anything because to do so
would be "too great a risk for me." This shows that fear of reprisal
is "an important, although secondary consideration" in failure to
disclose wrongdoing, the report says.

-- The Washington Star, 15 April 1981, page A-5.

9. Break down barriers between staff areas. People in research, design,

purchase of materials, sales, receipt of incoming materials, must learn about

the problems encountered with various materials and specifications in production

and assembly. Otherwise, there will be losses in production from necessity for

rework caused by attempts to use materials unsuited to the purpose. Everyone in

engineering design, purchase of materials, testing materials and testing per-

formance of a product, has a customer, namely, the man (e.g., a plant manager)

that must try to make, with the material purchased, the thing that was designed.

Why not get acquainted with the customer? Why not spend time in the factory,

see the problems, and hear about them?

A new president came in: talked with the heads of sales, design, manufac-

turing, consumer research, etc. Everybody was doing a superb job, and had been doing so for years. Nobody had any problems. Yet somehow or other the company was going down the tube. Why? The answer was simple. Each staff area was suboptimizing its own work, but not working as a team for the company. It was the new president's job to coordinate the talents of these men for the best good of the company.

A common problem is caused by a rush into production. The factory made up six items, and incurred no problem. Salesmen, showing the prototypes, piled up orders. The outlook was bright. Production of hundreds of items on a mass basis, however, was another matter. Stoppages, adjustments, and small changes in style and specifications, which required explanation and assent from customers, solved the problems, but with severe loss of time and with increases in cost. More teamwork at the start would be better: see the problems all the way through.

Management often complicates the work of the people in design by making last minute changes in style and engineering, after the plans are submitted, and production is ready, leaving to the design and production engineers only a few weeks to do a year's work.

Teams composed of people in design, engineering, production, and sales, can accomplish important improvements in design of product, service, and quality, and reduction of costs. Such teams could be called QC-Circles in management.

10. Eliminate exhortations & numerical goals for the work force. Eliminate targets, slogans, pictures, posters, for the work force, urging them to increase productivity, sign their work as a self-portrait, etc. ZERO DEFECTS is another. Would you sign your work? No: not when you give me defective canvas to work with, paint not suited to the job, brushes worn out. Posters and slogans like these never helped anyone to do a better job. What is needed is not exhortations but a road map to improvement, management's obligation.

WHAT TOP MANAGEMENT MUST DO TO IMPROVE PRODUCTIVITY

10a. eliminate work standards mgt. by numbers, MBO, etc.
10b. "

It was reported that one company, one of the most successful in the United
States, assembled top management of their 240 top suppliers, to tell them that
beginning three months from now this company will accept no defective parts.
This sounds great. The only trouble is that such a program can only be a farce.
How will the purchaser know that he is receiving no defects? How will he know
how many defects he has received? He can not learn by inspection, and he would
have no evidence about defective parts and materials till things go wrong on
the production line or on the customer's premises. He will then learn that his
program failed, and he may never know why.

"Do it right the first time." This has a lofty ring to it. But how could
a man make it right the first time when the incoming material is off gauge, off
color, or otherwise defective, or if his machine is not in good order, or the
measuring instruments not trustworthy? I fear that this solution to all problems is merely another slogan, a cousin of zero defects.

An example of a useless poster is shown in Fig. 2; man running upstairs:
increase productivity. Such posters help nobody.

Devoid of ideas by which to improve productivity, but desperate to do
something, management's course of action may be publication of new goals and
new work standards. The quotation on page 312 from Goethe may have wider
application than he thought.

Fig. 2. Man running upstairs

Chapter 2

I saw in the cafeteria of a company the charts in Fig. 3. Great idea. Set goals. Give people something to work toward. These are typical. What do they accomplish? Nothing. Wrong: their accomplishment is negative.

The improvement in production at the 20th week, perhaps obvious from the chart, arose from installation of two new machines. The chart had nothing to do with the improvement, except to record it. The new goal for production will not increase the contribution of the production workers; it will instead create questions and resentment amongst them. Their first thought is that the management is never satisfied. Whatever we do, they ask for more. No wonder the record of results has been pretty uniform:

1. Failure to accomplish the goal.

2. Increase in variability.

3. Increase in proportion defective.

4. Increase in costs.

5. Demoralization of the work force.

6. Disrespect of the management.

Such posters never helped anybody to do a better job. Like work standards, they fail to improve the potential of man and machine.

Posters that explain to everyone on the job what the management is doing month by month to improve the system, to make it possible to improve quality and productivity, not by working harder but by working smarter, would be a totally different story: they would boost morale. People would understand that the management is taking some responsibility for hangups and defects.

An individual will of course have his own goals. A man may set his heart on a college education. He may resolve to study harder to pass a course or an examination. I resolve to finish this chapter before morning: I give myself a deadline. Goals are necessary for you and for me, but numerical goals set for

WHAT TOP MANAGEMENT MUST DO TO IMPROVE PRODUCTIVITY

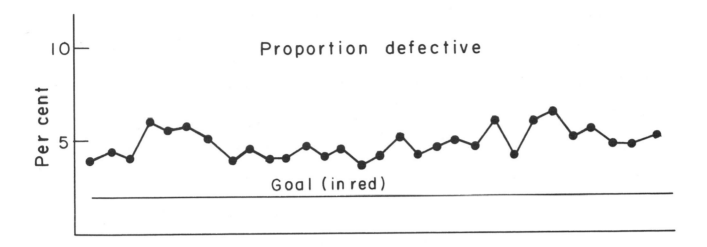

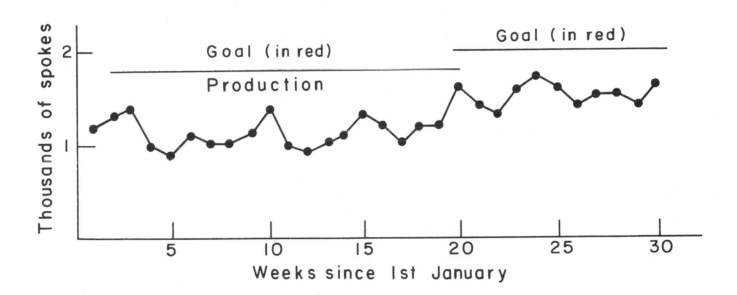

Fig. 3. Chart for weekly production and proportion
defective. The goals were set by industrial engineering.
In my opinion, they are demoralizing and ineffective.

other people, without provision for a road map to reach the goal, have effects opposite to the effects sought. They generate frustration and resentment. The message that they carry to everyone is that the management is dumping their responsibilities on to the work force. Why advertise the helplessness of management?

Slogans stress quality, but measure people on numbers.

The company will of course have a goal, namely, never-ending improvement.

Internal goals set in the management of a company are usually a burlesque. Examples: (1) Decrease costs of warranty by 10 per cent next year; (2) Increase sales by 10 per cent; (3) Cut by 10 per cent the number of employees in every division. A natural fluctuation in the right direction (usually plotted from inaccurate data) is interpreted as success. A fluctuation in the opposite direction sends everyone scurrying for explanations and into bold thrusts whose only achievements are frustration and more problems.

11. <u>Eliminate work standards and numerical quotas.</u> (Work standards are also known as measured day work.) These quotas take account only of numbers, not quality. A work standard is a fortress against improvement of quality and productivity. I have yet to see a work standard that includes any trace of a system by which to help anyone to do a better job.

I have heard that incentive pay in the steel industry in the United States is based on the total tonnage turned out, regardless of how much of the product is turned back into the furnace as unusable.

As usually used, work standards are a guarantee of inefficiency and high cost. For example, a work standard may contain an allowance of 10 per cent for defective items, and 20 per cent for scrap. Work standards guarantee that the company will get the specified amount of defective items, and the specified amount of scrap, and never improve.

WHAT TOP MANAGEMENT MUST DO TO IMPROVE PRODUCTIVITY

Someone said to me, "I could make 106 in six hours, but if I did, the standard would become 106 per day, and everyone would have to meet it." The management is locked in, no provision possible for improvement.

One will see any day in hundreds of factories, men and women standing around the last hour or two of the day, waiting for the whistle to blow. They have completed their quotas for the day; they may do no more work, and they can not go home. Is this good for the competitive position of American industry? These people are unhappy doing nothing. They would rather work.

A bank that I worked with had just engaged a consulting firm to set work standards. The consulting firm came up with figures on the number of customers that a teller ought to handle in an hour, the number of computations of interest and penalty that someone ought to compute in an hour, and a figure for every other activity, but not a word about quality of workmanship, and no aid for improvement.

A man in the service division of a manufacturing company discovered that a technician that ignores his quota of four calls per day, and instead, does not leave a job till he is satisfied that he has done it with credit to himself, regardless of the time required, will earn for the company better profit than someone that rigidly meets his quota. The reason is obvious: a job done well will lead to fewer calls to come back and do it right. There is no longer an acceptable excuse for such outdated ideas about supervision.

An additional gain, intangible, but possibly of even greater importance, is that he builds up goodwill for the company. He also gains his own self-respect for good work.

A work standard is sometimes purposely set high, by the management, to weed out people that can not meet it. She who falls short of the rate finds that her pay for the day also falls short.

Chapter 2

"The job is to make 155 pieces per day. I can't come near this figure--and we all have the problem--without turning out a lot of defective items." She must bury her pride of workmanship, or lose pay and maybe also her job. It could well be that with intelligent supervision and help, and with no inherited defects, this operator could produce on the average and with less effort 165 good items in a day, maybe even more.

Piece work is more devastating than work standards, if such a thing were possible. The hourly worker on piece work soon learns that she gets paid for making defective items and scrap--the more defectives she turns out, the higher her pay for the day. Where is her pride of workmanship?

In some plants, it is true, an hourly worker on rate gets docked for a defective item that she produces. This may be a cruel system. Who declares an item to be defective? Is it clear to her and to the inspector--both of them-- what constitutes a defective item? Would it have been declared defective yesterday? Did the operator create the defective item, or the system?

More to the point, what made the item defective? The operator, or the system? (See the next section, and Ch. 10.)

So long as a given number of units constitutes a day's work, with no provision built into the job for improvement of quality and productivity, there will be no improvement of either one.

Work standards, rates, and piece work are manifestations of inability to understand and provide appropriate supervision.

The loss to American industry from work standards, rates, and piece work must be appalling.

Management that is interested in raising dividends might well take immediate, strong interest in eliminating work standards, rates, and piece

WHAT TOP MANAGEMENT MUST DO TO IMPROVE PRODUCTIVITY

work, and the barriers that stand between the hourly worker and his pride of workmanship (Point 12).

There is no piece work in Japan.

12. <u>Remove barriers that hinder the hourly worker</u>. The hourly worker in America is under handicaps that are taking a terrific toll in quality, productivity, and competitive position. Barriers and handicaps rob the hourly worker of his birthright, the right to be proud of his work, the right to do a good job. These barriers exist in almost every plant, factory, company, department store, government office, in the United States today. Only the management can remove these barriers.

How can anyone take pride in his work when he is not sure what is acceptable workmanship, and what is not, and can not find out? Right yesterday; wrong today. What is my job?

The foreman is sometimes not helpful to a production worker that does not understand the job. Too often the foreman is rated on production, numbers, not on quality. He fears that this will be his last day here if he fails to produce his quota.

An hourly worker told me that instructions for every job where she works are printed and visible, but that nobody ever read them more than half way through. Anyone by the time he is half way through is already so confused that he is afraid to go on; he could only be more confused.

How can an hourly worker take pride in his work when there are problems with inspection—inspectors not sure what is right; instruments and gauges out of order, and the foreman pushed from above to meet a daily quota of numbers, not quality?

How can he, when he must spend time trying to correct or hide defective workmanship or off-gauge material, in a previous operation, or handling damage?

How can he, when his job is to produce X items as a day's work (work standard), good, defective, and scrap, all combined willy nilly?

How can he, when the machine is out of order, and no one listens to his plea for adjustment?

How can he, when, after stopping his machine to adjust it because it was making only defective product, the foreman comes along and orders him in two words, "Run it." In other words, "make defective product."

> The man (hourly worker) that told me about this incident described it as failure of communication.

> "Failure of communication? You understood what the foreman said, didn't you?" To the foreman, only the numbers count, defective plus non-defective combined. How can the foreman meet his quota with a machine sitting idle, waiting for adjustment? Who is at fault? Management.

How can she take pride in her work when she must spend a substantial fraction of her time changing tools, "soft, low quality," she explained.

"But the company saves money by buying cheap tools," I remarked. "Yes," she said, "and loses 10 times what they save because the tools wear out and use up our time."

"But you get paid for your time; what is the problem?"

"I could turn out much more work were it not for those poor tools."

<u>Hourly worker (recorded)</u>: The superintendent is afraid to make a decision. If he does nothing, he has nothing to explain to his superiors. No explanation is required of a man in management for doing nothing. How can anything improve if he passes the buck?

"What about productivity?" I asked him (the hourly worker).

"We can't get productivity when the conveyor is not working right, and we have to handle most of the stuff by hand. The stuff is hot and raises blisters if we handle it by hand as fast as it comes out. We have to slow down. We can't get any action from the management."

"How long has this been going on?"

"Seven years."

More on problems of the hourly worker appear here and there in the book: see, for example, page 54.

In another instance, hourly workers told me about the machine that they were trying to use, bought new two years ago, still a disappointment. Other hourly workers showed me machines badly maintained. The maintenance man had for years cannibalized discarded machines instead of using new parts.

Barriers against realization of pride of workmanship may in fact be one of the most important obstacles to competitive reduction of cost and improvement of quality in the United States.

How big a job is it for management to remove these barriers? In the first place, this question has no answer except eternity where the management is totally unaware of the problem (so far, in my experience, everywhere). Most companies, once the management sees videotapes or listens to audiotapes of meetings with hourly workers, and becomes aware of the problem, will require three to five years, even when the management is shocked and determined. Some companies will require ten years. Some people in management are paralyzed by the problem.

There are other losses from incompetent supervision, as if poor quality and low productivity were not by themselves enough cause of loss. For example, it is fairly well known that the average number of days off with pay for accidents on the job go sky high under poor supervision.

The hourly worker is deeply aware of the need for quality. To him, quality means his job. He also understands why productivity increases as quality goes up (p. 1). He can not understand why the management talks about quality but does nothing about it--in fact, impedes it.

The fact is that management can have both quality and numbers by providing road maps to quality and eliminating barriers that confront the hourly worker.

There is much talk about involvement of employees, quality of work life, communication, motivation, and other poetic words. What is needed is involvement of management: get the management involved. Employees will become involved, and quality of work life will improve, once management takes on their job of restoring dignity to the hourly worker.

Another example. Salaried employees took over production during a strike of hourly employees. The manager of a department reported that he found machines out of order, some sadly so, some badly in need of maintenance, one a candidate for outright replacement. Production doubled when he tuned up the machines. Were it not for the strike, he should never have known about the sad state of the machines, and production would have continued at half the capability of the process. "Well Hal," I said, "you know whose fault it was, don't you?" Yes, he knows. It won't happen again. He assured me that from now on, there will be a system by which employees may report trouble with machines or with materials and that these reports will receive attention.

A control chart in the hands of a supervisor in any of the cases described under Point 12 would show an inordinately high proportion of items to be defective, and would thus detect the existence of problems. It would require little imagination on his part to learn what these problems are. Tippett's ratio-delay studies, commonly known in this country as work sampling, would detect an inordinate amount of downtime. Whether the supervisor or anyone else in management would take action to remove the problems so detected is another matter. (References to Tippett and to Marvin Mundel and others appear at the foot of page 255.)

13. <u>Institute a vigorous program of education and training</u>. Management has a new job; so has everybody else. As we have seen, everybody in the purchasing department has a new job.

Improvement in productivity means that fewer people will be needed for some lines of work. At the same time, however, more people will be needed in other lines. Education and training will fit people into new jobs and new responsibilities. So-called quality control departments must adjust themselves to new responsibilities. There will be (e.g.) fewer inspectors year by year as quality improves. People that have been engaged in quality control, quality assurance, and in inspection, with their wealth of knowledge about materials and instruments, and with skills that they have developed, by acquiring new knowledge about management, and with education and refresher courses in simple but powerful statistical techniques, will render indispensable service to their companies. They will be needed for improvement of inspection, for use and maintenance of instruments, and for improvement of comparability of quality between vendors and purchasers, as well as by the purchasing department as it changes character (Point 4).

Management's new job is embodied in the 14 points. It is necessary for management to learn also some rudiments of statistical theory and application.

Education in simple but powerful statistical techniques is required of all people in management, all engineers and scientists, inspectors, quality control managers, management in the service organizations of the company, such as accounting, payroll, purchase, safety, legal department, consumer service, consumer research. Engineers and scientists need rudiments of experimental design.

Chapter 2

Five days under a competent teacher will suffice as a base. The five days, at the discretion of the teacher, might include brief study of factorial designs and some theory of reliability.

Only a teacher with the equivalent of a master's degree in statistics, and who has worked years in industry, is qualified for this teaching. Home study and original research published in a reputable journal constitute qualifications in lieu of a formal degree.

This program is not an instant affair, nor is it ever finished. It is costly. One bottleneck is the shortage of competent statisticians for teachers.

Universities, with guidance from competent consultants, may attempt to provide continuing education for theoretical statistics, slanted toward the needs of industry. It is possible that one in 500 of the people that take such courses may decide to spend the necessary extra ten years in a university and as an apprentice to become a statistician.

It is obvious that control charts and any other statistical calculations in the hands of the production workers would be meaningless in the presence of problems like those described under Point 12. For example, what meaning could be attached to a control chart or to any other statistical calculation made on the work of a man that is forced to make defectives, or when he is not clear what the job is? He already knows very well what the trouble is.

The first step is for management to remove the barriers that rob the hourly worker from his right to do a good job (Point 12).

Anyone who supposes that quality, productivity, and competitive position can be achieved by massive immediate use of control charts and other statistical techniques by hourly workers will doom his own career and carry his company along with him.

WHAT TOP MANAGEMENT MUST DO TO IMPROVE PRODUCTIVITY

Where conditions are clean, however, training of a judicious selection of people in the hourly work force, and foremen, in simple statistical methods such as control charts will help them to do better work, with less effort and with even greater satisfaction of pride. A few hours under a competent teacher is usually sufficient as a start for hourly workers and foremen that wish to learn and adopt the method. Again, instructors should have proper qualifications.

Management must institute a vigorous continuous program for retraining employees in new knowledge and new skills, to keep up with changes in model, style, materials, methods, and—at times, if advantageous—new machinery.

14. Create a structure in top management that will push every day on the above 13 points. Top management will require guidance from an experienced consultant, but the consultant can not take on obligations that only the management can carry out. Part of his duties would be to teach statistical methods, to develop teachers (Ch. 17).

It is easy to make this recommendation, but it is another story to carry it out, owing to the severe shortage of competent statisticians that are willing to undertake duties of the kind required for successful practice.

An experienced consultant would work with a statistician of the corporation (or company), and would have as his aim creation in the corporation of a structure that would in time be able to carry on satisfactorily without the consultant. Everybody doing statistical work would have a chance to learn and improve his ability. The length of time required would depend on the ability of the permanent statistical head. Two or three years should suffice. Some advice on statistical organization appears in Chapter 17.

He who is not willing to engage competent advice along with assistance that
the man may require, will delay his advance in quality and productivity, and
competitive position. Everyone in a company needs a road map toward constant
improvement in knowledge and effectiveness.

D. SOME ADDITIONAL PRINCIPLES FOR PURCHASE OF MATERIALS

Single purchase contrasted with continuing purchase. It is important for
managers of purchasing to understand the difference between the two problems now
to be described. Company A has been in business for some time, and provides
continuing evidence of statistical process control. Company B has not process
control.

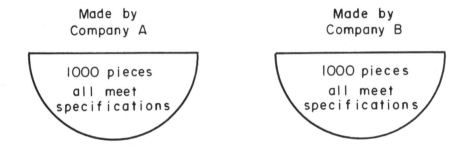

Fig. 4. Two lots, made by two different companies, all pieces good.

Problem 1. You wish to purchase 1000 pieces of xbae. You make calls to
companies A and B to explain the specifications. Each company submits 1000
pieces of xbae; all good, so the companies claim. You satisfy yourself, by your
own inspection, that indeed all 2000 pieces meet your specifications. Which
lot would you buy? Toss a coin?

There may be characteristics that are important to you, but which are not
covered in your specifications. There may be other characteristics that you
would wish to avoid, and your specifications may not protect you. There may be

persuasive arguments in favor of Company A. For example, the distribution of the important quality-characteristics of the 1000 parts made by Company A will be narrower than the distribution of those made by Company B. Uniformity is nearly always an important characteristic of whatever you buy.

In contrast, one could expect the distribution of the same important quality-characteristic in the 1000 pieces made by Company B, if he has not process control, to be pretty ragged from one specification to the other.

If the price offered by Company B is the lower of the two, it would be wise to enquire how this could be, as Company A's cost will be lower. It is possible that Company B can offer to you a bargain because he has the material on hand from a cancellation, or picked up a bargain.

Problem 2. Now, we come to a totally different problem. You plan to purchase 1000 pieces of xbae every week. Your requirements in this problem point definitely to selection of Company A. There are a number of reasons. The distribution of the important quality-characteristic of the xbae produced by Company A is predictable (Fig. 5). It will be steady week after week. If the distribution falls within your specifications, you can eliminate inspection of incoming items except for routine observations and comparisons for identification. You will note from the control charts that came along with the product, far better than any amount of inspection can tell you, what the distribution of quality is, and what it will be tomorrow.

If a distribution overlaps a specification, as at C in Fig. 5, you will have a sound basis for deciding by the theory in Chapter 13 whether to change your specifications or to accept some defective material and take the consequences, or try to screen out the defectives.

There is another important point about Company A. His product will improve with time. He has statistical control, and his engineers, chemists, and other experts will be innovative, creative. The purchaser of product from Company A will be a beneficiary of continual improvements of quality and of decrease in cost of production. His other customers will also be beneficiaries. He makes a contribution to better material living for everybody.

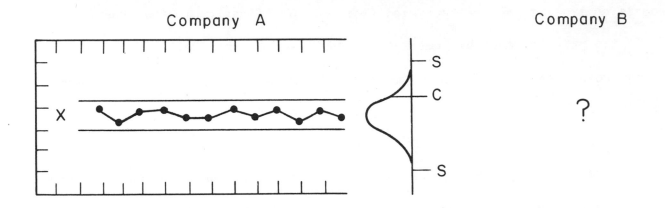

Company A   Company B

Fig. 5.a. $\bar{x}$-chart for a critical quality-characteristic. The size of the sample was n = 4. Hence the distribution of individual parts (shown by the curve) was twice the spread of the control limits for $\bar{x}$. If the specifications are at S, S, the output of Company A requires no inspection. If a specification were at C, then some items would be defective, and the upper tail of the distribution above C would show the proportion defective.

Fig. 5.b. About Company B we know nothing.

Types of gaps in information about the performance of incoming materials.

Any batch of material sent to a plant falls into one of four categories.

1. Used in production with no problem.

WHAT TOP MANAGEMENT MUST DO TO IMPROVE PRODUCTIVITY

2. Used in desperation, being unsuited to the requirements of manufacture and finished product, invariably with waste of material or cost of rework, or both. Example: a block, dished out at the top. Should be flat for cement. Requires rework before use. Another example is a panel (veneer or hide) of non-uniform color. Some of the material must be discarded, with loss of time and material, or risk that the finished product will be condemned.

In another example, there was only one vendor capable of supplying the right material, but to meet a large contract, the company ordered the same material from other vendors, which, as it turned out, were not able to produce the grade desired. This material was used, nevertheless, in desperation, with the consequences of rework and waste.

3. Totally unusable, in the judgment of the plant manager. A way to decide what to do on this problem is to call a meeting attended by the plant manager and the buyer, possibly also by an expert from the laboratory. These men may decide:

That the plant manager was justified in his complaint, the material is unfit for use; return it to the vendor.

Or

That he should try harder to use the material.

Or

That the trouble lies not in defective material, but in specifications that did not make sense for the use intended. Hold the material for other uses, or try to sell it; possibly sell it back to the vendor (usually at a loss).

4. Material in inventory. Examples: (1) Material bought, held for use. (2) Customer cancelled the order before work started. Example: Customer contracted for 2000 items; there is enough material for only 1000; he can not use 1000, and can not wait for attempts to procure more material, so he cancels

the order. (3) The product would reach the customer too late: the season will be over: customer cancels the order.

There are several possible solutions to this class of item. One is to sell it back to the vendor. Another is to put it into inventory, hoping to find use for it later. Still another is to call up your competitor: he may be looking for precisely this material.

A cross-section of American industry would show, I believe, that the only categories understood and documented are Categories 3 and 4, materials declared by the plant manager to be totally unusable, and material put into inventory or returned to the vendor.

In my experience, Category 3 is very small, less than one per cent of the dollar-value of materials bought. The dollar value of Category 2, large as it may be, must be far less than the waste of effort spent in trying to use it.

Example in respect to Category 2. It occurred in a factory that makes electrical equipment. The most visible and absorbing activity seemed to be inspection. "What proportion of your capital equipment is invested in gauges, instruments, and computers?" I asked.

"About 80 per cent," was the answer, "including printing of reports."

"What proportion of your payroll goes for inspection?"

"Between 55 and 60 per cent. We have to be sure of our quality. We have a reputation to maintain."

A memory chip on each finished piece of apparatus held information that could print out the serial number of every one of the 1100 parts in the piece of apparatus, with indication of whether this item was accepted on first test, or was a replacement for items that had failed.

Because of so much inspection, the engineer in charge explained to me, we don't need quality control.

WHAT TOP MANAGEMENT MUST DO TO IMPROVE PRODUCTIVITY

Later, in a meeting with union representatives, two of the women present enquired thus: "Why do we have to spend so much of our time straightening out these plastic plates before we can work on them? A third of them come in warped."

"Why do they come in warped?" I asked.

"Handling damage, we think."

"What difference does it make to you? You get paid by the hour."

"Yes, but we could turn out more work if we didn't have to spend our time straightening out those warped plates," and couldn't I do something about it?

"How long have you had this problem?," I asked.

"I have been screaming about it for three years, but nothing has happened."

One may wonder what she and her people thought of the management, taking no heed of her cries for help to eliminate this cause of waste.

Later on with the top management, it was possible to enquire why it is that with 80 per cent of your capital equipment in gauges, instruments and computers printing piles of machine sheets, and with 55 per cent of your man hours going for inspection, no one except the production workers knew about the warped plates? You are trying to build quality by inspection--the wrong way.

You are concerned because one of your best customers is looking around for a supplier for lower prices and better quality. You may lose a good customer. You can't blame him. Your prices are high because of waste of human effort and because of huge expense in equipment for inspection and storage of information that nobody can use.

E. PROBLEMS OF ONE OF A KIND *

Many products are one of a kind. A home that one buys is one of a kind.
So is a rug, and the grand piano. A job shop is a producer of one of a kind.
A certain model of automobile is one of a kind: once in production, little can
be done about resistance to purchase, any more than one can remodel a battleship
once built. A company may build six aeroplanes of specified design, or 37 of
them. They are one of a kind. A building, once under construction, is pretty
well fixed. Changes are costly.

Machinery, once bought, becomes a fixture. So it is with a home, a grand
piano, a building, an automobile, an aeroplane.

Special care needed in planning. When a factory sets off to make a large
number of items, one can expect to throw away the first half dozen or so or
even more in a learning period. Many more parts may have to be made before the
desired quality is stabilized. But in the making of one of a kind, planning
must be much more thorough. Put another way, the most important observation to
make in respect to one of a kind is that extreme care must go into the plans.
Changes are costly or impossible.

How do you test a battleship? The only answer is that it is too late.
Care is needed more than ever in making one of a kind. Plans and purchase of
materials have only one chance.

It is amazing to observe the vast amount of knowledge that can be put into
the mechanical and electrical contrivances, such as an aeroplane or in a hotel,
or in a hospital, and to observe also what little thought the design engineers
gave to the customer.

---

* I am indebted to my friend William A. Golomski of Chicago for my education
in most of the ideas presented here.

If people in engineering design would do their work as if they had no chance to make any change, once the product goes into production, they might do a better job.

> There may be in any of these examples repeated operations from one house to another, from one building to another, from one contract to another, etc. These repeated operations may lend themselves to statistical aids such as control charts.

Example 1. The engines of the aeroplane started. We shall soon be off the ground, Nashville to Washington. All was in readiness except for nine people standing in the aisle looking for their seats. The flight attendant begged them to sit down, anywhere. Why were they standing? They were trying to find their seats. The numbers that designate the aisles were too small for easy visibility, and obscured by lights besides. Who could make an aeroplane at a cost of several million dollars, yet give no attention to the passenger? Somebody did. Who would buy it? Somebody did.

Example 2. Ask anyone knowledgeable in the aeroplane business about the difficulty to transfer luggage from one airline to another in the airport in San Francisco. A passenger makes a connexion; the luggage does not. The luggage follows, sometimes at huge cost to the airline and at great inconvenience to the passenger. Who would design an airport without reference to the problem of transferring luggage from one airline to another? Somebody did. The airport cost enough.

Example 3. Here is a hotel (Fig. 6), almost new, the lights placed so that the keyholes for the doors are in darkness. Customers complained, but the manager was helpless. He inherited the problem. He can not rebuild the hotel. Customers conquered the problem by sense of touch. No one, so far as I could learn, spent the night in the corridor, failing to gain access to his room.

Fig. 6. Lights in the corridor of a hotel obscure keyholes.

What architect would be so completely oblivious to the customer? One was.
What purchaser of the building would have the same failing? One did.

Example 4. Some hotel rooms are constructed so that the blast of air for
air conditioning or for heat blows on to the occupant of the bed, and there is
no escape. The only solution is to apply minmax theory: bear the breeze, or
turn it off and roast or freeze, depending on the temperature of the season.
What architect would ignore the customer? One did. What owner of a hotel would
ignore the customer? One did.

Example 5. Why do companies that own hotels spend millions of dollars
for furnishings without reference to the need of occupants? Some guests are
businessmen that need to do some writing. What they find in a room is a beautiful round low-down table for cocktails; no semblance of a desk for writing.
Chairs especially designed for discomfort. What can the manager of the hotel
do about it? Nothing: it is too late.

Example 6. A conveyor belt, two feet off the floor, carries glass jars
of food. Jars fall off, break, and spill messy contents on to the floor. Some
of the mess runs under the conveyor. To clean it up, a man must be under two
feet in height or else crawl on his knees and broken glass to reach under the

WHAT TOP MANAGEMENT MUST DO TO IMPROVE PRODUCTIVITY

conveyor. What architect or engineer would suppose that there would never be need to clean house? One did.

Example 7. What company would build an aeroplane with no individual reading lights for passengers? The aeroplane costs millions of dollars, and is well designed (I hope) with respect to engineering and aerodynamics, but no one thought in advance about the passenger. What airlines would buy several of these aeroplanes without thought of the needs of the passenger? One did.

Example 8. A job shop furnishes a good example of production of one of a kind. Factories that turn out clothing, shoes, handbags, turn out a few thousand items on a contract. A factory may turn out only one of a kind. The toolroom in a large factory producing prototypes is an example. Excellent results come from intense attention to plans and to purchase of materials. There are, in any job shop, repeated operations, turning, welding, riveting, stitching. Productivity can be improved in these operations by the methods of process control.

Chapter 3

OBSTACLES AND PROBLEMS

My people are destroyed for lack of knowledge.--Hosea 4: v.6.

A. OBSTACLES

<u>The big obstacle: lack of constancy of purpose</u>. Much of American industry is run on the quarterly dividend. A president is brought in by the Board of Directors for this very purpose. Constancy of purpose is impossible in such a climate. Until and unless top management establishes constancy of purpose for service, and makes it clear that everyone in the company can work without fear toward this purpose, efforts of other people in the company, however brilliant be the fires that they start, can only be transitory.

Announced intentions to improve quality fail in some instances because the management is unwilling to direct sufficient funds into education, and is unwilling to pay the price for competent teachers and consultants. Improvement of quality is not for the curious, nor for the faint-hearted.

Even where top management has announced with full commitment constancy of purpose toward quality and productivity, other people in the company may be perplexed and skeptical. I hear these questions:

How long will this program last? What will be the program three years from now? Will a new president come in and undo all that we can accomplish?

The following letter illustrates doubts and perplexities.

I am manager of one of our plants. There are 5 plants in this region, 19 plants in the U.S. The district manager is only concerned with his own record, being a candidate for the next president. To him, the numbers are all important--high profit; quality not to stand in the way of high production. He is on a cost cutting program: cut maintenance, cut education, cut research.

For myself, I shall be promoted at the end of two more years; otherwise I will leave the company.

My question is, what can I start now that will continue to help quality and productivity in my company after I leave this job.

Perhaps education of all management in the 14 points and in simple, powerful statistical methods would be a good answer. This education would last everyone forever, wherever he goes. The writer's loose attachment to his company is clear. Other types of enquiries come in the mail:

The quandary is whether we as one division in our corporation can be successful with statistical control of quality without the active involvement of superiors.

I fear that the answer is no, unless this man is endowed with total authority for his division.

Many of the people in attendance at seminars for management are delegates, top management being too busy to learn what their job is, forgetting that efficiency and effectiveness are different qualities. Also, there is always the hope that the problems will somehow go away. "Jim, I wish for you to attend the seminar, and give me a 15-minute briefing when you return."

The big problem for top management and for anyone else in management may be difficulty to make any kind of change. This difficulty may in fact amount to paralysis.

Mobility of top management. A company whose top management is committed to quality and productivity, with roots, does not suffer from the uncertainty and bewilderment. But how can top management be committed to any policy when their tenure is only a few years, in and out?

A friend in Japan, whose knowledge of industry in Japan and the United States is unquestioned, made the remark in conversation that, "America can not make it." The reason that he gave is the mobility of American management, not taking root in the company, but instead building up personal reputations for even greater mobility.

People need time to learn how to work together. Men may require ten to fifteen years to learn to appreciate each other's achievements and potential, and to absorb enough knowledge from and about each other to form a working pool. I can testify that some of the happiest and most fruitful relationships with clients required ten to fifteen years to develop. Had we broken off our relationship at the end of ten years, we should never have known the bond of friendship and effectiveness of efforts that we now enjoy.

The job of management is inseparable from the welfare of the company. In and out, from the management of one company to the management of another is no longer something that American industry can afford.

Failure of management to get involved with problems of production. There is much talk about how to get employees involved with quality. The big problem is how to get the management involved. Management must remove the obstacles that rob the hourly worker of his birthright--namely, the right to pride of workmanship (page 43). Management must remove fear throughout the company (Point 8).

As mentioned on page 45, this is in my judgment a three to five year program in companies in America that are ostensibly well managed--more like ten years for others.

The economic loss in quality and productivity and competitive position from the obstacles that stand in the way of production workers is stupendous.

Production, service, and competitive position suffer from the supposition that management need not possess substantive or technical knowledge, and need not understand problems of design of product and production: that a good manager in one spot can be a good manager wherever good management is needed.

OBSTACLES AND PROBLEMS

Obsolescent curriculum in schools of business. In respect to turnover in management, in and out, it may be worthwhile to point out that some schools of business lead students to suppose that for success they must be marketable, so that they may go into a company, perform miracles, and expect a call to go to another company for more miracles.

Students learn little about their limitations and deficiencies. They are led to suppose that they are ready to manage.

It is a fact that anyone might pass with high marks all the courses offered today in schools of business, and yet be helpless against the problems of low productivity and high costs that afflict American industry.

The teaching of trades and skills, such as the art of negotiation, taught now in some schools of business, is not education. The best place to learn a trade or a skill is to work for some good company, under masters of the art, and get paid while you learn.

Insulation surrounding top management. A perennial question in people's minds is how to reach their top management, to acquaint them with the fact that the company is in trouble, and that there are courses of action to take to regain competitive position.

I have no formula on how to reach top management. If the top management do not know that the company is in trouble, and that there is a plan available for top management, there is little that anyone can do for them. In my own practice, I observe the rule to work with a company only on invitation of the top management, and only on a long-term basis, and only if they will engage a competent consultant to work with me and to carry on (Ch. 17).

I have a suspicion, in some cases of complaint about inability to reach top management, that the man's efforts to persuade his top management may be his own failure to understand the responsibilities of top management for quality and productivity. In other instances, fear may be the root cause. A man may be afraid to argue tenaciously with someone on a higher level. It is good to remember what General Leslie E. Simon taught me in 1936 and onward, "If you can't argue with your boss, he is not worth working for."

Search for examples. Improvement of quality is a method, transferable to different problems and circumstances. It does not consist of procedures on file ready for specific application to this or that kind of product.

It is not unusual for a consultant to receive an enquiry for examples of success in a similar product line. One man enquired if statistical methods had ever been used in the manufacture of wheelchairs. Another enquired about compressors for air conditioners: did I know of any application? Another man enquired about the management of a hospital: would statistical methods apply? One could only conclude that he knows little about hospitals. Another wondered about application in a large accounting firm. Another man wondered if quality control had ever been used in the manufacture of automobiles, as if he had never heard of Japan's automobiles. A banker wondered about application in banks. How could he be a banker and not know about William J. Latzko's work at the Irving Trust Company? (Ch. 12)

There is prevalent the supposition that quality control is only for large companies and for large operations. This is not so. Small companies, including job shops, are in fact most responsive to learning and use of new ideas. For one thing, the management is on the job.

Our problems are different. A common disease that afflicts management and government administration the world over is that, "Our problems are different." They are different, to be sure, but the principles that will help to solve them are universal in nature.

OBSTACLES AND PROBLEMS

Hope for instant pudding.* An important obstacle is the supposition that improvement of quality and productivity is accomplished suddenly by affirmation of faith. Letters and telephone calls received by this author disclose prevalence of the supposition that one or two consultations with a competent statistician will set the company on the road to quality and productivity-- instant pudding. "Come, spend a day with us, and do for us what you did for Japan; we too wish to be saved." And they hang up in sorrow. It is not so simple: it will be necessary to study and to go to work. One man actually wrote to me for my formula, and the bill therefor.

A magazine, much read by American people, published in 1981 in its section on business and economics an article on Japan. The author of the article spoiled his otherwise splendid piece of writing by saying in effect, "Dr. Deming went to Japan in 1950 and gave a lecture, and just look what happened." A million readers, I surmise, must have been misled into the supposition that it is all very simple for American industry to copy the Japanese.

An example of expectation of quick results without effort and without suffi- cient education to the job is exemplified in a letter received by Dr. Lloyd S. Nelson, statistician with the Nashua Corporation, which reads as follows:

> The President of my company has appointed me to the same position *major*
> that you hold in your company. He has given me full authority to *chemical Co.*
> proceed, and he wishes me to carry on my new job without bothering
> him. What ought I to do? How do I go about my new job?

Appointment of someone to the same job that Dr. Nelson has will not create another Dr. Nelson. The president's supposition that he can resign from his obligations is another fallacy. This is an example of someone in favor of quality, but not willing to go to work on it.

---

* A term aptly used by James K. Bakken of the Ford Motor Company.

One of the lecturers at the meeting of the Bank Administration Institute held in Atlanta in January 1982 advised every bank to establish a productivity department, to measure productivity. Unfortunately, measurement of productivity does not improve productivity. Announcement of policy to improve productivity will accomplish nothing. It will be just more meaningless words.

Barriers that rob the hourly worker of pride of workmanship. We saw examples on page 43. Other examples appear here and there elsewhere in the text. It is management's responsibility to remove these barriers. This is a 5-year job in some companies; 10 years in others. In some companies, it can never happen without a complete turnover in the management.

Hourly workers have the idea that only they are concerned about quality and productivity. To them, quality and productivity mean their jobs. They tell me that, in contrast, no one in management ever lost his job because he failed to act on quality. They accuse the management of not being serious about quality. It is easier in management to do nothing about quality.

This obstacle, by which the hourly worker is deprived of his right to do good work and to be proud of himself, may be the single most important contribution of management to poor quality and loss of market, save for failure to act on Point 1.

The problem has its origin in the supposition that a manager need not know anything about the problems of production.

Difficulty to change. People in my seminars have told me that their top management are aware that there are some new ideas in the air about quality and productivity, but that people in management have difficulty to make any kind of change. It is simpler to keep busy and to improve efficiency on routine work, in the hope that the big problems will go away.

OBSTACLES AND PROBLEMS

Many figures; no information. Quality control to some people means periodic review of reports on productivity, and on quality shipped out; also perhaps on costs of warranty. To other people, quality control means piles of machine sheets. Such figures are like statistics on accidents. As we noted earlier, they tell us all about accidents except how to reduce their frequency and severity.

Unfortunately, the function of quality assurance in many companies is too often to provide hindsight, to keep the management informed about the amount of defective product produced week by week. Figures that show what happened in the past, in such form that they can not be used for detection of special causes and measurement of common causes, have little or no use.

> I never saw so many figures, yet we still don't have the figures that we need.--Heard in a board meeting in Washington, 26 December 1962.

Poor teaching of statistics. Too many teachers of statistics look backward, still teaching and applying the theory of enumerative problems to analytic problems that they do not understand. Students learn inefficient methods such as analysis of variance (which often buries 90 per cent of the information at hand), tests of the null hypothesis, and probability levels of significance. Unfortunately, these mathematical exercises provide no basis for action, and no basis for prediction of the results of the next experiment, which is of course the only question of interest in a study aimed at improvement of performance of a process, or of product. It is time for statisticians to awaken to the needs of science and industry of today. I quote:*

> Challenges face statisticians today as never before. The whole world is talking about safety in mechanical and electrical devices (in

---

* W. Edwards Deming, "On probability as a basis for action," The American Statistician, vol. 29, 1975: pp. 146-152.

automobiles, for example), safety in drugs, reliability, due care, pollution, poverty, nutrition, improvement of medical practice, improvement of agricultural practice, improvement in quality of product, breakdown of service, breakdown of equipment, tardy busses, trains, and mail, need for greater output in industry and in agriculture, enrichment of jobs. The consumer requires month by month ever greater and greater safety, and he expects better and better performance of manufactured articles. The manufacturer has the same problems in his purchases of materials, assemblies, machines, and use of manpower. He must, in addition, know more and more about his own product. What is due care in manufacturing? What is malpractice in medicine?

These problems can not be understood and can not even be stated, nor can the effect of any alleged solution be evaluated, without the aid of statistical theory and methods. One can not even define operationally adjectives like reliable, safe, polluted, unemployed, on time (arrivals), equal (in size), round, random, tired, red, green, or any other adjective, for use in business or in government, except in statistical terms. A standard (as of safety, or of performance or capability) to have meaning for business or legal purposes, must be defined in statistical terms. (More on this in Chapter 15.)

Our troubles lie entirely in the work force. The supposition is prevalent the world over that there would be no problems in production or in service if only our production workers would do their jobs in the way that they were taught. Pleasant dreams. The workers are handicapped by the system, and the system belongs to management.

It is a new and incomprehensible thought to a man in an executive position that management could be at fault in the production-end. Production and quality, in the view of management, are the responsibilities of plant managers and production workers. Research into faults of the system, to be corrected by management, is not what a manager is trained for. Result: faults of the system get no attention, the production worker gets the wrong attention. Rejections and high costs of production continue.

It was Dr. Joseph M. Juran who pointed out long ago that most of the possibilities for improvement lie in action on the system, and that the production workers can reduce variation only a limited amount.

OBSTACLES AND PROBLEMS

> There is here (in Czechoslovakia) the same widespread unsupported assumption that the bulk of defects are operator-controllable, and that if the operators would only put their backs into it, the plant's quality-problems would shrink materially.--Joseph M. Juran, Industrial Quality Control, vol. 22, May 1966, p. 624.

We saw earlier the improvement achieved in the system for making coated paper (Ch. 1).

Dependence on final inspection on a mass basis. Mass inspection does not do the job. Scrap, downgrading, and rework are not corrective action on the process. They do not guarantee quality of incoming lots, nor of outgoing lots, and they still less--not at all--improve the process that will produce future products.

a. Inspection does not improve quality, nor guarantee quality. Inspection is too late. The quality, good or bad, is already in the product. As Harold F. Dodge said, "You can not inspect quality into a product."

b. Mass inspection is unreliable, costly, ineffective. It does not make a clean separation of good items from bad items.

c. Inspectors fail to agree with each other until brought into statistical control. They fail to agree with themselves. Test instruments, cheap or costly, require maintenance and study. Examples appear in Chapter 10. Routine inspection becomes unreliable through boredom and fatigue. A common excuse of a foreman or of a plant manager, when confronted with data on the number of defectives that he has made, is that the instruments used for the tests are unreliable. Automatic inspection and recording require constant vigil.

d. In contrast, the inspection of small samples of product for control charts to achieve or to maintain statistical control can be a professional job. Inspectors of vendor and customer have time to compare their instruments and test, to learn to speak the same language.

Inspection under pressure, with a high vacuum on the production side, as when a contract must be finished and shipped tonight or tomorrow, is a farce: anything passes inspection, whether it is coming in or going out.

Incidentally, 200 per cent inspection, as usually carried out, is less reliable than 100 per cent inspection for the simple reason that each inspector depends on the other to do the job. Divided responsibility means that nobody is responsible.

My friend David S. Chambers told me about a printing company that proofread everything 11 times. Why do you think the manager called on Mr. Chambers for help? You guessed it: he was plagued with mistakes and complaints from customers. None of the 11 proofreaders had a job: each one depended on the other 10 to do it.

Newspapers across the country in August 1982 bore the news that a nine year old girl failed to find a toy in the package of popcorn that she had purchased. To the maker and distributor of the popcorn, the omission seemed impossible, as every package goes through three inspections to make sure that it contains a prize. The fact is that three inspections ensure omissions, as no one has full responsibility.

Courts of law may be impressed today by three inspections. Two decades from now, three inspections will, in the eyes of the law, be evidence of negligence.

The following excerpt from the Cincinnati Post for 18 November 1981 provides a further illustration of results of divided responsibilities.

GETTING IT STRAIGHT

The names of Greiwe Interiors Inc. and of Richard F. Greiwe/Group III were misspelled 11 times in our story about Cincinnati firms which are celebrating centennials this year. The errors were committed by the reporter and escaped two editors who prepared the article for print.

The Cincinnati Post hates to make mistakes, but human and mechanical errors do get published from time to time. We want to know about our mistakes and make corrections, if necessary. If you spot an error, please telephone the metro desk at 352-2727 or write us at 800 Broadway, Cincinnati 45202.

Repeated inspection on samples of product, on a regular basis, by use of the same testing machine, to learn how well the machine repeats itself, and to maintain it in statistical control, is another story, a mark of good quality control.

OBSTACLES AND PROBLEMS

Put on four more inspectors. This is one way a company sought solution to a problem in quality--a sure road to more trouble.

I have encountered here and there inspection on an incentive basis--the more you inspect, the more you earn. What is the inspector's job? Is he responsible to discover all defects, or just some of them? It would be hard to imagine a surer way to let defective parts slip through.

Inspection for extra high quality. It would be wrong to suppose from the foregoing sections that inspection is never necessary nor effective. My point is that the original work, and inspection as well, if inspection there be, must be carried out under appropriate supervision, with recognition of responsibilities.

There are instances in manufacturing and in service where elimination of mistakes and defects is vital. Spindles on a front axle of an automobile may undergo 100 per cent inspection for reasons of safety. Calculations in a bank must be rigidly correct. Prescriptions must be filled accurately in the pharmacy. Tariffs, as many as 10,000 in one book, put out by a Rate Bureau, must be accurate, including the names of the carriers.

The principle to adopt under such extreme circumstances is that it would be better to turn out no work at all today than to turn out a single mistake. This philosophy is extreme, but it makes the point. Inspection, 100 per cent, is necessary in most of these circumstances, but under the same philosophy. The management must understand that this is a job for quality, not a production job.

An example is in the verification of punching of cards. Let two punchers both do the work in parallel, and let the machine compare the results, flagging differences. Even this procedure is not foolproof. Both punchers may have misread a figure that they both had to guess at.

In the case of computations, interest, penalty, and other transactions in a bank, 100 per cent inspection (or review or verification, as one might prefer to call it) could be carried out by making the computations in parallel, to be followed by comparison by machine of the two sets of results, both with again a possibility of failure from illegible figures. If the computations require that figures be placed on the original documents (as in the computation of divisions on interline abstracts in rail traffic), then it would be necessary that verification start off with a clean copy of the original document.

Extreme care must accordingly be exercised in 100 per cent inspection (or review) to eliminate a common cause or interaction between the original work and the inspection. Thus, for example, in transcribing, punching, or making calculations from figures (such as interest due on a loan), supervision must make it clear to everybody concerned that absolutely no work is to be done on a figure that is not clear. There must be no possibility of reading 8 as a 5, for example. If a figure is not totally clear (unfortunately a matter of judgment), then the document must be laid aside for the supervisor to investigate by study of backup papers or at times by a lengthy search, possibly with letters, telegrams, and telephone calls.

If interaction between the original work and the review be totally eliminated, and if both the original work and the review work were subject to a process average of one mistake in 1000 documents, then the two together would accomplish a process average of $1/1000^2$ or $1/1,000,000$.

Failure to use data from inspection. We have encountered summaries of data from inspection. There is also, more prevalent, no use at all of figures generated by inspection. Data that are filed and eventually thrown away are waste of a wealth of basic information. One will find companies using elaborate

OBSTACLES AND PROBLEMS

plans of acceptance, based on Military Standard 105D or on a Dodge-Romig table, usually with no understanding of the economies involved, making no use of the data from inspection to improve the process and eliminate need of inspection.

In a recent experience in a factory where an inspector looked at every joint, I enquired into the proportion of joints that he found to be defective. "Very few." I asked for data. "We don't keep any record" (whereupon I wondered about the basis for "very few"). The answer depends on the causes of the rare defectives that are encountered. Unfortunately, this answer is not forthcoming without statistical tests.

An impression that defectives are few can be costly. Statistical use of the record, were one kept, would detect existence of special causes of defectives, whether few or many. These causes, once removed, would leave only faults of the system, which when corrected might eliminate the need for inspection. The inspectors' talents could then be put into maintenance of testing equipment.

A curious failure to use information, even when it is posted, is also encountered here and there. For illustration, the product was an important component to go into a nuclear power plant. A large chart was posted to show for each component the number of defective tubes that required replacement. The superintendent explained to me that this chart was not a control chart; it was merely a record for information only (Fig. 7).

He had missed the fact (a) that this chart was in fact a simple but powerful statistical tool known as a run chart; (b) that it showed 11 successive points (14-24 July) at or below the median, almost surely indication of a special cause (or causes) of quality better than usual. Once identified, these causes could be studied in an attempt to improve quality henceforth. Or, the conclusion of

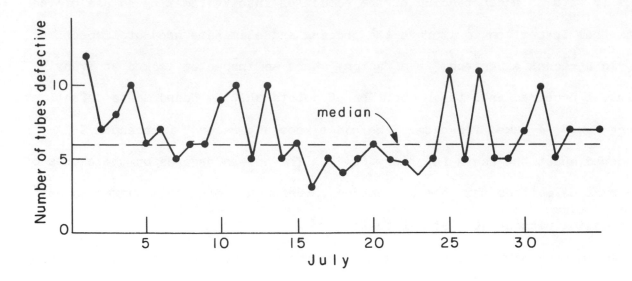

Fig. 7. A chart for the number of tubes found defective. A run of 11 points at or below the median occurs at
14-24 July, indicating a special cause of better quality
over this period.

the study could well be that the system for the inspection of tubes had gone bad
over the period of time that covered the 11 points.*

"We installed quality control." No. You can install a new desk, or a
new carpet, or a new Dean, but not quality control. Anyone that proposes to
"install quality control" unfortunately has little knowledge about quality
control.

---

* The interpretation of runs and of other statistical charts is sometimes
tricky. See A. Hald, STATISTICAL THEORY AND ENGINEERING APPLICATIONS (John
Wiley, 1965): pp. 338-360. I prefer to take a moving stretch of 30 to 60
points as background for a run chart for a process not in statistical control.

Quality control, to be successful in any company, must be a learning process, year by year, top management leading the whole company. As the president of a large corporation (one of my clients) put it, statistical quality control will last here as long as I am around. He had the right idea. There are no short cuts.

The unmanned computer. A computer can be a blessing. It can also be a curse. Some people make good use of computers. Few people are aware, however, of the negative input of computers. Time and time again, in my experience, when I ask for data on inspection, to learn whether they indicate that the process is in control, or out of control, and at what time of day it went out, and why, or ask about differences between inspectors and between production workers, or between production workers and inspectors, in an attempt to find sources of trouble and to improve efficiency, the answer is, "The data are in the computer." And there they sit.

People are intimidated by the computer. They can't tell it what data or charts they need: instead, they take whatever the computer turns out, which is reams of figures.

A large company produces wheels in one of their plants. Every wheel is subjected to a uniformity test. (Engineers and physicists will recognize a uniformity test as a measure of the running balance of the wheel.) We suppose here that the instruments that perform and record the results of the tests are reliable. The plant manager finds on his desk every morning a statistical summary of the tests of yesterday's production:

-- The average quality of the uniformity tests, by style of wheel.
-- The standard deviation of these tests.
-- The standardized 4th moment coefficient of these tests.
-- The number of defective wheels (the number that would not be accepted by the customer, for example).

Officials of this company supposed that this summary was quality control. It cost enough. Actually, this information is a total loss to the plant manager. At first, he would try this change and that change, only to be hopeful one day when the number of defective wheels decreased, despondent the next, when the number of defectives went up. After a time, he sensibly ceased to pay any attention to the report. He decided that he had had enough problems without, in addition, this nonsense dumped in his lap every morning.

Why throw away a wealth of information in the data of inspection that could be used to improve the process? The same electronic machinery could place on the manager's desk every morning a control chart, or a run chart, that would show him whether the process was in statistical control. It would show, for example, when trouble occurred, at 10 o'clock yesterday. "Ah, just when we dumped in that batch of graphite from the new vendor. Maybe that caused the trouble."

In other words, sense could be made from these costly figures from inspection if the figures were mixed with brains.

It is my advice that many companies ought to take a hard look at their so-called information-systems. Stacks of machine-sheets are not information in useful form. An information-system, to be useful, would produce a report on a page or two to indicate where trouble occurred recently, plus charts to show the effect of attempts to eliminate the trouble and to improve the system. Micro-films and storage-systems are not the best answer to the so-called explosion of information. A better answer is reduction of tons of figures to a few meaningful pages and charts.

> "I'm buying another $3,000,000 machine," a Vice President of a large insurance company said to me, to which I remarked, "What you need around your place is $300,000 worth of brains."

OBSTACLES AND PROBLEMS

I told this joke at a lecture one time at American University. Afterward, a dozen people stayed a while to talk, and a Mr. Edward R. Kingman made this pungent observation:

It is easy to buy $3,000,000 worth of hardware. Any of four companies will be delighted to write up the purchase order for me. They know exactly how to do it. They can convince your management that you can not live without this purchase. All that you have to do is to sign your name to the purchase order. But to buy brains--that requires knowledge, and there is no one to help you to write a purchase order for brains. There are no specifications and no catalog of candidates--in fact, no candidates.

Purchasing departments must learn new careers. This is a temporary obstacle, which is melting away as buyers learn about process control and how to apply statistical methods in their own work.

The supposition that it is only necessary to meet specifications. Specifications can not tell the whole story. The supplier must know what the material is to be used for. For example, a specification for sheet steel of a certain composition and thickness is not sufficient for the inside door panel of an automobile. The inside panel must undergo a considerable amount of stretching and warping. If the supplier knows that the steel will be used for the inside panel, he may be able to supply steel that will do the job. Steel that merely meets the specifications can cause a lot of trouble.

A programmer has a similar problem. She learns, after she finishes the job, that she programmed very well the specifications as delivered to her, but that they were deficient. If she had only known the purpose of the program, she could have done it right for the purpose, even though the specifications were deficient.

The problem is not merely to find good vendors for good parts. Two vendors may both be able to meet your requirements for statistical evidence of quality, and both make superb product. There may nevertheless be a problem in change-over from the cylinder heads made in the United States to cylinder heads made in Italy. Both are of excellent quality, but five hours are required to change from one to the other.

A still more serious problem exists in the manufacture of complex apparatus, such as a fibre glass cable to run from one city to another. The system requires more than a good cable. It requires repeaters and loading coils, carrier equipment and filters, and a myriad of other essential items of equipment. These items are not bricks and mortar to be put together by a skilled workman. They must be designed together, tested over and over in small subassemblies, modified as required, then in a multitude of bigger subassemblies, and so on.

Anyone who has bought his computer equipment from several sources can testify to problems. Whatever happens, any trouble is always laid to some other part of the equipment, made by someone else.

My friend Robert Piketty of Paris put it this way. Listen to the Royal Philharmonic Orchestra of London play Beethoven's Fifth Symphony. Now listen to some amateur orchestra play it. Of course, you like both performances: you enjoy home-grown talent. Both orchestras met the specifications: not a mistake. But listen to the difference. Just listen to the difference!

The aim in production should be to continually improve the process to the point where the distribution of the chief quality-characteristics of parts and materials is so narrow that the specifications are lost beyond the horizon. This is happening in Japan.

<u>Anyone that comes to try to help us must understand all about our business</u>. All evidence points to the fallacy of this supposition. Competent men in every position, if they are doing their best, know all that there is to know about their work except how to improve it. Help toward improvement can

OBSTACLES AND PROBLEMS

come only from some other kind of knowledge. Help may come from outside the company, combined with knowledge already possessed by people within the company, but not being utilized.

B. NOTES MADE BY A STATISTICIAN ON HIS ROUNDS

Heard and seen

1. The customer's specifications are often far tighter than he needs. It would be interesting to ask a customer how he measures the items that he says must conform to his specifications, and why he needs the tolerances that he specifies.

2. We rejected a load of material and returned it to the vendor. He sent it back to us, and this time our inspection passed the lot. He learned in a hurry what to do. In fact, our two drivers met each other over coffee on the road, we returning a load, they returning a rejected load to see if it would pass on second trial.

3. Figures on the amount of rework do not provide a signpost on how to reduce it. They do provide, however, a basis for understanding the magnitude of the problem. Anyone can see what rework is costing us, and that we would be justified in spending a lot of money to learn how to reduce it substantially.

4. Our budget allows us 6 per cent for rework. Just think how profits of the company would soar if we had no rework! The allowance of 6 per cent provides no incentive to do better. It becomes a work standard: meet it, but don't beat it.

5. A complicated machine requires a special oil, expensive. The plant manager had orders to cut expenses. He did. He bought oil locally from a dealer at a big saving. Result: repairs $7500.

6. Machine out of order, but running, turning out product, every piece wrong, yet usable. Final product, blemished. The operator had reported three times that this machine was out of order, but nothing had yet happened.

7. There are 1100 parts on each circuit board. By terms laid down by the government, every piece must be inspected by four people, and signed, the fourth one being the government's inspector. This means 4400 signatures for one circuit board. We have more trouble with the signatures than with the circuit boards. For example, all four men failed to inspect a part. We have to bring all four men back here to inspect the part and sign the record. All four men inspected a part, but one of them failed to sign for it. Where is he?

8. Foreman to production worker in response to question: "Just do your job."

9. Woman on the job held up by wrong count. She was making a batch of 24 items. A box of a certain part turned up one short. Result: 35 minutes lost for search for a part of the right size.

10. Samples of shoes sent out; orders are coming in. Production is ready to start, but for one hitch: the purchasing department can not find material to match well enough the color and texture of the samples. No one had foreseen this difficulty.

11. We shipped to the customer a machine. I looked at it on the customer's premises, before he started it up. I could see that it would leak abrasive. I did not wish to tell the customer that it was defective. I told a man in our service department about it. He said that he knew that it would leak, but that he could do nothing about it, because the people in engineering design would not believe him until it failed in operation. It failed, and brought down upon the customer delay of five weeks. He is withholding $10,000 for loss in production. (Related to me by Miss Kate McKeown.)

OBSTACLES AND PROBLEMS

12. Somebody in engineering made an error in design, in the nature of an oversight, so that the flighting on an auger that carries abrasive to an elevator continued past the elevator's boot and on to a bearing, and on through the seal. This happened three times. Finally, a service engineer discovered the cause of the problem and simply reversed several inches of flighting. There is no system by which these troubles may be reported. The manufacturing department continues right along with the same construction. Servicemen continue right along to make the necessary correction at every installation. The people in engineering may never learn about the fault.

13. Operator running four lathes simultaneously. "Before I had the control chart, I could not tell what I was doing. I could only learn later: too late. We were making one defective item out of ten. Now I can see what I am doing before it is too late. The three of us on the three shifts use the same chart. We do not need to make adjustments when we come on the job. We can see where we are at. We are now making no defectives. I am happier." "Why are you happier?" "Because I am not making any defects now."

14. A housing authority put up one hundred dwelling units in an area for low-cost housing. The government engaged three inspectors to report on the construction, once it was finished. When winter came, occupants of dwelling units found bills for heat in the neighborhood of $300 per month, not fitting to the bank accounts of occupants of low-cost housing. Why was the cost of heating so high? No insulation in the attic, was the answer. All three inspectors declared that they were aware of the failure of the builder to put in insulation in the attic, but each one decided not to make note of the failure, as he was sure that the other two inspectors would not observe it, and he wished not to discredit his colleagues.

15. We have been making brake lining all these years, and we never understood what we were doing, nor what brake lining the customer wished to have. We had many arguments; in fact, nothing but, though he did take our brake lining, such as it was. Perhaps he had no other source to depend on. We decided a few years ago to work together, to develop operational definitions of what he wished to have, and what we could make. Of course, this was a big job, because brake lining is measured by many characteristics. We now furnish to the customer $\bar{x}$- and R-charts for the chief characteristics of the brake lining that he buys from us, and we have no problems.

16. Before.

--   1.15 per cent of parts produced were scrapped.

--   13 per cent of parts produced required rework because of oversize or undersize diameters.

--   The cutting operation was not capable of producing parts within the specification of .05mm, even though it was in statistical control. The problem thus required action on the system.

--   The operator's test of every part that he produced did not halt production of defective items.

After.

--   Three parts in 10,000 are rejected for being oversize or undersize.

--   Repair and scrap are nil.

--   First-run capability and productivity have improved by incorporating the machining of this diameter at an existing multi-wheel grinding machine.

--   Tools at the turning operation have been eliminated. They are no longer required.

--   The life of the grinding wheel for this characteristic is now considerably longer than it was.

17. The process was in control, but it was producing one defective item in seven (cam shafts). We relied on inspection to find the defective items. Everybody had his own idea about what was wrong.

OBSTACLES AND PROBLEMS

We changed the process; used grinding instead of cutting. Rejects descended to 7 in 10,000.

At this level, the instruments used for inspection may introduce uncertainty of this magnitude.

Next step: improve instruments and the process of grinding.

We discovered that the instrument was off slightly, giving false indications. We are now producing zero defects.

18. We tried QC-Circles amongst the hourly workers, without first educating the management into their responsibilities to remove obstacles reported. We learned our lesson the hard way: our QC-Circles disintegrated.

19. Our quality control department takes care of quality. The rest of us don't need to worry about it.

20. An airline cut out first class on some aeroplanes, put in three seats for second class where there had been two seats for the first class, but left the overhead lights as they were--two lights for three passengers, not one of the two lights in the right spot for the new arrangement. An example of disregard for the customer to save expense.

21. We have for 25 years been working on problems, and not on the processes that caused the problems.

Chapter 3

C. AMERICAN MANAGEMENT HAS MISSED THE POINT.

THE POINT IS MANAGEMENT ITSELF.

By Yoshi Tsurumi

American managers have been impressed, especially after touring Japanese businesses. Over the past year hundreds of businesses in this country have experimented with quality control circles. Yet very few of the fifty large Japanese manufacturing firms here have extensively used quality control circles. Most Japanese managers know that the establishment of them is not the first but the last step in building a corporate culture that will support a company's total commitment to product quality and high productivity.

No concept has been more misunderstood by American managers, academics, and workers than productivity. For workers in America a call for increased productivity carries with it the threat of layoffs. Managers understand productivity to be an economic trade-off between efficiency and product quality. Business-school courses on management are often watered down to numerical games of inventory control and production flow in which financial budgeting and tight control are oversold as effective management tools. On production floors and in corporate offices, sociological verbiage has replaced a basic understanding of human behavior.

Attempts to cope with the human side of labor have often been superficial. American managers have come up with solutions both to soothe emotions and to boost lagging production. Workers now greet these management fads with skepticism, having seen too many of them come and go. Background music and suggestion boxes and psychological counseling were tried and abandoned. These efforts are just naive attempts, workers say, to get them to work harder. Are quality control circles any different? they ask, especially after one electronics firm that had acted on the idea abruptly laid off workers so it could meet its budgeted profit.

OBSTACLES AND PROBLEMS

General Motors' solution to its productivity problems was to promote belatedly a quality control manager to the rank of executive and to initiate a "quality of work life" program, which included employee participation groups similar to the Japanese quality control circles. But GM still lays off its workers during a decline in sales or when certain product lines are discontinued. And U.S. auto companies tend to shift costs and risks of business adjustments to society at large. It is true, however, that under employee participation groups, incidences of both absenteeism and union grievance have decreased.

In Japan, when a company has to absorb a sudden economic hardship such as a 25 per cent decline in sales, the sacrificial pecking order is firmly set. First the corporate dividends are cut. Then the salaries and the bonuses of top management are reduced. Next, management salaries are trimmed from the top to the middle of the hierarchy. Lastly, the rank and file are asked to accept pay cuts or a reduction in the work force through attrition or voluntary discharge. In the United States, a typical firm would probably do the opposite under similar circumstances.

Quality control circles can never replace management's fundamental responsibility to redefine its role and rebuild the corporate culture. As long as management is quick to take credit for a firm's successes but equally swift to blame its workers for its failures, no surefire remedy for low productivity can be expected in American manufacturing and service industries.

Big Japanese corporations treat human resources as their most renewable resources. The hiring, the training, and the promotion of employees and managers are the responsibility of the corporation as a whole. Even a chief executive officer does not dangle the threat, implied or otherwise, of firing a subordinate. Instead, it is management's job to encourage working toward the shared goals of the firm by helping to satisfy the human needs of job satisfaction and self-fulfillment.

One Japanese plant manager who turned an unproductive U.S. factory into a profitable venture in less than three months told me: "It is simple. You treat American workers as human beings with ordinary human needs and values. They react like human beings." Once the superficial, adversarial relationship between managers and workers is eliminated, they are more likely to pull together during difficult times and to defend their common interest in the firm's health.

Without a cultural revolution in management, the quality-control-circle alternative will not produce the desired effects for American private and public corporations. Nor can anyone guarantee that job security for the rank and file would be enough to produce high productivity and product quality. However, without a management commitment to the personal welfare of its workers, it will be impossible to inspire employees' interest in company productivity and product quality. With guaranteed job security, management's job becomes far more difficult and challenging.

For the first time in its history, the United States faces the job of managing economic growth with an increasing scarcity of capital, raw materials, energy sources, managerial skill, and market opportunities. There are strained business-government relations and antagonistic management-employee relations. It is not going to be easy for the U.S. to learn Japan's secret.*

---

* Condensed from Dr. Tsurumi's article in The Dial, September 1981. I am deeply indebted to Dr. Tsurumi for the privilege to include in this book his enlightening article. I am also indebted to the publishers of The Dial.

OBSTACLES AND PROBLEMS

Chapter 4

WHEN?   HOW LONG?

Whoso removeth stones shall be hurt therewith; and he that
cleaveth wood shall be endangered thereby.--Ecclesiastes 10:v.9.

Rehearsal of some of the problems. We live in a society dedicated to
dividends, organization, decision, orders from top to bottom, confrontation
(every idea put forth must win or lose), and all-out war to destroy the
competition at home or abroad. Take no prisoners. There must be winners, and
there must be losers. This may not be the road to better material living.

We live in an era in which everyone expects to see an ever-rising standard
of living. A little arithmetic sometimes helps to clarify thinking. Whence
cometh the ever-increasing supply of worldly goods that build up an ever-
increasing supply of food, clothing, housing, transportation and other services?
It is difficult to understand how any economic upturn of importance can take
place in the United States till products made there become competitive at home
and abroad.

The only possible answer lies in better design and greater productivity.

Better management can bring improvement in both. The big question is, how
long will it be until top management becomes active in their responsibilities?
and then how long?

Can the management of a company adopt constancy of purpose for product and
service in the future as the prime reason for existence of the company, and hold
on to their jobs long enough to get started on this road?

Obstacle to constancy of purpose. Constancy of purpose to stay in business,
to provide jobs for our people, by planning now for product and service that

will have a market in the future, is vital, as earlier pages have explained. However, there are obstacles. Anyone that sets off on this course runs the risk of being dismissed for using funds that could otherwise be put into dividends. An example was recorded in Business Week for 15 March 1982. A man who had been engaged by a large company to lead plans for the future was dismissed because the dividends for the fourth quarter of 1981 took a dip.

Can stockholders understand that some part of earnings might well be plowed into plans for the future, into maintenance, into alterations of machinery and plant, into research, education, training? Would there be a stockholders' revolt if funds were used to keep the company in business?

Management has led stockholders to believe that dividends are a measure of management's performance. Some schools of business teach their students how to maximize profits. It may well be that stockholders are smarter than management. That is, stockholders, including managers of pension funds invested in industry, may be far more interested in growth and in future dividends than in today's dividends.

How long? How long will it take to change the climate? An advertising agency changed in a decade an entire nation with respect to one commodity.* Could an advertising agency change a nation's views on quick profits, to give to management a new outlook, and a chance to adopt constancy of purpose? If yes, how long would it take? A decade? Two?

A big ship, traveling at full speed, requires distance and time to turn around.

_____

* Edward Jay Epstein, "Have you ever tried to sell a diamond?" Atlantic, February 1982: pp. 23-34.

WHEN? HOW LONG?

How many years will pass before economists learn the new economics, and teach it? A decade?

How many more years will pass by before government regulatory agencies learn that the forces of competition for price do not solve the problems of quality and of service: that competition that destroys service may not be a desirable aim of regulation? Two decades? Three?

Regulatory agencies, victims of mandates that are not clear, not knowing how to take into account the interest of the public, may meanwhile continue to make it difficult for industry to improve productivity. They may wreck our system of telephone communication (best in the world) and transportation (whatever is left of it) under the tenet that competition for price is good for all. Hard lessons lie ahead.

The history of recent years is replete with examples of government regulations that were born of good intentions, but which wound up far deadlier than the disease that they were supposed to cure.--Editorial, Business Week, 3 July 1978, page 112.

But the problems of antitrust extend beyond that of a changing environment. Enforcement often loses sight of what should be the predominant question. How do we make America more productive? ... We still need further improvements in the ratio of intelligence to body weight in antitrust matters.--Lester C. Thurow, in Newsweek, 18 January 1982, page 63.

An additional factor (that inhibits productivity) is government regulation, which requires business to spend huge sums and man hours in complying with affirmative action, safety, and other programs. The cost of regulation to American business in 1976 alone was estimated at approximately $30 billion.

We all know about the miles and miles of red tape that banking has had to deal with. The Truth in Lending Act is a classic example. We have also had to hire huge legal staffs to cope with the red tape. --Leland S. Prussia, Chairman of the Board of the Bank of America, at the meeting of the Bank Administration Institute in Atlanta, 25 January 1982.

Chapter 4

Let us reflect further. Even when the management of a company embarks in earnest on the 14 points for quality, productivity, and competitive position, advancement will at the best appear to be sluggish. One must allow five years for the purchasing department to learn their new job and to put it into effect, namely, to shift from (a) search for lower prices and award of business to the lowest bidder, to (b) purchase based on evidence of quality as well as on price. Concurrently, a company may embark on other improvements, such as to cease dependence on mass inspection and reduction of the number of vendors to those that deliver their product along with statistical evidence of process control. Other points of the 14 will also require time, even in companies where the management has removed obstacles to constancy of purpose.

Companies with good management will require five years to remove the barriers that make it impossible for the hourly worker to take pride in his work. Many companies will require ten years.

When? It may be obvious to anyone, on reflection on the obstacles that we have seen, that a long thorny road lies ahead in American industry--10 to 30 years--to settle down to an acknowledged competitive position. This position along with the associated standard of living that lies ahead may be second place, may be fourth.

By that time, products that have been the backbone of export may dwindle or vanish, while new products swell forth from companies that are putting faith and resources into their own future.

Agricultural products have been helpful the past few years in our balance of trade: without them the deficit would be much larger than it is. Will soil and water hold out?

WHEN? HOW LONG?

It might be of interest to note that the business of agriculture has become ever more and more efficient to the point where today only three people in 100 in the United States are engaged in producing food, surplus and all. People in agriculture have never lost a chance to adopt immediately any possible practice that would improve efficiency. Incidentally, innovation in agricultural practice comes largely from experimental stations the world over, all of which use statistical methods for efficiency and reliability of tests.

In contrast, most of industry in the United States, especially the service industries, have been slow to adopt new knowledge and new methods.

Agriculture might become even more productive if governmental support of prices were removed.

Quick gains illusory. It is easy to be misled by quick gains, and to rest easy, supposing that the job is finished. This is what happened in the United States in 1942-1950. Brilliant fires here and there wrought by zealous applications of techniques burn out unless top management plows ahead on the 14 points for long-term planning.

Survival of the fittest. Who will survive? Companies that adopt constancy of purpose for quality, productivity, and service, and go about it with intelligence and perseverance, have a chance to survive. They must, of course, offer products and service that have a market. Charles Darwin's law of survival of the fittest, and that the unfit do not survive, holds in free enterprise as well as in nature's selection.

Actually, the problem will solve itself. The only survivors at the end of two decades will be companies with constancy of purpose for quality, productivity, and service.

Chapter 5

QUESTIONS FOR SELF-EXAMINATION

I held my tongue and spake nothing. I kept silence, yea, even
from good words, but it was pain and grief to me.--Psalm 39, v. 3

Purpose of this chapter. This chapter consists of questions that will
provide to management and the statistician a basic understanding of the problems in a company. These questions assist management's preparation for the
first meeting with the statistician, and they serve as well for continued
self-appraisal.

Preamble. The questions asked here will not be clear without some background. They should not be answered in a hurry. Some of them will require
time.

The questions

1.a. Has your company established constancy of purpose?

b. If yes, what is the purpose? If no, what are the obstacles?

c. Will this stated purpose stay fixed, or will presidents come and go?

d. Whom does your president answer to? Whom do your Board of Directors
answer to?

2.a. How do you define quality of one of your products or services? How
can you tell if your product is good?

b. Have you an operational definition for quality? That is, how do you
know whether you have achieved quality? (Take any one or two of your products
for illustration.)

c. In summary, what operational definitions of satisfactory quality have you formulated for assemblies, prototypes, and final products?

3.a. What is your program for development of new product and new service for the future?

b. How do you plan to test your new designs or ideas?

4.a. What do you know about the problems of your customers in the use of your products? What tests do you make of your products in service?

b. How do your customers see your product in relation to competitive products? How do you know? What data have you?

c. Why do they buy yours? How do you know? What data have you?

d. What problems or dissatisfaction do customers see in your product? How do you know? What data have you?

e. Same for the competition. How do you know?

5.a. Do your customers think that your product lives up to their expectations? What did your advertising and your salesmen lead your customers to expect? More than you can deliver? How do you know?

b. (If applicable.) Are your customers satisfied with the service that you or your dealers provide? If yes, what is satisfactory about it? The quality of workmanship? The lag between your call and appearance of the serviceman? How do you know?

6. What inspection or verification are you carrying out

-- On incoming materials?

-- In process?

-- Of final product?

Do not try to answer this question for every one of your products. Answer it for only three or four important products, or for three or four production lines.

7.a. How reliable is your inspection at each of these points? How do you know?

b. What data have you to show whether your inspectors are in line with each other?

c. What about your test instruments, or rather, your use of them? Can you present evidence of statistical control of the system of measurement or classification, visual? or by instrument?

8.a. Where is inspection being carried out where Chapter 13 would indicate that no inspection would minimize total cost?

b. At which points are you carrying out no inspection where by the theory of Chapter 13 you ought to inspect in order to minimize total cost?

9.a. What records do you keep of these inspections? In what form? In the form of control charts or run charts? If not, why not?

b. What other use do you make of the records that you keep?

c. If you keep no records, why don't you?

d. If you keep no records at some point, why don't you cut the inspection there?

10.a. How much material that goes into the production line is used in desperation by the production manager (invariably with waste of material or rework or both)? Try to answer the above question for two or three important production lines. How often do you encounter examples like these:

-- Material that met the specifications but was not suited to the process or to the finished product?

-- Inspection of an incoming material was considered to be necessary, but inspection was hurried or skipped, owing to high vacuum on the production side?

QUESTIONS FOR SELF-EXAMINATION

b. How much incoming material turns out to be totally unusable in the judgment of the production managers? (Again, for two or three important production lines.)

c. What system have you for report and correction of these problems?

11.a. Are you paying for defective product from your suppliers?

b. Who pays for defective incoming product? (Answer: you do.)

12.a. Does your purchasing department stick to the lowest bidder? If yes, why? and what is this policy costing you?

b. Does quality come into consideration? How?

c. Are your requirements of quality effective?

13.a. Do you have 2, 3, or 4 or more suppliers for the same part or material? If yes, why?

b. Would it be better to have one supplier for any one part or material? If yes, why do you have more than one? Can you obtain quality and statistical evidence of quality from each of several suppliers?

14.a. At which points do you use data from inspection (i) to detect by control charts or other statistical techniques a special cause of variation? (ii) to learn what proportion of the problems of rejection, waste, and productivity, belong to the system (the responsibility of management)?

b. What changes have you made recently in the system? What led you to this change? How do you know whether your efforts to alter the system had any effect, and in which direction?

15.a. What arrangements have you with your suppliers for receipt from them of evidence of statistical control, so that you may safely decrease inspection? What help are you giving to your suppliers?

96.

b.   What cooperative work are you carrying on with your suppliers to make sure that you are both talking about the same kind of centimeter, and same kind of test?

16.a.   What are you doing to make quality (and productivity) everybody's job, including management?

b.   Do you know the loss that ensues from a defective item or defective product or of a mistake at any point along the line?

17.   Are you still using Military Standard 105D or Dodge-Romig plans for purchase of materials? Why, in the light of Chapter 13?

18.   What proportion of your costs are chargeable to defects inherited from previous operations?

19.   What proportion of the troubles that you have with quality and productivity are the fault (i) of the production workers? (ii) of the system (management's responsibility)? How do you know?

20.   How much loss do you attribute to handling-damage (i) along the production line, (ii) in packing, transportation, installation? What data have you on these problems? What are you doing about them?

21.   What are you doing to improve the training of new employees?

22.   What are you doing to help employees that have been on the job a while?

23.a.   Do your people that are engaged in training understand when an employee is trained, and when he is not yet trained?

b.   Do they know that they have only one chance? That an employee once trained in statistical control can not be helped by further training in the same procedures?

24.   Do you depend on work standards? If yes, have you thought of a better way?

QUESTIONS FOR SELF-EXAMINATION

25.   Are you guilty of setting numerical goals for productivity and for proportion defective? Can you explain why? Did any such goal ever help anyone to do a better job?

26.   What are you doing about statistical education of your

— Management?

-- Engineers?

— Chemists, physicists?

-- Plant managers?

-- Foremen and supervisors?

-- Production workers, clerks, punch-operators, etc.?

-- Purchasing department?

-- People engaged in product testing, in consumer research, and in redesign of product?

-- Financial department?

-- Payroll department?

-- Personnel department?

— Data processing department?

27.   If you have a competent statistician in your company, are you making maximum use of his knowledge and ability? Is he teaching statistical methods to your management, engineers, chemists, physicists, production workers, foremen, supervisors, purchasing agents, in your department of commercial research and design of future product? Do you send him to statistical meetings? Is he working throughout your company to find problems and to find causes and results of corrective action? Is he working on all your problems of design, quality, procurement, specifications, testing of instruments? Does he have authority and responsibility to look anywhere in the company for problems, and to work on them? If not, why not?

28.a. Are you trying to set up your statistical work in conformity with Chapter 17?

b. If you have no competent statistician, what efforts are you putting forth to find one to help you with your problems of quality, productivity, procurements, redesign of product?

c. What effort have you made to discover people with knowledge of statistical theory right in your own company, and give them a chance to move into statistical work under competent leadership?

d. What are you doing to encourage these people to continue their studies of statistical theory?

29. What is your plan and what are you doing about it for removal of barriers that rob the hourly worker of his pride of workmanship?

Chapter 6

A VIEW OF HOW QUALITY BEGAN IN JAPAN

Do not confuse your wits with wisdom.--Tiresius to
Dionysus, in Euripedes's THE BACCHAE.

Wisdom sounds foolish to fools.--Dionysus to Cadmus,
in Euripedes's THE BACCHAE.

A. THE FOUR FORCES

Motive for this chapter. The whole world is familiar with the miracle of
Japan, and knows that the miracle started off with a concussion in 1950. Before that time, the quality of Japanese consumer goods had earned around the
world a reputation for being shoddy and cheap. Yet anyone in our Navy will
testify that the Japanese knew what quality is. They simply had not yet bent
their efforts toward quality in consumer goods.

Suddenly, Japanese quality and dependability of consumer goods turned upward
in 1950 and by 1954 had captured markets the world over. The new economic age
had begun. What forces caused the explosion in Japan? Answer: the four forces
in Fig. 8.

1. Japan's statisticians. Japan's statisticians had learned and
contributed new theory for enumerative studies for censuses as well as for
current reports on the labor force, nutrition, housing, and agricultural
production, and had also made important contributions to design of experiment
and to other lines of research. Work and conferences with them during 1947
on studies of nutrition, housing, agricultural production, fisheries, and
demographic characteristics, naturally expanded into industry. Japan's

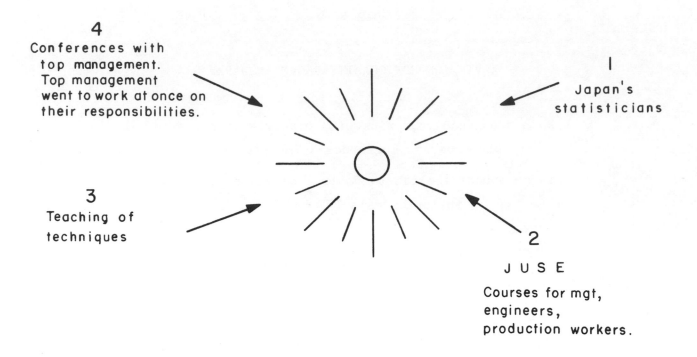

Fig. 8. Four forces came together in 1950 in Japan to
cause the explosion in quality and productivity.

statisticians might become their country's most important resource. Men from

the Bell Telephone Laboratories, on detail to the Central Communications Section

of General MacArthur's Headquarters, reinforced this thought and procured for

Japanese statisticians and engineers journals and books on the statistical

control of quality. As I understand it, the men of JUSE produced in Japan at

least one pamphlet on quality control, but it received only weak circulation.

A number of Japanese statisticians thus acquired some appreciation for the

contribution that statistical methods might make to Japanese industry. Some of

the men had already by 1950 seen successful application.

The men from the Bell Laboratories explained to members of JUSE
that statistical methods had improved accuracy of American weapons.
My friend Dr. E. E. Nishibori, listening to them, came forth with the
remark: "Yes, I know something about that. Six fire bombs landed on
my house during the war, and they were all duds."

2. <u>The Union of Japanese Science and Engineering</u>. This Union (better translated as society or Gesellschaft), known by its telegraphic code, JUSE, was formed in 1947 by Kenichi Koyanagi, the aim being reconstruction of Japan. Dr. Nishibori gave in 1949 under auspices of JUSE a short course in statistical methods in industry. The next step was to bring in a foreign expert. The invitation came in 1949.

3. <u>Teaching of techniques</u>. The first series of lectures commenced in June 1950, with the teaching of elementary, powerful statistical methods. Four hundred engineers took these courses in the summer of 1950. The content of the courses, and the method of teaching, opened up new ways to build statistical knowledge into the education of engineers. The text used was the pamphlet, "Guides for Quality Control," listed at the end of Chapter 7.

4. <u>Conferences with top management</u>. Statistical methods took fire in America around 1942, following a series of ten-day intensive courses for engineers, initiated by Stanford University on a suggestion from this author.* The war department also gave courses at factories of suppliers. Brilliant applications burned, sputtered, fizzled, and died out. What the men did was to solve individual problems. Control charts proliferated, the more the better. Quality control departments sprouted. They plotted charts, looked at them, and filed them. They took quality control away from everybody else, which was of course entirely wrong, as quality control is everybody's job. There was no

---

* W. Allen Wallis, "The Statistical Research Group," <u>Journal of the American Statistical Association</u>, vol. 75, 1980: pp. 320-335, page 321 in particular.

structure to teach management their responsibilities. Attempts by Dr. Holbrook Working, one of the instructors in the ten-day courses given in America in 1942-45, to reach management by inviting them to come to the course for half a day, were noble but ineffective.

It was vital not to repeat in Japan the mistakes made in America. Management must understand their responsibilities. The problem was how to reach top management in Japan. This hurdle was accomplished through the offices of Mr. Ichiro Ishikawa, president of the great Kei-dan-ren (Federated Economic Societies), and president of JUSE.

Mr. Ishikawa understood. He sent telegrams to all men in top management to ask them to come to the Industry Club. They all came. Further conferences with top management were held that summer of 1950, and still more on two trips to Japan in 1951; more in subsequent years. The subject of these conferences was the responsibility of management to institute constancy of purpose toward service, to improve the system through all stages of production, and to manage the use of statistical quality technology company-wide, from procurement of materials to the consumer, consumer research, innovation, and redesign of product. The simplified flow diagram in Fig. 9 was helpful in the conferences with top management. The message to put before them was that management must understand that the consumer is the most important part of the production line. It will be necessary for Japanese management to stand behind the performance of product. They must look ahead and design new products and services. They must work with vendors to improve the uniformity and dependability of incoming materials: teach them the improvement of quality as you learn it. This was, of course, the natural Japanese way of doing business. Management must give rigid attention to maintenance of equipment and to instructions and gauges (Chs. 10 and 13).

A VIEW OF HOW QUALITY BEGAN IN JAPAN

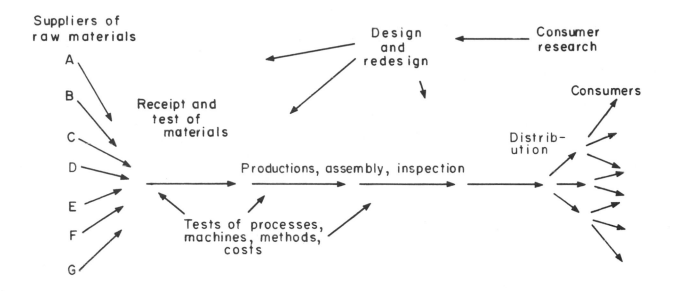

Fig. 9. Production viewed as a system. Improvement of
quality envelops the entire production line, from incoming
materials to the consumer, and redesign of product and service for the future. This chart was first used in August 1950
at a conference with top management at the Hotel de Yama on
Mt. Hakone in Japan. In a service organization, the sources
of A, B, C, etc., could be sources of data, or work from preceding operations, such as charges (as in a department store),
calculation of charges, deposits, withdrawals, inventories in
and out, transcriptions, shipping orders, etc.

Everyone in the company must attack improvement of quality, not just the

problems that walk in, but as a plan of knowledge by which to find problems and

the causes thereof. It will not suffice to have some brilliant successes here

and there. Disjointed efforts and successes here and there will have no

national impact. In short, efforts toward improvement of quality must be total.

Chapter 6

They must:

-- be COMPANY-WIDE.

-- be NATION-WIDE.

-- embrace EVERY ACTIVITY--procurement, design, instrumentation, manufacturing, consumer research, marketing, redesign.

Japanese management went to work with understanding of their responsibilities. Quality became at once in 1950 everybody's job.

B.   CONTINUATION OF EDUCATIONAL EFFORT

Expansion of education to management, engineers, foremen. JUSE, with confident support of Japanese industry, expanded on a vast scale education of management, engineers, and foremen, in rudiments of statistical methods for improvement of quality, and advanced statistical theory to statisticians and engineers. The plague of barriers that rob the hourly worker of his pride of workmanship in American companies today was zero or at a low level in Japan. Hourly workers could thus learn to make, understand, and use control charts.

The teaching of consumer research, with an introduction to modern methods of sampling, began in January 1951. The students divided themselves into teams for door-to-door enquiries into the needs of households for sewing machines, bicycles, and pharmaceuticals.

Dr. Joseph M. Juran made his first visit to Japan in 1954, at the request of JUSE. His masterful teaching gave to Japanese management new insight into the meaning of quality and management's responsibility to achieve it.

Between 1950 and 1970 JUSE taught statistical methods to 14,700 engineers and thousands of foremen. Courses in statistical quality technology for management at this writing are booked to capacity, in fact with a waiting

A VIEW OF HOW QUALITY BEGAN IN JAPAN

period of seven months. Courses in consumer research, taught by Japan's foremost statisticians, are in equal demand.

   Further notes in respect to top management in Japan. The first hurdle to overcome with top management in Japan in 1950 was the general supposition that it would be impossible for them to compete with industry of America and Europe in view of the reputation for shoddy quality of consumer goods that Japan had earned. The year 1950 was the beginning of a new Japan in quality. I predicted in 1950 that Japanese products would within five years invade the markets of the world, and that the standard of living in Japan would in time rise to equality with the world's most prosperous countries.

   Japanese management could not understand the basis for this prediction. Some of them have told me in recent years that their only hope in 1950 was that they might, in time, recover to the economic level that they had before the war. Top management in Japan nevertheless went to work with fervor and hope on innovation and in the production line (nothing unusual in Japan), and beat my prediction. Statistical symbols and methods became in Japan a second language for everybody, including hourly workers.

   The basis for my confidence in this prediction was (1) observations on the Japanese work force; (2) knowledge and devotion to their jobs of Japanese management, and their eagerness to learn; (3) faith that Japanese management would accept and carry out their responsibilities; (4) expansion of education by JUSE.

   Encouragement from immediate results. Mr. Keizo Nishimura of the Furukawa Electric Company reported within six months reduction to 10 per cent of its former level the amount of rework in insulated wire in the cable plant at Nikko, and equal success in the manufacture of cable; also great reduction in the frequency of accidents. Productivity soared.

Mr. Kenichi Koyanagi (deceased 1965), founder and Managing Director of the Union of Japanese Science and Engineering, reported at the meeting of the American Society for Quality Control in Rochester in 1952, great strides in quality and output that had been made by 13 Japanese companies within a year and a half after the first courses of 1950. These 13 reports were every one written by men in top management.* These men were out in the plants at work. Examples follow.

Mr. Gohei Tanabe, President of Tanabe Pharmaceutical Company, reported that within a year after the conferences of 1950, through improvement of the process, his company was producing three times as much PAS (para-aminosalicylic acid) as they had been getting earlier with the same people, same machines, same plant.

Fuji Steel Company reported reduction of 29 per cent in the fuel required to produce a ton of steel.

Examples like this spread the word throughout Japan that improvement of quality means improvement of the process, which in turn improves the product and productivity.

Year by year, the Japanese have advanced their understanding and use of statistical methods, company-wide and nation-wide, and have learned them and absorbed them in the Japanese way, and have given them back to the world in a demonstration of industrial might and service to the consumer never known before.

It has been said that all Japanese industry has achieved the best practice in the control of quality. This is not so. Five of the horrible examples

---

* Kenichi Koyanagi, "Statistical quality control in Japanese industry," report to the Congress of the American Society for Quality Control held in Rochester, 1952.

A VIEW OF HOW QUALITY BEGAN IN JAPAN

recorded in this book, of what not to do, came from Japan--from big companies, not small ones. There are still some large companies in Japan and a lot of small ones that depend too much on 100 per cent inspection, not sure of their quality.

Some companies in Japan, as in America, have plants that are located far away from courses in statistics. One company in Kyushu is solving the problem by arranging for a teacher to come weekly from Hakata.

C. QC-CIRCLES

QC-Circles. A fifth force was added in 1960, the formalization of QC-Circles by Dr. K. Ishikawa. A QC-Circle is the natural Japanese way of working together. Dr. Ishikawa brought to the attention of management the importance of making full use of the successes of small groups of workers in the elimination of special causes of variability of product, and in improvement of the system, through changes in tools, changes in design, and in scheduling and even in alterations of the production process. Accomplishments of a QC-Circle in one spot may well have wide application throughout the company and in other companies. It is the responsibility of management to carry the fire from one success to another.

A QC-Circle uses simple statistical techniques such as scatter diagrams, Pareto diagrams (feature or Ishikawa diagrams), control charts, to discover which possible sources of trouble that they can govern are most important, and to eliminate them (usually one at a time).*

---

* Kaoru Ishikawa, GUIDE TO QUALITY CONTROL, Asian Productivity Organization, Tokyo, 1980. Obtainable in the United States from Unipub, 345 Park Avenue South, New York 10016.

I venture the opinion that QC-Circles have little chance of success in a climate of insecurity where people that work in a place have a suspicion that they will be dumped when business slacks off.

A QC-Circle requires months to get into action. One can imagine the hopelessness, when business picks up, of trying to reconstitute a QC-Circle, composed of new employees and old ones and some rehired. The motto of Tokai Rika Company reads as follows:

    We will never separate ourselves from an employee
or from a subscriber (customer or supplier).

This same sentiment pervades Japanese industry. No elaboration of reasons why Japanese workers work for the good of the company is necessary. It is also important to note that the bond between vendor and purchaser is almost as strong as the bond between employee and company, with the same mutual trust between them.

The journal Quality Control For The Foreman, established in 1960 by JUSE and edited by Dr. K. Ishikawa, enables QC-Circles all over Japan to learn from each other. Exchange visits to other companies, and regional conventions of QC-Circles, stimulate interest of members. The national convention in Tokyo brings 1800 members together from all over Japan, from the total spectrum of products and services. Leaders of QC-Circles that have achieved extraordinary results are selected by their companies for group tours, arranged by JUSE, to plants in America and in Europe.

One of the hundred reports given at the national convention of the QC-Circles held in Tokyo in November 1980 was an explanation of how with rearrangement of work, five people now do the same work that previously required seven.

A VIEW OF HOW QUALITY BEGAN IN JAPAN

Translated, 100 people can now do the work of 140. Forty people did not lose their jobs: they merely transferred to other work.

Contributions like this help to put the company in better competitive position, with the ultimate result that the company will need more employees, not fewer.

A QC-Circle can not thrive if no one in management is eager to listen to a suggestion and to take action on it. A QC-Circle can not thrive when barriers rob hourly workers of dignity and of their right to pride of workmanship.

What about QC-Circles in America? QC-Circles should be spontaneous, with appreciation of management, but not pushed. Most QC-Circles in America are, I fear, management's hope for a lazy way out, management in desperation. QC-Circles are a raging disease in America, and are even worse in some other countries. They can accomplish nothing unless the management is prepared to act on suggestions from the QC-Circle. This is a rare circumstance, I fear.

Unfortunately, most reports of successful results from QC-Circles in the United States are rediscovery of the Hawthorne effect.* It burns out.

The best place to start a QC-Circle in America is with the management. For example, managers of purchasing need to follow through the production lines the materials that they purchase. This would call for a QC-Circle consisting of purchasing, production, research, engineering design, and sales. Many companies already have a QC-Circle in management but never thought of them as QC-Circles. QC-Circles composed of supervisors and inspectors are excellent, and will be spontaneous with a little encouragement. The letter that follows has been helpful to the author.

----

* Fritz J. Roethlisberger and William J. Dickson, MANAGEMENT AND THE WORKER (Harvard University Press, 1939).

Chapter 6

In the seminars, many participants asked about QC-Circles (QC-C).
Besides, I have heard that many plants in the world are now starting
QC-Cs. Many executives and managers might be possessed with serious
illusion that, if they succeed in establishing QC-Cs they could solve
major problems in their plants. Then, they would not begin any
management improvement activities for quality by themselves. There is
no doubt that QC-Circles are a very powerful force to solve problems
in quality and productivity at the operational level, but it should be
well understood that a QC-Circle is not a cure-all. Defects are
caused not only by faulty operation of workers, but also usually more
seriously and frequently by poor design, poor specifications, poor
education and training, poor arrangement and maintenance of machines,
and so on. These are all problems of management, which a QC-Circle can
not solve.--Excerpt from a letter from my friend Dr. Noriaki Kano of
the University of Electro-Communications, Tokyo.

The reader will recall also similar remarks by Dr. Tsurumi, page 84.

Chapter 7

THE TWO BASIC SOURCES OF IMPROVEMENT

For indeed, he that preaches to those that have ears but hear not
makes of himself a nuisance.--Geoffrey Chaucer, The Tale of Melibeus.

My two ears ache from all your worthless speech.--
Geoffrey Chaucer, Prologue to Melibeus.

A. SPECIAL CAUSES: COMMON CAUSES: IMPROVEMENT OF SYSTEM

Purpose of this chapter. We have already seen in a number of examples how
simple but powerful statistical techniques point to the type of action that
will lead to reduction of waste and improvement of productivity and competitive
position. There will be more examples in this chapter and in later chapters.
The main aim in this chapter is to summarize some of the essential points about
statistical charts. This book is not a book on techniques. The aim is,
instead, only to show where techniques fit into the education of top management
for improvement of quality and productivity and competitive position. The
reader who wishes to pursue study of techniques is advised to place himself
under the guidance of a competent teacher, with help from some of the pamphlets
and books listed at the end of this chapter.

We saw a run chart in Chapter 1, Fig. 1. It indicated that any substantial
improvement must come from a change in the system, the responsibility of
management. We take a look now at a portion of another run chart, Fig. 10, a
simple exhibit of the number of miles per gallon from one filling to another of
the tank on a vehicle. The points vary from one filling to another, sometimes
close to the average, sometimes well above the average, sometimes below. The
average of 25 miles per gallon had already been established for warm weather.

Suddenly, the mileage dropped below average on nine successive fillings. Nine
points fell below the average. What was the cause? Two or three successive
points below the average, or above, we might expect, but nine points indicate a
special cause of variation.*

The explanation of the special cause could be any or a combination of a
list of possibilities--cold weather (perhaps on a trip to the mountains), water
in the gasoline, short runs, spark plugs. New spark plugs brought the mileage
back to its historic level.

Many companies that own automobiles and trucks (2,000,000? in the U.S.)
keep an accurate record of miles traveled and of gallons of fuel purchased.
They could make good use of the data. A simple run chart could be kept up to
date on each one by the driver for indication of trouble. A chart might
enchant the driver and open up a new world to the owner.

A statistical chart detects the existence of a cause of variation that lies
outside the system. It does not find the cause.

A run chart is not an instant indicator. A trend of seven or eight points,
or a run of seven or eight points below or above the average, will usually
indicate a special cause.

There are other kinds of charts, some of which we have already seen in
action. A control chart of $\bar{x}$ or for R, or both, will usually detect a special
cause or a change in the system with less data than a run chart will require.

---

* Shewhart used the term <u>assignable</u> cause of variation where I use the term
<u>special cause</u>. I prefer the adjective <u>special</u> for a cause that is specific to
some group of workers, or to a particular production worker, or to a specific
machine, or to a specific local condition. The word to use is not important;
the concept is, and this is one of the great contributions that Dr. Shewhart
gave to the world.

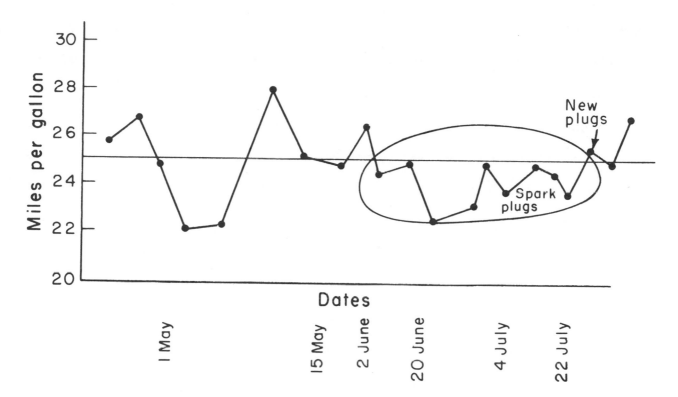

Fig. 10. Portion of a run chart for miles per gallon
between fillings of the tank. The run of nine points below
the average detected a change. The cause was bad spark
plugs. This example was furnished by Messrs. Frank
Belchamber and Robert B. M. Jameson of Nashua Corporation.

What is more, $\bar{x}$- and R-charts will detect a shrinkage in spread (shift to
greater uniformity), which is not easy to see on a run chart. Once statistical
control is achieved, improvement from then onward will depend almost totally on
efforts of engineers, chemists, and other experts to improve the process in any
way possible. We learned this in Chapter 1.

A first lesson in application of statistical theory. Courses in statistics
often commence with study of distributions and comparison of distributions.
Students are not warned in classes nor in the books that for analytic purposes
(such as to improve a process), distributions and calculations of mean, mode,

standard deviation, chi-square, t-test, etc., serve no useful purpose for improvement of a process unless the data were produced in a state of statistical control. The first step in the examination of data is accordingly to question the state of statistical control that produced the data. The easiest way to examine data is to plot points in order of production to learn whether any use can be made of the distribution formed by the data.

As an example, we turn attention to a distribution that appears to have all the good qualities that one could ask for, but which was misleading, not just useless. Fig. 11 shows the distribution of measurements made on 50 springs used in a camera of a certain type. Each measurement is the elongation of the spring under a pull of 20 g. The distribution is symmetrical, and both tails fall well within the specifications. One might therefore be tempted to conclude that the process is satisfactory.

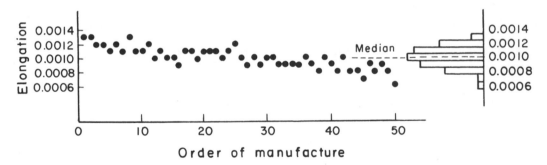

Fig. 11. Run chart for 50 springs tested in order of manufacture. The data form a symmetrical distribution, but when plotted in order of manufacture they show that the distribution is useless. The distribution would not, for example, tell us what specifications might be met. The reason is that there is no identifiable process.

However, the elongations plotted one by one in the order of manufacture show a downward trend. Something is wrong with the process of manufacture, or with the measuring instrument.

THE TWO BASIC SOURCES OF IMPROVEMENT

Any attempt to use the distribution in Fig. 11 would be futile. The standard deviation of the distribution, for example, would have no predictive value. It would tell nothing about the process, because there is no stable process. Analysis of variance, t-test, and other statistical techniques taught in the books would be not only useless but misleading. Such methods are inefficient: they bury important information in the data. Most computer packages for analysis of data, as they are called, provide flagrant examples of inefficiency.

We have thus learned a very important lesson in statistical analysis—look at the data. A few minutes with pencil and paper will answer most of the questions that one could ask of the data.

We learned another simple lesson on pages 2 and 5: plot the points; don't just compute the average.

The two sources of improvement. Improvement of a process can come from removal of a special cause of variation or from action on the system.

Constant improvement is management's responsibility. Most causes of low quality and productivity belong to the system.

Special causes of variation, detected by a point that falls outside a control limit.

The term common causes for faults of the system was used first, so far as I know, in a conversation held about 1947 with Dr. Harry Alpert (deceased), on the subject of riots in prisons. The term appeared in print in 1956.*

Simple statistical techniques separate out the responsibilities for action into different levels of administration. A point beyond a control limit, or a sustained, important difference between accident-rates in two areas, a trend or a run, all point to the existence of a SPECIAL CAUSE of variation NOT COMMON to all the lots or to all the areas involved.

---

* W. Edwards Deming, "On the use of theory," Industrial Quality Control, vol. viii, No. 1, July 1956: pp. 12-14.

One of the main aims in improvement of quality is to reduce variation of product. The only safe guide to the cause of variation, to detect the existence of a special cause, is use of statistical signals. The naked eye looking at figures is not a safe guide: it is a hazard. Judgment is always wrong with a perfect track record.

The discovery of a special cause of variation, and its removal, are usually the responsibility of someone who is connected directly with some operation. It is his job to find the cause, and to remove it. In the case of accident rates, a significant difference indicates the existence of causes specific to a certain area.

As we learned in Chapter 2, however, any attempt to use statistical techniques under conditions that rob the hourly worker of his right to pride of workmanship will lead to disaster.

In contrast, there are common causes of defectives, of errors, of low rates of production, of low sales, of accidents. These are the responsibility of management. A list of common causes appears further on. Poor sales may stem from a faulty product, or from unwarranted high price. The worker at a machine can do nothing about causes common to all machines. He is responsible only for the special causes chargeable to him. He can not do anything about the light; he does not purchase raw materials; the training, supervision, and the company's policies are not his.

Common causes (faults of the system) stay on the job until corrected or reduced (Juran). Elimination or reduction of common causes can be effected ONLY BY ACTION OF MANAGEMENT. Special causes, in contrast, come and go and return, unless apprehended and eliminated.

Confusion between common causes and special causes leads to frustration of everyone, and leads to greater variability and to higher costs, exactly contrary to what is needed. Unaided by statistical techniques, man's natural reaction to trouble of any kind, such as an accident, high rejection rate, stoppage of production, is to blame the operators. Anything bad that happens, it might seem, is somebody's fault.

"Bill," I asked of the manager of a company engaged in motor freight, "how much of this trouble (shortage and damage) is the fault of the drivers?" His reply, "All of it," was a guarantee that this level of loss will continue until he learns that the main causes of trouble belong to the system, which is for Bill to work on.

The usual explanation offered by the man on the street for recall of automobiles is careless workmanship. This is entirely wrong. The fault, where there is any, lies with management. The fault may be in the design of some part, or in failure of management to listen to the results of tests, being too eager to put a new product on to the market before the competition beats him to it. Management may disregard early warning from tests conducted by the company's own engineers, and reports of trouble from customers. No amount of care or skill in workmanship can overcome such fundamental faults in the system.

The boost in morale of the production worker, if he were to perceive a genuine attempt on the part of management to work on the 14 points of Chapter 2 and to hold the production worker responsible only for what he can govern, and not for handicaps placed on him by the system, would be hard to overestimate.

Ups and downs often lead management into costly mistakes. For example, at the headquarters of a railway, high-priced officials were concerned about the performance of the company's agent in Minneapolis. He sold last week only three carloads to a certain shipper (meaning that three loaded cars would move over the tracks of this railway). The year before during this same week he had sold four carloads to this shipper. What has happened? The men were ready to send off to the agent a telegram to ask for an explanation, but were halted by a brief exposition on the nature of variation. Agents of railways all over the country spend time explaining small variations in sales like this. They would make more sales if they would spend their time calling on shippers instead of trying to explain to headquarters nonsensical reasons for small variation. The fact is that constant sales week to week would indicate that the man had juggled his report to smooth out the variation, and to avoid setting new standards.

Spindles halt in a spinning mill. The cause of a halt could be mechanical trouble in the spindle, or it could be a fault in the yarn. The manager had been keeping track of breakage, and had directed the efforts of the mechanic toward spindles that broke down most during the preceding week. What he needs to know is whether a spindle is in need of attention or whether the efforts of the mechanic should be directed toward maintenance of all spindles on a rotation basis. A run chart would show whether there are cycles or runs. For example, it might disclose a problem with some kind of yarn.

Let r_i be the number of halts for Spindle i over a specified run, such as 40 hours. (A change of yarn or of specification would end the run.) If the run chart shows pretty good statistical control, then a suggestion might be to plot the distribution of $\sqrt{r_i}$ for every spindle. Compute Average $\sqrt{r_i}$. Useful limits for the distribution of $\sqrt{r_i}$ would be

$$\sqrt{Av\ r} \pm 1.5$$

A spindle that falls beyond the upper limit raises a question. It may have had special usage or it may be in immediate need of special maintenance. A spindle below the lower limit is an extra good spindle, or had special usage. (The square-root transformation is explained in almost any book on statistical theory: cf. the list of books at the end of this chapter.)

THE TWO BASIC SOURCES OF IMPROVEMENT

Spindles that do not fall outside the above limits are simply spindles, to take their turn at regular maintenance.

"We rely on our experience." This is the answer that came from the manager of quality in a large company recently, when I enquired how he distinguishes between the two kinds of trouble, and on what principles. This answer is self-incriminating: it is a guarantee that this company will continue to pile up about the same amount of trouble as in the past. Why should it change?

Experience without theory teaches nothing. In fact, experience can not even be recorded unless there is some theory, however crude, that leads to a hypothesis and a system by which to catalog observations.* Sometimes only a hunch is sufficient theory to lead to useful observation.

Wrong style of supervision: incentive to employees. It was rumored that a large airline offered to the employees thereof an increase in pay of 3.5 per cent if earnings on gross revenue exceed two per cent in any year, with reduction of pay in bad years. The plan led to disappointment. Revenue went down a one-way street. The most that the employees could contribute was little.

This was a plain case of confusion of common causes with special causes. The big contribution to better performance must come from the management. The management provided no guidance, no plan for improvement of the system.

Statistical control. Sound understanding of statistical control is essential to management, engineering, manufacturing, purchase of materials, and service. Stability, or the existence of a system, is seldom a natural state. It is an achievement, the result of eliminating special causes one by one on statistical signal, leaving only the random variation of a stable process.

---

* C. I. Lewis, MIND AND THE WORLD ORDER (Scribners, 1929), page 195.

A stable process, one with no indication of a special cause of variation is said to be, following Shewhart, _in statistical control_. It is a random process. Its behavior in the future is predictable. Of course, some unforeseen jolt may come along and knock the process out of statistical control. A system that is in statistical control has a definable identity and a definable capability (cf. "Capability of the process," _infra_).

The control limits to use on a chart are calculated from actual data from inspection. The rules for calculation of control limits are simple, and are explained in any textbook on quality control.

> Some people accept also some designated pattern of points as indicative of a special cause, such as two successive points inside a control limit, but close to it. Search for patterns can be over-done. It is necessary to state in advance what the rules are for indication of a special cause. One can always concoct a pattern that will indicate anything desired, once the chart is in hand.

Statistical control of instruments and gauges. A recorded measurement is the end-product of a long series of operations from raw material on forward, plus the operation of measurement at some stage of the product, and the record thereof. As is emphasized in numerous places in this book, statistical control of the process of measurement is vital: otherwise there is no measurement.

Will this instrument give about the same results next week on 100 items as it gave today? What if we change operators? This subject reappears in Chapter 10 on supervision, and in Chapter 13 in connexion with costs of inspection. The reader may wish to consult the book by Harry Ku listed at the end of this chapter, and the book by the Western Electric Company, pp. 84 ff. (excellent).

Control limits are not specification limits. Control limits, once we have achieved a fair state of statistical control, tell us what the process is, and

THE TWO BASIC SOURCES OF IMPROVEMENT

what it will do tomorrow, and not necessarily where we wish the limits to be. The control chart is the process talking to us.*

The distribution of a quality-characteristic that is in statistical control is stable and predictable, day after day, week after week. Output and costs are also predictable.

Moreover, as Mr. William E. Conway pointed out, engineers and chemists then become innovative, creative, toward improvement of the process, once they see it in statistical control. They sense the fact that further improvement is up to them (Ch. 1).

Without statistical methods, attempts to improve a process are hit and miss, with results that usually make matters worse.

Specification limits are never shown on a control chart. Some textbooks, admirable in many ways, are in error in this respect. So-called "reject limits" in some books will be avoided by the reader that wishes to understand the meaning of statistical control.

Control limits do not set probabilities. The calculations that show where to place the control limits on a chart have their basis in the theory of probability. It would nevertheless be wrong to attach any particular figure to the probability that a statistical signal for detection of a special cause could be wrong, or that the chart could fail to send a signal when a special cause exists. The reason is that no process, except in artificial demonstrations by use of random numbers, is steady, unwavering.

As already stated, the function of a control chart is to minimize the net economic loss from the two mistakes described above, viz., over-adjustment and

---

* Eloquently stated thus, by Irving Burr in his book cited at the end of this chapter.

Chapter 7

under-adjustment. This it does very well. It will of course fail with some rare frequency to detect a special cause when it exists (or existed), and it will sometimes indicate existence of a special cause when none can be found. The record, however, is magnificent: the control chart will do its job if it is interpreted with knowledge and care.

<u>Statistical control helps to meet specifications economically</u>. Maximum and minimum limits for the specification of a product are by themselves a costly and unsatisfactory guide to the production worker.* Thus, specification limits for an outside diameter to lie between 1.001 and 1.002 cms tell the production worker that a diameter of 1.0012 cms meets the specification, but it is no help to him in an attempt to produce fewer defectives and to increase his production, both of which he can accomplish with less effort with the aid of statistical methods.

The production worker's job description should therefore, for best economy, help him to achieve statistical control of his work.* With or without the aid of engineering, he will reach the right level and will continually reduce the spread of individual items. Under this system, his output will meet the specifications and in fact leave them beyond the horizon, eliminating the cost of inspection. Workers that are in statistical control but whose output is unsatisfactory can be transferred and trained in other work (Ch. 10).

---

* This was the theme of a talk given by Dr. Joseph M. Juran years ago at a meeting of the Metropolitan Chapter of the American Society for Quality Control (New York). For a published reference, I cite Irving Burr, "Specifying the desired distribution rather than maximum and minimum limits," <u>Industrial Quality Control</u>, vol. 24, No. 2, 1967: pp. 94-101.

THE TWO BASIC SOURCES OF IMPROVEMENT

Partial list of common causes of variation and of wrong spread, wrong level.

Responsibility of management. The reader may supply other examples, appropriate

to his own plant and conditions.

— Poor design of product

— Failure to remove the barriers that rob the hourly worker of the right
to do a good job and to take pride in his work

— Poor instruction and poor supervision (almost synonymous with
unfortunate working relationships between foremen and production workers)

— Failure to measure the effects of common causes, and to reduce them

— Failure to provide the production workers with information in
statistical form that shows them where they could improve their performance
and the uniformity of the product

— Incoming materials not suited to the requirements

In a recent experience, leather would in one trial in three fail
to stick to plastic as intended by the design of the product. The
trouble, as it turned out, was too much grease in the leather. A
change in the specifications for leather removed the trouble. This
was a simple change in the system. (Incidentally, the manager declared that turnover dropped dramatically when he made this change.)

— Procedures not suited to the requirements

— Machines out of order

— Machines not suited to the requirements

— Settings of the machines chronically inaccurate (fault of the crew
responsible for settings)

— Poor light

— Vibration

— Humidity not suited to the process

— Mixing product from streams of production, each having small variability, but different levels

— Uncomfortable working conditions: noise, confusion, unnecessary dirt,
awkward handling of materials, unnecessary extremes of heat or cold, poor
ventilation, poor food in the cafeteria, etc.

— Shift of management's emphasis from quantity to quality, back and forth,
without understanding how to achieve quality

Another common cause is management's failure to face the problem
of inherited defective material. Defective items or subassemblies fed

into one operation from a previous operation in the same company, or from the outside, are demoralizing. No matter how well the operator performs his own work, the product will in the end still be defective. The multiplicative effect of intermediate defectives is disheartening. (More on this point in Chapter 10.)

B. TWO BASIC USES OF CONTROL CHARTS

1. <u>As a judgment.</u>* Was (past tense) the process in statistical control? Here, we look at a control chart to observe whether the process that made a particular batch of product was in statistical control. If yes, then we know, for the quality-characteristic that was plotted on the chart, the distribution of this quality-characteristic for individual items. We saw an example on page 5.

2. <u>As an operation (ongoing).</u>* To maintain the state of statistical control during production. Here the process has already been brought into statistical control (or nearly so, with only rare evidence of a special cause). We extend into the future the control limits on (e.g.) an $\bar{x}$-chart, and plot points one by one, perhaps every half hour or every hour. The up and down movements of the points are to be disregarded by the production worker unless they show a run (as for wear of tool), or unless a point falls outside the control limits.

Removal of a special cause of variation, to move toward statistical control, important though it be, is not improvement of the process. Removal of a special cause only brings the system back to where it should have been (quoting a lecture by Dr. Juran). As Dr. Juran also said, the important problems of improvement commence once you achieve statistical control.

Continual improvement of the system by the engineers may not take place. Improvement may be simple, some adjustment that will raise or lower the level

---

* The terms <u>As a judgment</u> and <u>As an operation</u> are Shewhart's terminology.

THE TWO BASIC SOURCES OF IMPROVEMENT

on the control chart, to lessen the risk of production of defective items. On the other hand, improvement may be difficult and complex, the possible aim being to lower use of certain materials (Ch. 1), or to shrink the spread between the control limits.

Two kinds of mistake on the job. There are two kinds of mistake that the production worker can make on the job:

1. Over-adjust. An example was the man that was running the coating-head (Ch. 1).

2. Under-adjust.

It is easy to establish a clean record on either mistake: never make mistake No. 1, or never make mistake No. 2. But in avoiding one mistake, one commits the other mistake as often as possible. There is no hope to avoid both mistakes all the time. What one must do, for minimum economic loss from both mistakes, is to commit each mistake only now and then, and not too much of one nor too much of the other. We need a rational scheme to regulate the frequencies of the two mistakes. This is precisely the function of the control chart. It provides a rational and economic guide to minimum loss from both mistakes.

Over-adjustment usually shows up on $\bar{x}$- and R-charts as sawteeth. No use can be made of such a chart. The operator tests a few items now and then, and adjusts his machine on the basis of ups and downs. He will never achieve statistical control until he leaves the machine alone for a period of time that is long enough to get a meaningful control chart.

Meanwhile, he is losing time by shutting down his machine too often, and he is actually creating unnecessary extra variability in his output, with danger of producing defectives. Several examples have appeared in foregoing chapters, with more to come.

Chapter 7

The two mistakes may be restated as two types of error that are inherent in any technique that is put to optimum use:

1. The chart may give a signal that a special cause exists when none exists, or when a cause can not be found. If a special cause exists, it will return and give you another chance. In other words, the chart may lead to over-adjustment.

2. It may fail to detect a special cause when one actually exists. In other words, the chart may lead to under-adjustment. The cause, if it exists, will return and give you another chance.

Some advice about control charts as an operation. The production worker requires only a knowledge of simple arithmetic to plot a chart. But he can not by himself decide that he will use a chart on the job, and still less can he start a movement for use of charts.

It is the responsibility of management to teach use of control charts on the job (ongoing) where they can be effective. As we learned in Chapter 2, a control chart in the hands of an hourly worker can be effective only if he is not afflicted with barriers that make it impossible for him to take pride in his work. Otherwise, control charts in the hands of hourly workers will have a short life.

A chart for a group has the deficiencies of a chart for a mixture (p. 150). A chart for each member of the group is sometimes helpful. The production worker, seeing a point outside control limits, can almost always identify at once the special cause, and eliminate it. Only the production worker and the foreman see the chart, unless the worker elects to make his chart public.

A chart for fraction defective for a group, prominently displayed to indicate a special cause shortly after it occurs, is usually helpful to everybody.

THE TWO BASIC SOURCES OF IMPROVEMENT

Proliferation of charts without purpose is to be avoided. One plant that I visited near Nagoya had on that day 241 $\bar{x}$- and R-charts. Every chart was useful. All charts are reviewed every two months; charts added, charts discontinued when they have achieved their purpose, reinstituted later if need be indicated.

Exercise 1. Show that over-adjustment in the extreme will explode the process. That is, if an operator adjusts the process whenever a point is higher or lower than the preceding point, the variation will go wider and wider.

Exercise 2. A manufacturer of carburetors for automobiles was using two tests. Test A: a cheap test with solid fuel, applied to every carburetor. Test B: expensive test, with gas, applied to a sample of 10 carburetors drawn from a lot. (No instruction about how to draw the sample of 10.)

Each carburetor in the sample of 10 is then tested by both methods. RULE: Compute the averages $\bar{A}$ and $\bar{B}$ for the 10 carburetors in each lot. If $\bar{A}$ is on the same side of $\bar{B}$ in three successive lots, adjust Test A to conformity, and proceed.

Explain what is wrong with this rule. In the first place, tossing coins would show $\bar{A}$ to be greater than $\bar{B}$ or less than $\bar{B}$ in one third of the tests. The rule therefore leads to woeful over-adjustment, the penalty being an artificial increase in the magnitude of disagreement between the two tests. Worse, the rule does not bring either test into statistical control, nor the difference between the two tests.

Example of over-adjustment. Fig. 12 shows in the upper panel a run chart of measurements on consecutive items. The operator continually adjusted her tool, trying to hold the specification. With aid of $\bar{x}$- and R-charts, she adjusted her tool only on statistical signal. The result was (1) much greater

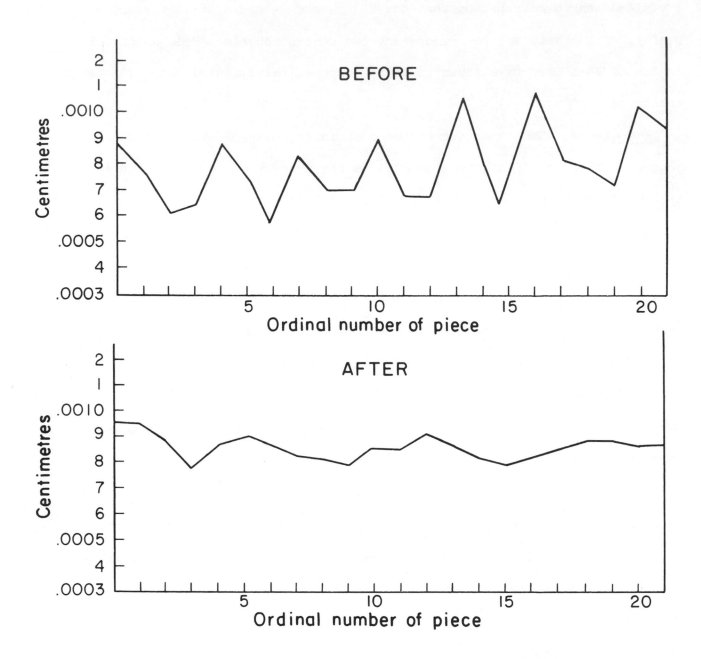

Fig. 12. Upper panel: result of over-adjustment. The operator adjusted her tool at every item, doing her best to hold the item to specification. Lower panel: greater uniformity is obvious with aid of $\bar{x}$- and R-charts that told her when to adjust her tool, and when to leave it alone.

THE TWO BASIC SOURCES OF IMPROVEMENT

uniformity in measurements; (2) substantial increase in production because she no longer spent time for adjustment.

Next step: cut down on the inspection: 100 per cent is no longer necessary. Inspect at some appropriate interval four consecutive items only for continuation of the $\bar{x}$- and R-charts.

Another example. The job in a certain staff area in a company that manufactures automobiles is to make monthly forecasts of sales. The men take into account many kinds of information. The forecast falls short or long, month by month, when compared with actual sales. The procedure for the next month had been to adjust the method up or down on the basis of this comparison. The reader may perceive that what the men were doing was guaranteeing that their method could never improve.

Capability of the process. Once a process has been brought into a state of statistical control, it has a definable capability. It will show sustained satisfactory performance on the $\bar{x}$- and R-charts. The specifications that it can meet are predictable.

A simple way to describe the specifications that it can meet is to measure up and down from the mean $\bar{\bar{x}}$ on the $\bar{x}$-chart $\sqrt{n}$ times the spread between the control limits for $\bar{x}$, where n is the size of the sample. An illustration appears on page 168. The spread between individual parts is also equal to $6 \bar{R}/d_2$.

The symbol d_2 is a number that depends on n, to be found in any book on the statistical control of quality. It is derived from the distribution of the range.* As an approximation, d_2 is very nearly equal to $\sqrt{n}$ up to n = 10.**

---

* The distribution of the range was published by L. H. C. Tippett, "On the extreme individuals and the range of samples taken from a normal population," Biometrika, vol. 17, 1925. An excellent book on the capability of the process is Masao Kogure, THEORY OF PROCESS CAPABILITY AND ITS APPLICATIONS (JUSE Press, Ltd., Tokyo; 1975 and 1981). Alas, in Japanese.

** Nathan Mantel, "On a rapid estimation of standard errors for the means of small samples," American Statistician, vol. 5, Oct. 1951: pp. 26-27. M. H. Quenouille, RAPID STATISTICAL CALCULATIONS (Hafner, 1959): pp. 5, 6, 7.

One could say in fact, in connexion with $\bar{x}$- and R-charts, that the R-chart, if in control, tells us the capability of $\bar{x}$. If a point on the $\bar{x}$-chart falls outside the control limits for $\bar{x}$, the process is not living up to its capability for $\bar{x}$. In other words, a special cause has turned up.

Advantages of stability or statistical control. A process that is stable, in statistical control, presents a number of advantages over instability. In statistical control:

1. The process has an identity; its performance is predictable. It has a measurable, communicable capability, as we saw in the last section. Production and dimensions and other quality-characteristics, including the number of defects, if any, remain nearly constant hour after hour, day after day.

2. Costs and quality are predictable. The management need not lose money on specifications that can not be met economically.

3. Productivity is at a maximum (costs at a minimum) under the present system.

4. The effects of changes in the system (management's responsibility) can be measured with greater speed and reliability.

Without statistical control it is difficult to measure the effect of a change in the system. More accurately, only catastrophic effects are easily observable.

5. A stable process provides sound argument for altering specifications that can not be met economically.

Other uses (brief mention). Improvement of inspection. This means experimental design for reinspection of small samples, or by interpenetrating samples in destructive testing, to improve the reliability of inspection and to learn how inspection can produce more useful results. Unreliable inspection can create havoc and demoralization of production workers by classifying good product as defective, and the converse. Unreliable inspection can lose future business: no one can calculate the cost of a defective item once it goes out on the market.

<u>Maintenance of standards</u>. This means statistical tests of instruments and gauges; training and supervision of use of instruments. Maintenance of quality of product, and quality-assurance, are highly intricate statistical problems; also highly intricate substantive problems.

Interlaboratory testing (closely allied with the quality control of instruments and gauges). This activity is important for both buyer and seller, else the buyer may pay too much for his material purchased, or the seller may receive too little. Both are entitled to a square deal. This activity is also important in a company that has several plants that make the same or nearly the same products.

<u>Another example of uses of a control chart as a judgment</u>. Examples appeared in Chapter 1. We now turn to another. An executive of a large mail order company came with the problem of high costs. He also came with data which showed the number of orders filled every half hour. Four half hours provided data for $\bar{x}$- and R-charts (Fig. 13) with n = 4. Once he saw how wide the control limits were for the output of orders, he made the remark that the control limits were too wide: he preferred less variation. But how would you achieve it? I asked. He surmised that you just draw new lines closer together. It was my obligation to point out to him that the control limits were only telling him what the process is, not what he wished it to be; that any reduction in variation in the future was entirely up to him. He must investigate possible common causes of variation and remove them. Any success in this endeavor would raise productivity and show narrower spread between control limits, which is what he wished to see.

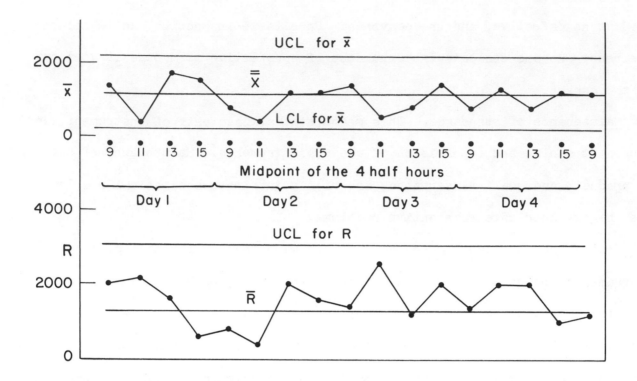

Fig. 13. The number of orders filled is recorded for each half hour. Each point in the chart comes from 4 consecutive half hours. $\bar{x}$ is the average number of orders filled in 4 consecutive half hours. R is the range between these 4 numbers. The calculation of control limits follows the usual formulas.

$$\bar{\bar{x}} = 1200 \qquad \bar{R} = 1372$$

For $\bar{x}$ $\quad$ $\begin{matrix}\text{UCL}\\\text{LCL}\end{matrix} = \bar{\bar{x}} \pm A_2\bar{R}$

$$= 1200 \pm .729 \times 1372$$

$$= \begin{matrix}2200\\200\end{matrix}$$

For R $\quad$ UCL $= D_4\bar{R} = 2.282 \times 1372 = 3131$

$\qquad$ LCL $= D_3\bar{R} = 0$

The numerical values of the constants

$A_2 = .729$

$D_3 = 0$

$D_4 = 2.282$

come from tables to be found in any of the books listed at the end of this chapter.

THE TWO BASIC SOURCES OF IMPROVEMENT

The cause of the wide variation, it turned out, was simple--variable backlog of orders: nothing to do some of the time, slavery at other times. The

management smoothed out the backlog, production increased, mistakes decreased--

everybody including customers happier.

One big payoff came in the dramatic reduction in complaints from
customers about delays. Five girls had been on the payroll to try to
explain delays. One girl now takes care of the calls and has half her
time left over for other work. Increase of customer satisfaction was
automatic. A concomitant payoff was an equally dramatic increase in
production from the same equipment. Nobody worked harder, only
smarter.

Decreased cost through reduction of inventory from better quality. Fig. 14

shows inventory in process month by month by month, including incoming parts

ready for use. The vertical scale is millions of dollars. The inventory was

$30,000,000 at the start of the program, $15,000,000 seven months later--

a decrease of $15,000,000. At current rates of interest, this would mean a

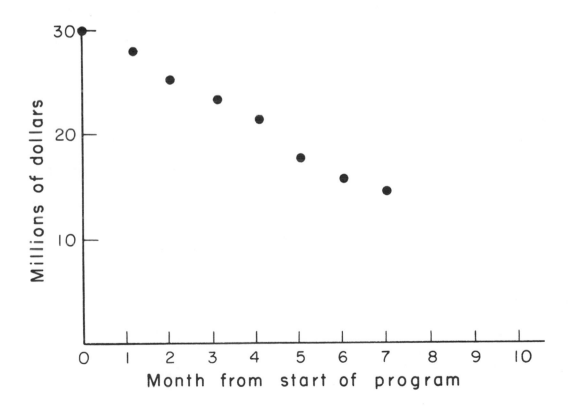

Fig. 14. Inventory decreases as quality and dependability improve.

saving of something like $6000 per day every day, including Saturdays, Sundays, and holidays.

What brought the decrease? Better quality of incoming materials, through cooperation with vendors; reduction in number of vendors; reduction of rework. It is no longer necessary to have on hand crippling allowances for defective parts. A more important factor is fewer parts waiting for rework. It is well known that rework piles up: No one wishes to tackle it. Another gain is floor space now free for other uses, owing to decrease in inventory and less rework.

More attention to orderly scheduling undoubtedly made substantial contribution.

Application to sales. A company receives reports from salesmen. Quarterly reports for the eight salesmen are shown in Fig. 15. Each salesman covers a territory in the Philadelphia area. What are the problems? Statistical thinking has something to offer on the problems. Some handicaps are undoubtedly common to all salesmen, problems of the system. It is possible that some salesmen are out of limits.

Now of course the company would wish to have a bigger slice of the pie for all its products. This would require action on the part of management in ways that are beyond the scope of this book, though three possibilities might be mentioned here, such as improvement in the efficiency of manufacture to permit lower prices, speedier and perhaps better and more dependable delivery, and perhaps better and more dependable quality. Would a wave of advertising help?

Salesmen No. 1 and No. 2 are having problems. No. 1 is low compared with the group on both Product A and B. No. 2 is low only on Product B. It would be unwise to jump to the conclusion that other men could do better in their areas. A first step for management would be to examine both the salesmen's

THE TWO BASIC SOURCES OF IMPROVEMENT

territories and their competition. Brand loyalty to another company's product
is sometimes a cause of low sales.

It is possible that the right kind of help to the low-volume salesmen could
push them upward in both products. The result could be a large and immediate
gain in profit in these areas, well worth much thought and effort on the part
of management on how to help the low-volume salesmen in particular.

A second step would be to have a talk with them and with the District Manager
and try to find out what the specific causes are. The conclusion might be, of
course, that the low-volume salesmen should be put into other jobs and replaced.

The company had a quota (a work standard) of $7200 per day. Does anyone
suppose that a salesman would ever report more than $7200 of business in one day?

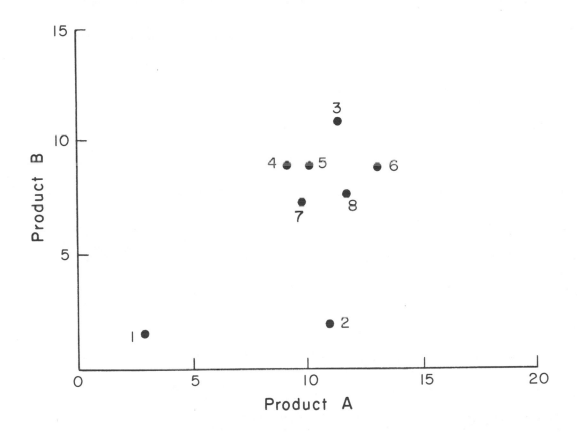

Fig. 15. Share of market in percentage (wholesale)
achieved by 8 salesmen in the Philadelphia area from Product
A and Product B. Each point is a salesman.

Chapter 7

<u>Example of use of a control chart during production</u>. The example in Fig. 16 is taken from the pamphlet, "Guides for Quality Control," listed at the end of this chapter.

Product: 2-ply woolen yarn

Characteristic: clean content after the yarn is cleaned

Unit of Measurement: per cent fat

Size of sample: n = 5

Periods of time 1, 2, 3, etc., are marked on the chart.

1. Control limits are computed from the data collected over this period. Statistical control had been established during previous weeks by elimination one by one of special causes of variation detected by the chart. The control limits for $\bar{x}$ are derived from the average range $(\bar{R})$ on the range chart, not shown here.

2. Change in scouring--started use of new cleaner.

3. Operator failed to hold specified alkali reading.

4. Faulty electrode on alkali meter--replaced.

5. Reduction in speed of yarn: not good.

6. Change in scouring--started use of still another cleaner.

7. Cause not determined.

8. Excessive residue of fat because of change in method. This explanation was not accepted at first by production unit. Corrected finally in August.

9. Period of experimental changes: results not good.

10. Started change in scouring equipment--counterflow.

11. Further changes and adjustments in equipment started here.

12. Process now appears to be in good statistical control at slightly lower level than in Period 1. Adjustments carried out in Period 11 appear to be successful. Control limits will now be recomputed over Period 12 for extension and use in the near future.

THE TWO BASIC SOURCES OF IMPROVEMENT

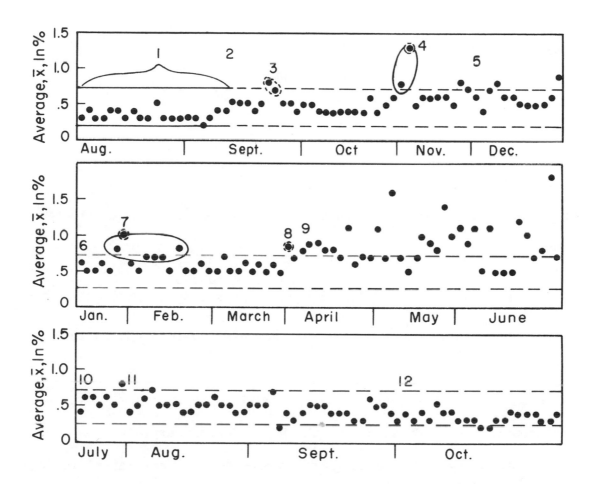

Fig. 16. Use of an $\bar{x}$-chart to find special causes of variation during production, on the basis of control limits established.

C. EXPERIMENT TO SHOW TOTAL FAULT IN SYSTEM *

Apparatus: Red and white wooden beads, 5 mm in diameter, in box.

TOTAL 4000

White 3200

Red   800

Paddle No. 2: 50 beveled depressions, 10 x 5. One scoop with the paddle pulls up 50 beads.

Advertisement on blackboard or on overhead projector, to draw volunteers from the audience:

> Vacancies seven: applicants must be
> willing to work. Educational requirements minimal.

Seven volunteers come forward. Six of them will go into apprenticeship; one will be appointed chief inspector.

Names go on the payroll; see table on page 141.

Apprenticeship, three days, during which the foreman explains the job. Instructions, taught by the foreman. Stir thoroughly the raw materials (beads). Scoop up a paddleful, the day's production. A red bead is a defective item. The foreman explains that we have work standards here, 50 items per day, red and white combined. We have also 700 per cent inspection. All six people and

---

* I learned this demonstration from Mr. William A. Boller of the Hewlett-Packard Company, who kindly introduced it in a seminar there.

THE TWO BASIC SOURCES OF IMPROVEMENT

the chief inspector will inspect every lot. All six people agree that they understand the job. All are ready for the first day's production. The results are in the table on page 141.

The foreman is aghast at the number of red beads produced the first day, and pleads with the workers to study every red bead, and try not to produce any the next day.

He is hopeful whenever one lot is better than the preceding one, and despondent when it is worse. Efforts to improve production, it seems, are effective one minute, a disappointment the next.

At the end of the third day, he puts their jobs on the line. The workers are, to be sure, meeting their quotas of 50 items per day, but the company is losing money on the defective items: our customer will not take red beads.

The fourth day is no better, and the foreman tells the workers that though they have done their best, their best is not good enough. This may be the only time for some of them to lose a job. He is sorry. Pick up your pay as you depart. He will have to advertise for replacements. The chief inspector is on salary, and will be retained for a while.

Everyone plots the chart for number of items defective (Fig. 17).

Interpretation of chart. The process exhibits statistical control, with no evidence of difference in performance between operators nor between days.

The operators have put into the job all that they have to offer.

The only way to eliminate defective items in the product is to eliminate the red beads from the system.

The control limits are extended into the future as prediction of the limit of variation to expect from the same process.

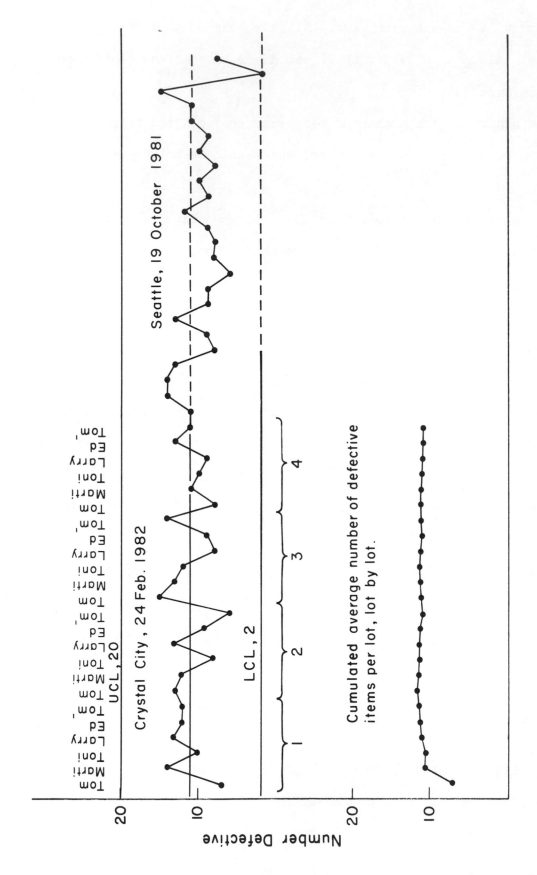

Fig. 17. Upper panel. Chart for number of defective items lot by lot, by name, by day. Projection of the control limits into the future is prediction of the variation to expect from the same process in future lots. Data from an experiment in Seattle are added to compare with the prediction.

Lower panel. Cumulated average number of defective items, lot by lot.

THE TWO BASIC SOURCES OF IMPROVEMENT

Crystal City, 24 February 1982

Record of number of defective items
reported by operator, by day

Lot size 50, each operator per day

Name	Day				
	1	2	3	4	All 4
Tom	7	13	15	8	43
Marti	14	12	13	11	50
Toni	10	8	12	10	40
Larry	13	13	8	9	43
Ed	12	9	9	13	43
Tom'	12	6	14	11	43
All 6	68	61	71	62	262

Robert, Chief Inspector

Computation of control limits

$$\bar{r} = \frac{262}{24} = 10.92$$

$$\bar{p} = \frac{10.92}{50} = .22$$

$$\begin{matrix} \text{UCL} \\ \text{LCL} \end{matrix} = \bar{r} \pm 3\sqrt{\bar{r}(1-\bar{p})}$$

$$= 10.92 \pm 3\sqrt{10.92 \times .78}$$

$$= \begin{matrix} 20 \\ 2 \end{matrix}$$

The experiment is stupidly simple, but it makes the point. Once people have seen it, they find red beads (sources of trouble) all over their companies.

Prediction. As the process appears to be in statistical control, we may extend the control limits into the future as prediction of the limit of variation of future lots, from other workers, same beads, same paddle. The points shown for the future come from a previous experiment with the same beads and same paddle, same foreman, different workers.

What are the data of the experiment? Use of an experiment, if it has any use, is for prediction of the results of future experiments. The data of an experiment, emphasized by Shewhart, are information that could assist prediction. What records need to be made about this experiment to assist prediction of future experiments?

Unfortunately, future experiments (future trials, tomorrow's production) may be affected by environmental conditions (temperature, materials) different from those that affect this experiment. It is only by knowledge of the subject matter, possibly aided by further experiments to cover a wider range of conditions, that one may decide, with a risk of being wrong, whether the environmental conditions of the future will be near enough the same as those of today to permit use of results in hand.

Incidentally, the risk of being wrong in a prediction can not be calculated--a point that is usually overlooked in the textbooks and teaching of statistical methods.

We recorded here the date and time, the names of the willing workers, the name of the chief inspector, a description of the beads, identification of the paddle (No. 2). What else might be important?

As the six hourly workers appear to form a statistical system (none beyond the control limits), we could perhaps hereafter, in another experiment, omit from the record their names. The paddle, however, is important. Another paddle (No. 1), used for thirty years, gives results that differ markedly from the results obtained by this paddle (No. 2). (See the figures for cumulated results shown in the next section.)

Other data of the experiment would be the supervisor, and his zeal to enforce the rule of thorough mixing of the raw materials (beads).

Cumulated average. Question: as 20 per cent of the beads in the box are red, what do you think would be the cumulated average, the statistical limit, as we continue to produce lots by the same process over many days?

The answer that comes forth spontaneously from the audience is that it must be ten, because 10 is 20 per cent of 50, the size of a lot. This answer is wrong. We have no basis for such a statement. As a matter of fact, the cumulated average for paddle No. 2 over many experiments in the past has settled down to 9.4.

The cumulated average for paddle No. 1, over hundreds of experiments over thirty years, with the same beads, is 11.3.

The paddle is obviously an important piece of information about the process. Would the reader have thought so, in the absence of data?

The same question can be stated in a different way: tell me some reasons why we could not expect the cumulated average to be 10. Answers: (1) Red pigment is different to the eye from white pigment. It feels different to the fingers, and obviously to the paddle. (2) The sizes of red and white beads may be different. Their weights may be different. Red beads are made by dipping white ones into red pigment, or is it the other way around?

The difference between the accumulated $\bar{r}$ and 10 is often alluded to by people in the audience as bias. No, this difference is not bias. It is the difference between two methods of selection: (1) mechanical, used here; (2) selection by random numbers.*

Exercise 1. Show that the spread of the control limits for the number of white beads, lot by lot, would be identical with the spread of the control limits for the red beads, already calculated. Show further that we have already plotted a control chart for the white beads. We only need to reverse the vertical scale; replace 0 by 50, 10 by 40, 20 by 30, 30 by 20, 40 by 10, 50 by 0. The control limits for the white beads will then stay right in place, 49 for the upper limit and 33 for the lower limit.

Exercise 2. Before any data were collected, it was a 50:50 bet that Marti would make more defective items in the four days than Toni would make. Afterward, there was no doubt about it. Suppose that the experiment is to be continued through another four days. Assume that the differences between the six operators continue to show good statistical control. There is a 50:50 chance that the two workers will reverse themselves on the second four days. Show that the chance is 50:50 that the cumulated number of defective items for Marti will again exceed those made by Toni over all eight days.

Sampling by use of random numbers. If we drew by use of random numbers 50 beads from the box, to form a lot, then the cumulated average, the statistical limit, would be 10. The reason is that the random numbers pay no attention to color, nor to size, nor to any other physical characteristic of beads, paddle, or employee. Statistical theory (theory of probability) as taught in the books for the theory of sampling and theory of distributions applies in the use of

---

* W. Edwards Deming, SAMPLE DESIGN IN BUSINESS RESEARCH (Wiley, 1960), Ch. 5.

THE TWO BASIC SOURCES OF IMPROVEMENT

random numbers, but not in experiences of life. Once statistical control is established, then a distribution exists, and is predictable. The big lesson is that in industry, substantive knowledge about the process (knowledge of engineering, chemistry, inspection, production, marketing) is vital. Statistical methods show substantive experts where their knowledge is vital and can be effective, and that statistical problems require statistical knowledge.

Difficulties in estimation of the process average. It is a fact that the limiting value of the cumulated $\bar{r}/N$, calculated from samples drawn from lots by mechanical methods, may not be a good approximation to the limiting value of $\bar{r}/N$ that would come from samples drawn by random numbers or from 100 per cent inspection of a random selection of lots. The samples in the experiment were drawn by mechanical methods (stirring the beads and then drawing a sample of $N = 50$ with the paddle).

It is in practice, we must admit, not always practicable to draw samples by random numbers. Samples may be drawn by the inspector, from top, bottom, middle, and throughout the lot in an attempt to get a good cross-section. In some circumstances, sampling from the bottom and from all but the top quarter of the lot may be time-consuming. To get a good sample it might be necessary to empty the lot into another container, holding out now and then a part for the sample for inspection.

None of these plans is a dependable substitute for random numbers. We must therefore accept the fact that in much practice the average proportion defective calculated from a series of samples however long will not be the same as the process average that would be calculated from samples drawn by random numbers, or from 100 per cent inspection by the same method of inspection that was used for the samples, and with the same instruments, same inspectors, same care.

Chapter 7

A change in the method of selection of samples, when mechanical selection or judgment selection is used, could well throw a point out of control. This is an artifact that one should keep in mind in the interpretation of a chart. (Pointed out to me by Mr. Dave West in Johannesburg.)

D. FURTHER REMARKS ON STATISTICAL CONTROL

Statistical control does not imply absence of defective items. Statistical control is a state of random variation, stable in the sense that the limits of variation are predictable. A process may be in statistical control, yet produce defective items. In fact, it could produce a high proportion of defective items. We saw this in the experiment with the red and white beads.

Intervention to change the system (to get rid of the red beads in the system) may be simple, or it may be complex and lengthy. A change in the average may be simple. It may require long experimentation (recall the example with the coated paper in Ch. 1). Reduction in spread is usually more difficult than change in level. Every problem is different from every other, and no rule should be attempted.

Fig. 18 shows $\bar{x}$- and R-charts for a process that was producing 20 per cent defective items. The distribution of individual items fell outside the specifications, 15 per cent on one side, 5 per cent on the other. (Specification limits are never shown on a control chart, except in connexion with inferred distribution of individual items, as in Fig. 5.a.)

Fig. 19 shows the $\bar{x}$- and R-charts plotted three months later, after much labor had been put in on changes and adjustments in the process in attempts to

THE TWO BASIC SOURCES OF IMPROVEMENT

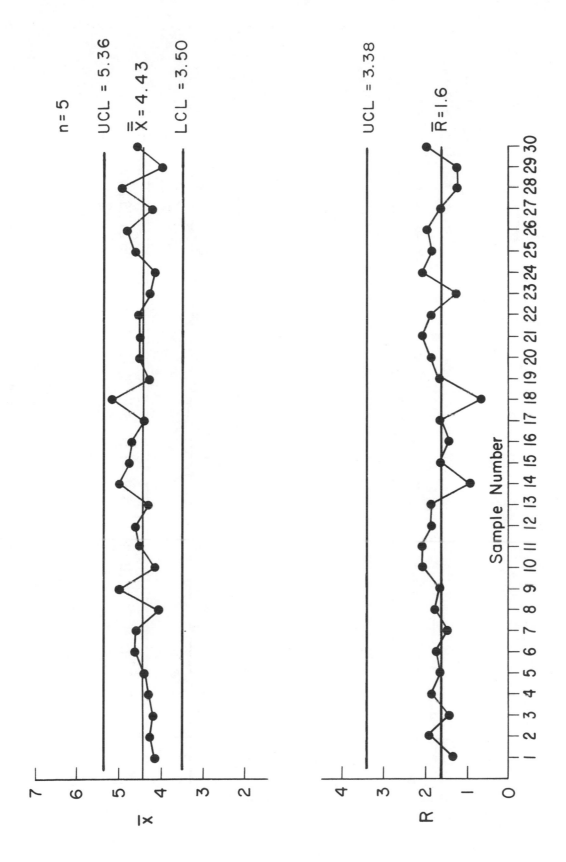

Fig. 18. The charts show that the process is in good statistical control.

However, it is making defective items.

148.

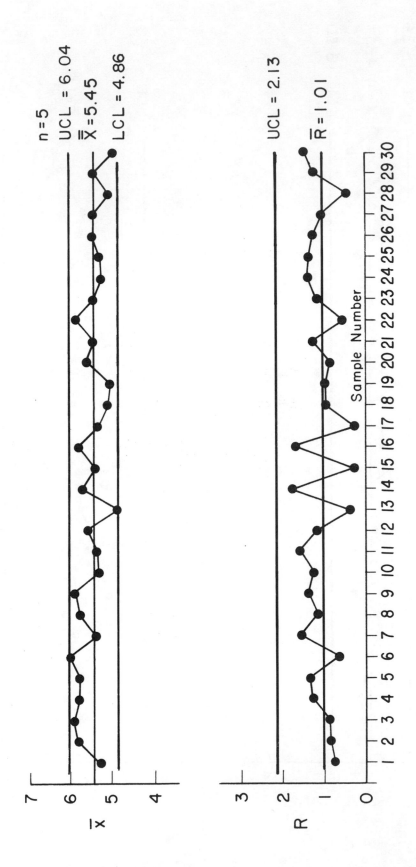

Fig. 19. Three months later. Study and changes in the process brought the average to a better level and shrank the variation. Result: no defective items now produced.

THE TWO BASIC SOURCES OF IMPROVEMENT

bring it into conformity with the specifications. The change in level from 4.43 to 5.45, coupled with shrinkage of variation, brought forth the desired results, zero defects.

We note that zero defects did not come about by shouting slogans nor by signing pledges.

Study of a mixture may obscure chance to improve. Let us think of three production lines, feeding their output into one channel. I like to think of three streams, feeding into a river, the mixture (Fig. 20). The mixture is the final product. If the three production lines are in statistical control, the mixture in the channel will also be in statistical control, even though the means of the three separate production lines be wide apart (Fig. 21).

In fact, if the material from the three production lines is thoroughly mixed, the variance of the mixture will be the total variance between items in all three production lines. Students of statistics will recognize the formula

$$\sigma^2 = \sigma_b^2 + \sigma_w^2$$

where σ^2 is the variance between items in the mixture, σ_b^2 is the variance between the means of the three production lines, and σ_w^2 is the average variance between items within the separate three production lines.

It follows that a road to reduction in the variability of the mixture is to bring the three streams to the same level, i.e., to a common mean. Next, if one of the streams has high variability, try to reduce it.

Even though the work of the group may be in pretty good statistical control, one or more members of the group may be out on a limb. Control charts for individuals, for a few days may discover that one or two people are in need of retraining or transfer. (Example on page 182.)

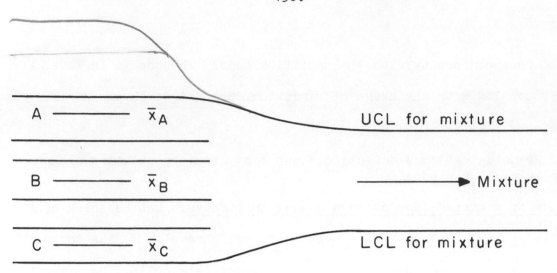

Fig. 20. Product comes in from three sources, all three in statistical control. The mixture from the three sources shows statistical control, but with wide spread.

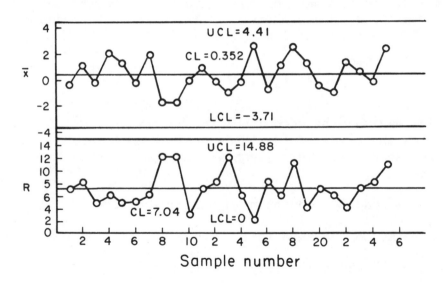

Fig. 21. The $\bar{x}$- and R-charts for the mixture show good statistical control, but they obscure the possibility that the three sources have different levels and spreads, and that much better uniformity might be fairly easy to achieve. A first step in reduction of the spread of the mixture is to bring the three streams to the same level, if possible. Next, work on Stream A to reduce its spread.

THE TWO BASIC SOURCES OF IMPROVEMENT

Nine grinding machines put the finishing touches on front axles. The mixture from the nine machines contained three per cent defectives on the average. Data from the individual machines showed that Machines No. 2 and 3 were making the defectives, being in need of fine tuning. When these two machines had the benefit of meticulous care, defective output of the battery of nine machines dropped to zero. Without data on the individual machines, all nine, improvement of the process would not have been accomplished.

In Fig. 34 on page 204 the mixture is all 11 welders. Study of the 11 welders separately showed that No. 6 was producing more than his share of faults.

In an example of looping, furnished to me by Professor David S. Chambers (next chapter), the combined output of 47 loopers was in reasonably good statistical control at 4.8 per cent downgraded and scrap. Individual charts for everybody disclosed the fact that seven women were making far more than their share of the faults. (Details in the next chapter, page 182.)

E. EXAMPLES OF COSTLY MISUNDERSTANDING

Example 1. Action line placed on chart by judgment, not calculated. As we have learned, the control limits on a control chart tell us what maximum variation to expect from the process as it is, not what we wish it to be. Suppose that a worker draws a line on a chart that shows day by day the fraction defective. He draws a line at (e.g.) 4 per cent, which seems to him to be a reasonable goal. A man showed me a point well above the line. Here, he said, was a point out of control.

Where are your calculations for the control limit?, I asked. "We don't make calculations; we just place the line where we think it ought to be."

Chapter 7

Some textbooks woefully mislead the reader by deriving control limits from specifications. This is just as bad as placement of a control limit by judgment.*

Such placement of a line, as substitute for a control limit, leads to over-adjustment or to under-adjustment, and perpetuates whatever troubles exist. As a sad comment, people discard the chart, misused in this manner, with the comment that "quality control does not work here."

No wonder. They never tried it.

Control limits are not specification limits, as already noted (p. 120). Wishing will not change the process. Action will.

Example 2. Same fault: Action limit set by manufacturer's rating. It is easier than one might suppose to fall into the trap of using judgment for an action limit. I quote here a letter received from the vice president of a company, pleased with the results of his efforts, but unaware that his methods are robbing him of quality and productivity that might be achieved with the same equipment and same people, given a better chance to exhibit their abilities. The manufacturer of the equipment might also be pleased to learn that his equipment could beat his claims, if given a chance. Here is the letter:

> In the last quarter of 1980, we reorganized and hired a consultant to teach and train through formal instruction and floor application the principles of effective supervision. We combined numerous jobs in both our salaried and hourly ranks. All standards were eliminated from our production people and we set floor standards based on the maximum speed of the equipment as specified by the manufacturer. When 100 per cent is not achieved, the floor supervisor has to identify reasons for per-formance less than maximum. Our maintenance, technical, and service personnel, work on correcting the identified problems.

---

* I thank Barbara Kimball of Cutter Laboratories, Los Angeles, for pointing out to me this error in a number of books. I have omitted these books from the titles shown at the end of this chapter.

THE TWO BASIC SOURCES OF IMPROVEMENT

Wrong way. His experts, using the manufacturer's claim for a control limit (action limit), were confusing special causes with common causes. There is no such thing as a machine by itself. Its variation and output are dependent on maintenance and on the operator. It is important to discover reasons why the performance of a machine varies with the operator, and to train the operators to uniformity defined by the control chart (invariably with increased output).

"The machine has a guaranteed quality. We know what it is. We know the capability of the process. We tested the machine before we bought it." This is only confession of failure to understand a machine.

Mechanical feedbacks of human effort, material, and machine time, that hold dimensions and other quality-characteristics within bounds are sometimes helpful but may be wasteful of human effort, material and machine time. They do not improve the system. They do not achieve statistical control at an economic level and spread. Better understanding of the effective use of feedback systems is important and management should not overlook the problem.

Example 3. Wrong use of distribution. More on the unmanned computer. This example illustrates futile use of a distribution where the aim was to improve the process to attain greater uniformity of the product. A distribution shows what happened the day before (emphasis on past tense). It indicates that something is wrong, but it offers no help toward improvement of the process. This example is typical of the mistake that is so often made when people are long on computers but are short on knowledge. Ingots of copper are extruded, red hot and sputtering. A machine cuts off ingots, the desired weight being 326 kgs. Every ingot is weighed automatically, and the data go into the computer.

The next step is electrolytic deposition of copper, the ingots forming the anode. An ingot that is too light wastes space in the electrolytic bath while the heavy ones finish.

The operator's job, seeing that the weight of an ingot is low, was to adjust his cutoff to increase the weight of the next ingot, and to take the reverse action for an ingot that is overweight. The automatic weighing contrivance plots at the end of the day a distribution of the weights of the ingots produced. The operator has in front of him the distribution of weights produced the day before (Fig. 22).

"What is the purpose of the histogram?" I asked.

"To show the operator how he is doing," was the answer.

"How long have you had the problem of nonuniform weights?" I asked.

"Ever since we started."

The fact is that the operator, by adjusting the machine up or down at every bar was actually widening the variance of the distribution of weights, another example of over-adjustment.

The next step was to explain to the men that the operator would achieve greater uniformity if he would construct a control chart and leave the machine alone except when the chart sends a statistical signal of a special cause: adjust it only on statistical signal.

The computer, in the above example, wastes material, human effort, and machine time.

It would not be wise, even though it be possible, to program a computer to plot the chart. It is much better for the operator to do it himself point by point, from data that flow in from the computer, as the weights of the ingots are recorded therein. By plotting the chart himself, he will take an interest in the process point by point.

THE TWO BASIC SOURCES OF IMPROVEMENT

One encounters instances in which somebody has bought a computer and accompanying software, for some colossal sum of money, with the understanding that it would supply information by which to achieve statistical control, only to learn that it will do no such thing. It seems that neither salesman nor purchaser understood what the computer must do to be useful.

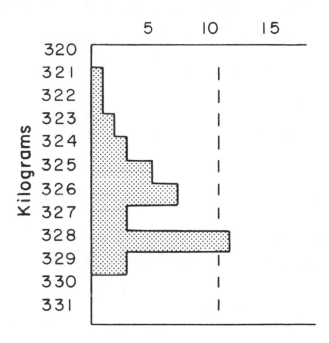

Fig. 22. Histogram of yesterday's production, constructed by automatic weighing and recording of every bar. The histogram shows the operator how he performed yesterday, but is no help to him toward achieving a narrower distribution about the desired average weight. The computer also printed the mean of the distribution, its standard deviation, skewness, and 4th moment coefficient, all of which were totally useless to the operator.

The engineer in charge had already explained to me that he does not need the statistical control of quality here, because he has 100 per cent inspection and a record of the weight of every ingot, and the operator adjusts the machine after every ingot is weighed. So wrong. Like so many people, well educated in many ways, the engineer in charge knew all about the job except what was important.

Chapter 7

An additional interesting statistical problem arises in consideration of the best (most profitable) weight above the mean beyond which to cut off the excess weight from an ingot. This problem is fairly straightforward, but we do not pursue it here. It would involve the distribution of weights, the cost of cutting copper off an ingot of excess weight, and the cost of extending the electrolytic process a sufficient number of minutes to finish up the heavy ingots in the electrolytic bath.

Be it noted that this problem has no solution unless the process is in statistical control. It is only in the state of statistical control that there will be a predictable distribution of weights to use as a basis for calculation.

Example 4. Deficiency in early stage of production. This example repeats a lesson already learned, but no harm will be done if we go through the lesson again.

Measurements on 10, 30, 40, or 100 pieces are examined to learn whether the process will do the job. The next step (wrong) is to examine the parts that fail, to try to discover the source of the trouble.

This is an example of failure of analysis of failure. A better procedure is to use statistical methods for a statistical problem, as follows:

1. Use the measurements to plot a run chart or other statistical chart (such as $\bar{x}$- or R-chart if there are enough data) in order of production to discover whether the process is in statistical control.

2. If the process is in statistical control, one may conclude that the defective parts were made by the same system that made the good ones. Only a change in the system can reduce the number of defective parts in the future. This might be a change in design of the part, or it might be a change in the method of manufacture. One of the first steps would be to examine the system

THE TWO BASIC SOURCES OF IMPROVEMENT

of measurement to see whether it is sufficiently standardized and in statistical control.

Seven or eight pieces, all showing a trend upward or downward, no reversal, would indicate pretty definitely that something is wrong with the process, or with the system of measurement.

A rational procedure with fewer than 15 or 20 pieces may well lead to difficulty in a logical answer to the question about the capability of the process. A smaller number sometimes nevertheless leads to a firm conclusion. Thus, if the entire initial run of 6 or 7 pieces all fail, one could conclude that the process is incapable of meeting the specifications, or that the system of measurement is out of order, or that the specifications should be relaxed.

3. If the chart shows lack of statistical control, then a search for special causes is the next step. Again, it would be wise to examine also the system of measurement.

Example 5. So obvious, so fruitless. The vice president of a huge concern told me that he has a strict schedule of inspection of final product. To my question about how they use the data came the answer: "The data are in the computer. The computer provides a record and description of every defect found. OUR ENGINEERS NEVER STOP till they find the cause of every defect."

The level of defective tubes had stayed relatively constant, around $4\frac{1}{2}$ per cent to $5\frac{1}{2}$ per cent for some years. Failure analysis had failed here because the engineers were confusing common causes with special causes. Every fault to them was a special cause, a breakdown of some kind, or a fault of the work force. Study of the product from a process that is in statistical control tells nothing about future product, except that a series of samples will furnish a basis for calculation of the limits within which future points ($\bar{x}$, R, p) will fall. Study of the defects in the product tells nothing. Like so much analysis of failure, the work of the engineers, only doing their best, was a failure.

To the customer, the manufacturer's efforts are appealing. It appears to the customer that the manufacturer is conscientious and is making every effort to reduce defective tubes in the future. This is so: he is. The only hitch is that these efforts are largely misdirected and are obviously not effective.

The same error, with equally good intentions, appeared in a proposal ascribed to the Nuclear Regulatory Commission, as reported by the Wall Street Journal for the 14th of September 1981, brought to my attention by Robert E. Lewis, writing in the New York Statistician, May-June 1982, page 8:

NRC STUDY RATES 15 NUCLEAR PLANTS 'BELOW AVERAGE'

By a Wall Street Journal Staff Reporter

Washington - Nuclear reactors at 15 of the nation's 50 power plant sites have failed on a Nuclear Regulatory Commission "report card" and will get closer attention from federal inspectors.

The NRC staff, based on studies concluded at the end of last year, found the 15 power plants "below average" in overall performance, including maintenance, radiation and fire protection and management control.

NRC spokesman Joseph Fouchard said, "...the purpose of the study was to make sure we focus our inspections on plants showing below-average performance."

Example 6. Loss from index of performance. Engineers in a company engaged in hauling general freight had developed so-called standards by which to measure the performance of the managers of their 70 terminals. Any manager that falls below 100 per cent must be delinquent in some way. Anyone above 100 per cent is doing his job.

This is the same mistake as the manager that examines only defective product in an effort to improve future product. What the management needs to investigate is the distribution of the indexes. Does the distribution form a system, or are there outliers? Study of correlation of performance with type of business handled might disclose reasons for what appears to be extra good performance or extra poor performance. For example, high ratio of inbound

THE TWO BASIC SOURCES OF IMPROVEMENT

freight to outbound freight might explain why some terminals show poor performance on profit. Thus, much more freight moves into most points in Florida than moves out: railway cars and trucks come north empty. The terminal manager is helpless against this ratio.

What the management was doing was to perpetuate their problems.

Example 7. I saw in a factory that makes tires the defective tires of the day, lined up for the engineers to investigate. More of the same thing that we just saw in the last example: same guaranteed continuation of trouble.

Example 8. I complained to the postmaster in Washington about mistakes in mail that came to my address. Everyone in the neighborhood, including me, it seemed, received envelopes addressed to other people. As I redelivered an envelope to an address not far away, I was met at the door by a woman just on her way out with an envelope in her hand addressed to me. An even trade. My complaint to the postmaster brought the following reply:

> Mistakes like the ones you point out are a source of irritation to us in the postal system, as they must be to you. This problem has been going on for years. We assure you that every mistake like the one that you mentioned is brought to the attention of the carrier at fault.

"Going on for years," is a confession that the fault lay in the system-- the fault of the man that wrote the letter. The trouble was apparently not localized by neighborhood, nor in time, nor was it specific to any one carrier. It will continue till the system undergoes fundamental revision to reduce the possibility of mistakes like those of my complaint. Meanwhile, the management blames the carrier. My complaint only caused hardship on the carrier.

F. FURTHER APPLICATIONS

Use of chart to measure combined faults of the system. Fig. 23 shows the fraction defective made by twenty production workers that performed essentially the same operation last month. It shows clearly that:

1. The output of the 20 production workers constitutes a stable, definable process, with a process capability.

2. The capability of the process is 2 per cent defective.

The production workers have put into their jobs all that they have
to offer. Improvement can come only from management, whose duty is now
clear: find and remove (or reduce so far as practicable) some of the
common or environmental causes of trouble, or accept the inevitable
continuation of 2 per cent defective.

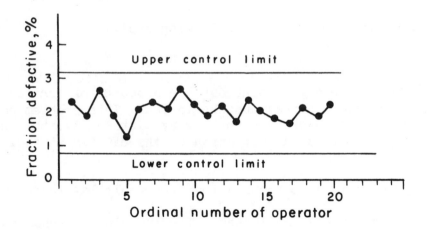

Fig. 23. Fraction defective produced by each of 20 operators. The points are in order of position. (All produced
about the same number of items.)

THE TWO BASIC SOURCES OF IMPROVEMENT

Computation of control limits

n = 1225, average production per man per month

$$\begin{matrix} UCL \\ LCL \end{matrix} = .02 \pm 3 \sqrt{\bar{p}\,\bar{q}/n}$$

$$= .02 \pm 3 \sqrt{.02 \times .98/1225}$$

$$= .02 \pm .012 = \begin{matrix} .032 \\ .008 \end{matrix}$$

<u>An example of benefit from studying the system and changing it.</u>

From the <u>Daily News</u>, Budapest, 29 May 1980

REVOLUTION IN MANAGEMENT

London (AP) - London's famous red buses scored a big productivity increase in the last six months and officials say that a "revolution in management" is the main reason.

London Transport which runs the publicly owned system attributes the improvement to the end of central control. The 5,500 buses on 300 routes were split into eight districts, each responsible for finances, repairs and complaints.

Scheduled mileage--the number of miles covered by buses on the road--increased by 10 per cent.

Waiting time at bus stops has been slashed and the number of buses off the road and waiting for repairs was cut from more than 500 to 150.

The buses now carry labels naming a district official to whom passengers can complain.

Next day in the same newpaper appeared an account of a speech by the First Secretary of Hungary, the Honorable Janos Kadar, with the heading:

LIVING STANDARDS DEPENDENT ON WORK-PERFORMANCE

...requirements of quality have to be raised. Proper work-performance must be demanded from everyone...

The Honorable The First Minister of Hungary had the right idea--better living depends on greater production. Top management in Hungary attended my

Chapter 7

lectures and learned about their responsibilities. They also learned not to expect much improvement in production from efforts of the work force, unaided by management.

People are part of the system. They need help. In spite of the fact that management is responsible for the system, or for lack of the system, I find in my experience that few people in industry know what constitutes a system. Many people think of machinery and data processing when I mention system. Few of them know that recruitment, training, supervision, and aids to production workers are part of the system. Who else could be responsible for these activities?

A man came from London. He was having problems, mainly in his billing department. His cash was low for two reasons: (1) He was behind in sending out monthly bills, mainly to big customers. His billing department had made so many mistakes in the past, especially to big customers, that he was afraid to send bills to them without many verifications. (2) Customers, especially big ones, were refusing to pay their bills for the last two or three months until errors in previous bills were cleared up.

He declared that the cause of these problems was careless work in his billing department; many mistakes between shipment of goods and the invoice.

1. Wrong item shipped: he has to pay the transportation both ways. Customer impatient; where is my machine?

2. Item shipped to wrong address: transportation to pay both ways. Customer impatient.

3. Invoice incorrect, such as no allowance for cumulated number of items purchased.

These errors created a multitude of debts and credits with mistakes. Bills for transportation mounted. He did not mention getting sued for loss of profit

THE TWO BASIC SOURCES OF IMPROVEMENT

for sending the wrong goods to a store for the Christmas season, but he had every other kind of problem. He claimed that the people that worked for him were the worst that anyone could pull together in London.

He could borrow money from the bank: he was a good risk, in spite of his problems, but to pay interest (18 per cent at that time) on what people owe you is not the way to get ahead.

All these problems would disappear, he said, when his new data processing machinery goes into operation, two years from now. Meanwhile, what can be done?

I assured him that he would encounter a whole new set of problems when his new data processing machinery starts up, unless he would take steps:

1. To simplify the system of charges for his product. It is too complicated. For example, elimination of rebate for cumulated purchase of a large quantity over a period of six months.

2. To provide better training and continual retraining. What do you know about the frequency of certain important errors? Where do they occur? What is the cause? Which workers contribute most of the errors? What workers are in statistical control? He had no answers to any of these questions. He was a manager.

It had never occurred to him that his people are part of the system, and that he is responsible for them and for answers to all these questions. System, to him, meant hardware, locations of warehouses, finance, etc. He went away an enlightened man, with a promise to engage a statistician in London to help him.

Five months later he returned, delighted. The most important mistake had tumbled from 39 per cent to 6 per cent, the second from 27 per cent to 4 per cent. He was on the way to further reduction.

Chapter 7

G. LIMITED SELECTION OF TEXT MATERIAL

Further study. The serious reader will take steps to improve his knowledge of statistical techniques.

There are many good books on control charts and on other statistical methods. The list that follows makes no claim for completeness. It may nevertheless be helpful. I have omitted books that contain serious errors, and are not suitable for self-study.

Guides for Quality Control (identified as A.S.Q.C. B1 and B2, American National Standards Institute, 1430 Broadway, New York 10018).

The reader is warned to skirt around suggestions for use of "reject limits for $\bar{x}$-charts," also to avoid "modified control limits."

The reader is already aware that chapters in textbooks on acceptance sampling are now outmoded.

I. W. Burr, ENGINEERING STATISTICS AND QUALITY CONTROL (McGraw-Hill, 1953).

W. J. Dixon and F. J. Massey, INTRODUCTION TO STATISTICAL ANALYSIS (McGraw-Hill, 1957).

A. J. Duncan, QUALITY CONTROL AND INDUSTRIAL STATISTICS (Richard D. Irwin, 1974).

D. Durand, STABLE CHAOS (General Learning Corporation, 1971).

A. S. C. Ehrenberg, DATA REDUCTION (Wiley, 1975).

E. L. Grant, STATISTICAL QUALITY CONTROL (McGraw-Hill, 1946, 1952, 1964, 1972. The later editions are by Eugene L. Grant and Richard S. Leavenworth.)

K. Ishikawa, GUIDE TO QUALITY CONTROL (Asian Productivity Organization, 1976); for sale by Unipub, 345 Park Avenue, New York 10010.

J. M. Juran and J. K. Louden, THE CORPORATE DIRECTOR (American Management Association, 1966).

J. M. Juran, MANAGERIAL BREAKTHROUGH: A NEW CONCEPT OF THE MANAGER'S JOB (McGraw-Hill, 1964).

H. H. Ku, et al, THE MEASUREMENT PROCESS (National Bureau of Standards, Special Publication No. 300, 1969; Government Printing Office, Washington 20402).

E. Kurnow, G. J. Glasser, and F. R. Ottman, STATISTICS FOR BUSINESS DECISIONS (Richard D. Irwin, 1959).

E. H. MacNiece, INDUSTRIAL SPECIFICATIONS (Wiley, 1953).

A. McF. Mood, INTRODUCTION TO THE THEORY OF STATISTICS (McGraw-Hill, 1950).

E. R. Ott, PROCESS QUALITY CONTROL (McGraw-Hill, 1975).

For study in basic statistics

E. M. Schrock, QUALITY CONTROL AND STATISTICAL METHODS (Reinhold, 1957).

W. A. Shewhart, THE ECONOMIC CONTROL OF QUALITY OF MANUFACTURED PRODUCT (Van Nostrand, 1931; American Society for Quality Control, 1980).

W. A. Shewhart, STATISTICAL METHOD FROM THE VIEWPOINT OF QUALITY CONTROL (The Graduate School, Department of Agriculture, Washington, 1939). (Reprinted by Marcel Dekker, New York.)

L. E. Simon, ENGINEERS' MANUAL OF STATISTICAL METHODS (John Wiley, 1941).

G. Taguchi, ON-LINE CONTROL DURING PRODUCTION (Japanese Standards Association, 1-24 Akasaka 4-chome, Minato-ku, Tokyo 107, 1981).

L. H. C. Tippett, STATISTICS (Oxford University Press, 1944).

L. H. C. Tippett, THE METHODS OF STATISTICS (Wiley, 1952).

M. Tribus, RATIONAL DESCRIPTIONS, DECISIONS, AND DESIGNS (Pergamon Unified Engineering Series, 1969).

W. A. Wallis and H. V. Roberts, STATISTICS: A NEW APPROACH (The Free Press, 1956).

Western Electric Company, STATISTICAL QUALITY CONTROL HANDBOOK (1956).

W. J. Youden, EXPERIMENTATION AND MEASUREMENT (National Science Teachers Association, Washington, 1962).

W. J. Youden, STATISTICAL METHODS FOR CHEMISTS (Wiley, 1951).

THE TWO BASIC SOURCES OF IMPROVEMENT

Chapter 8

MORE EXAMPLES OF IMPROVEMENT OF THE SYSTEM

For in much wisdom is great grief: and he that increaseth
knowledge increaseth sorrow.--Ecclesiastes 1, v. 18.

Purpose of this chapter. We now study some examples to illustrate how
statistical methods may tell us what proportion of the trouble in production
could be eliminated by changes in the system, sometimes easy to accomplish,
sometimes not.

Example 1. This example illustrates how a small change in the system could
virtually eliminate the possibility of defective items. The ordinates in
Fig. 24 are the means ($\bar{x}$) of samples of n = 3 for tests of uniformity of
finished wheels. The test is the running balance of the wheel. Observations:*

1. The production worker is in a state of control with respect to his own
work (which is the only work that he is responsible for). No point falls outside the control limits.

2. He is under the handicap of the system. He cannot beat the system and
the capability of his process: he will once in a while produce a defective
wheel, even though he is a good worker and in a state of control.

3. He is meeting the requirements of his job. He can do no more. He has
nothing further to offer.

4. The main trouble lies in the system. The central line in Fig. 24,
which falls at about 125 gram-cms, represents the contribution of the system to

---

* From my paper, "On some statistical aids to economic production,"
Interfaces, vol. 5, August 1975; pp. 1-15.

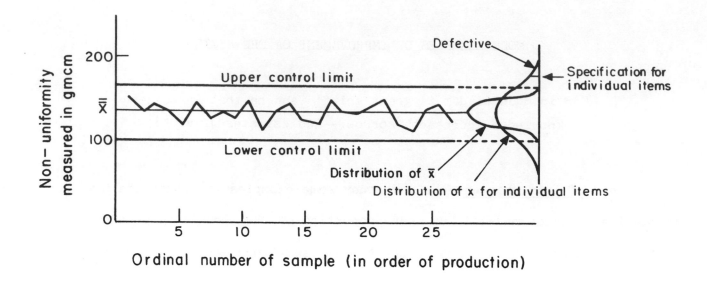

Fig. 24. Chart for $\bar{x}$ for test of uniformity of wheels
turned out by a production worker.

the total trouble. This handicap is built in. If the faults of the system
were reduced to 75 per cent of their present level, the upper tail of the
distribution of individual pieces would drop well below the specification limit,
and the entire production would be accepted; economies in production would be
realized.

Simple action by the supervisor of this production line lowered the entire
distribution. No wheels thereafter fall above the upper specification.

The reaction of management on the above paragraphs was the usual one,
namely, that they did not have in mind this kind of quality control when they
went into it. They were looking for everything to clear up, once the production
workers put their best efforts into the job. Eventually, however, patience
paid off.

Example 2. The second example deals with a service industry, motor freight.
Drivers of trucks pick up shipments and bring them into a terminal for reload

MORE EXAMPLES OF IMPROVEMENT OF THE SYSTEM

and onward movement. Other drivers deliver. A large company in motor freight may have anywhere from ten to forty terminals in or near large cities. There is a long chain of operations between the request of a shipper to the carrier (usually by telephone) to come and pick up a shipment, and placement of the shipment on the platform of the carrier, ready for reload and line-haul to the terminal that serves the destination of the shipment. Every operation offers a chance for the driver to make a mistake. The table shows 6 types of mistakes, plus all others. Although the frequency of mistakes is low, the total loss is substantial.

In mistake No. 1, the driver signs the shipping order for (e.g.) 10 cartons, but someone else finds, later on in the chain of operations, that there are only 9 cartons; one carton missing. Where is it? There may have been only 9 cartons in the first place; the shipping order was written incorrectly; or, more usual, the driver left one carton on the shipper's premises. Let us list some of the sources of loss from mistake No. 1:

1. It costs about $25 to search the platform for the missing carton, or to find the truck (by now out on the road) and to search it.

2. It costs $15 on the average to send a driver back to the shipper to pick up the missing carton.

3. It costs $10 to segregate and hold the 9 cartons for the duration of the search.

4. If the carrier does not find the carton, then the shipper may legitimately put in a claim for it. The carrier is responsible for the 10th carton. Its value may be anywhere from $10 to $1,000, with the possibility of an amount even greater.

It is obvious that mistake No. 1 may be costly. Any one of the 7 mistakes will on the average lead to a loss of $50. There were a total of 617 mistakes on the record, and they caused a loss of $31,000 for claims alone. Multiplied by 20, for 20 terminals, the total loss from the 7 mistakes was $620,000. (This amount is a minimum. It does not include the expenses of searches nor administration. Moreover, some mistakes are not included in the total of 617, but they nevertheless cause loss.)

The 7 types of mistakes

Type of mistake	Description
1	Short on pick up
2	Over on pick up
3	Failure to call in (by telephone) on over, short, and damaged cartons on delivery
4	Incomplete bill of lading
5	Improperly marked cartons
6	Incomplete signature on delivery receipt
7	Other

There were 150 drivers that worked all year long. Fig. 25 shows the distribution of the 150 drivers by number of mistakes, all 7 mistakes combined.

We postulate the following mechanism, which will distribute errors at random to drivers. We imagine a huge bowl of black and white beads, thoroughly mixed. Each driver scoops up a sample of 1,000 or more (the number of trips that an average driver makes in a year), and returns the beads to the bowl for more mixing. The total number of mistakes in Fig. 25 is 617, and there were 150 drivers. An estimate of the mean number of mistakes per driver would be

$$\bar{x} = 617/150 = 4.1$$

MORE EXAMPLES OF IMPROVEMENT OF THE SYSTEM

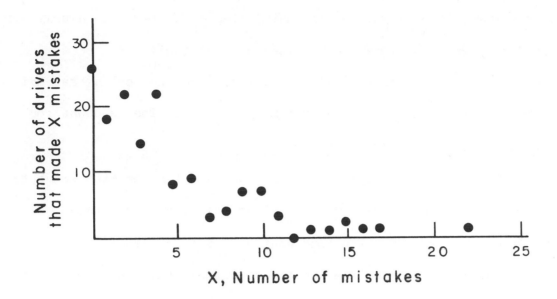

Fig. 25. The distribution of drivers by number of
mistakes, all 7 errors combined.

Upper and lower limits may be calculated as

$$4.1 + 3\sqrt{4.1} = 11 \qquad \text{(upper limit)}$$

and

$$4.1 - 3\sqrt{4.1} \text{ gives } 0 \qquad \text{(lower limit)}$$

We interpret the upper limit to mean that a driver that made more than 11

mistakes in the year is not part of the system. He contributes more than his

share. He is a special cause of loss.

There are two groups of drivers:

A. Drivers that made more than 11 mistakes.

B. Drivers that made fewer than 11 mistakes.

What have we learned from this simple statistical model?

1. The 7 drivers with more than 11 mistakes accounted for 112/617 or 18 per cent of the mistakes. They might reduce their rates of mistakes to average if they knew that they were outliers, and if they were at fault.

2. Drivers that made fewer than 11 mistakes measure the losses that arise from the system itself. They make the system what it is. They account for 100% - 18% = 82% of the mistakes.

No problem with people is simple. It would be wise for the management to defer criticism of Group A, to determine first whether these drivers worked unusually difficult routes, or extra long routes. As it turned out, they had.

Here we encounter an important lesson in administration. This company had been sending a letter to a driver at every mistake. It made no difference whether this was the one mistake of the year for this driver, or the 15th: the letter was exactly the same. A letter sent to a driver in Group B is demoralizing: the driver's interpretation thereof is that he is blamed for faults of the system.

One might pause here in passing to ask a question: what does the driver who has already received 15 warnings, all alike, think of the management?

And what about a driver that made only one or two mistakes during the period of study, and who may have made none or only one during the preceding six months? He receives the same letter as the man that has already made fifteen mistakes during the period of study. What does he think of the management?

> A man in one of my seminars related the fact that any policeman in his home city receives for every complaint against him, the same letter, no matter whether this was the first complaint in years, or the 10th within a few weeks. Good management?

Example 3. A small manufacturer of shoes was having trouble with his sewing machines, rent of which was very costly. The operators were spending a lot of their time rethreading the machines, a serious loss.

MORE EXAMPLES OF IMPROVEMENT OF THE SYSTEM

The key observation was that the trouble was common to all machines and to all operators. The obvious conclusion was that the trouble, whatever it was, was common, environmental, affecting all machines and all operators. A few tests showed that it was the thread that caused the trouble. The owner of the shop had been purchasing poor thread at bargain prices. The loss of machine time had cost him hundreds of times the difference between good thread and what he had been buying. Bargain prices for thread turned out to be a costly snare.

This was an example of getting rooked by the lowest bidder and being taken in by price alone without regard to quality or performance.

Better thread eliminated the problem. Only management could make the change. The operators could not go out and buy better thread, even if they had known where the trouble lay. They work in the system. The thread was part of the system.

Prior to the simple investigation that found the cause, pedestrian but effective, the owner had supposed that his troubles all came from inexperience and carelessness of the operators.

Example 4. Number of mechanics needed in the tool room. The job of the tool room is to make machines (especially prototypes), to modify existing equipment, and to take care of emergencies from breakdown of equipment in use anywhere in the whole plant. The foreman was sometimes caught short with not enough mechanics to take care of emergencies. On other days, there were few emergencies, and his people could devote a lot of effort to development.

About how many emergencies occur per day, on the average?

He had no figures, but a possible number could be 36, perhaps 40.

On the supposition that breakdowns are independent, not chain reactions, the number of breakdowns day by day will form a Poisson distribution. If the average number is 36, the standard deviation of this distribution will be $\sqrt{36} = 6$. The number of mechanics needed to meet any emergency would be

$$36 + 3\sqrt{36} = 54$$

If the average number of breakdowns per day were 40, he would need to prepare for 58 emergencies, not 54. The upper limit is sensitive to the average and to cycles.

If he is willing to get caught short only now and then, possibly once in two months, he could use the upper 2-sigma limit, which would be

$$36 + 2\sqrt{36} = 48$$

This limit is also sensitive to the average and to trends and should be increased by 4 if the average were 40, not 36.

The next step would be to compile figures day by day for a few weeks, and plot a run chart to examine the distribution for randomness.

Example 5. Pellets of iron ore are loaded into railway cars. The cars move past the loader at about 4 mph.

Desired: more uniform loads (net tons per car).

A loader manipulates the mechanism for loading the cars, trying to achieve uniformity of weight. Uniformity is desirable for several reasons. It is feasible, for a customer that orders some large number of cars such as 100 or more in a week, to compute the total weight of the order, and the cost of transportation, by use of a sample of 10 or 15 cars. Use of the sample decreases the cost of weighing the cars, and it also speeds up the movement of cars in the yards. The capacity of every car should be utilized, but not over-done. Pellets piled too high in a car may fall off and be lost as the train goes around a curve. Loss of half a metric ton of pellets in this way from a car was not unusual.

MORE EXAMPLES OF IMPROVEMENT OF THE SYSTEM

Fig. 26. Railway cars, as they pass by, are loaded with hot iron ore pellets. The plate at A smooths out the mountains and valleys in the top surface of the pellets as the loaded cars move by it. The result is improved uniformity and greater tonnage per car. Heavy loads are desirable, also uniformity in weight. These requirements were difficult to achieve prior to installation of the strong steel plate at A.

How can greater uniformity be achieved?

Why had not the engineers thought of this before? They had supposed that the loader, if she tried hard enough, could shrink the variation. Their thoughts had not before turned to the possibility that the system could be changed.

Example 6.* Improved production of stockings. Here, the management looked ahead and foresaw that costs would overtake revenue in the near future and the company would move into the non-profit category unless something were done soon. Any plan that would increase the proportion of first grade of stocking would

---

* I have borrowed this example from an unpublished paper written by my friend David S. Chambers.

increase net revenue and put the company into better competitive position, even at current volume. There were other reasons to improve production: workers were paid by the piece, with a penalty of two pieces for every bad piece made, and the company had to pay the difference between a worker's pay for the week and the minimum wage, if she fell below it. Any increase in productivity would help the worker as well as the company. Initial steps:

1. The big step was that the manager saw trouble ahead, and sought help from a statistician (David S. Chambers).

2. The second step was indoctrination of the management.

3. Then, on advice of Professor Chambers, the company sent twenty supervisors to a ten-week course at the University of Tennessee, $2\frac{1}{2}$ hours per week.

Incidentally, this course gave twenty supervisors their first chance to get acquainted and to talk about their problems.

4. After the training sessions were finished, the supervisors were asked by the management to try to make some applications of the principles learned and to prepare a report on the results achieved.

The report was presented at one of the weekly foremen's meetings which had been initiated during the training period. Management wished these meetings to be a forum for exchange of ideas between the operating personnel and they were successful. It was the first indication to supervisors that their work was important to the management and to the plant. They developed teamwork and interest that had been totally lacking heretofore. This group was, in effect, a QC-Circle composed of supervisors, a hitherto untapped resource.

5. After several meetings of supervisors had been held, the consultant recommended, as a start, a study of the problems of the looping department. The main reason for choice of this department was that (1) there appeared to be problems there, (2) the supervisor had learned the philosophy of quality

MORE EXAMPLES OF IMPROVEMENT OF THE SYSTEM

control, and (3) had ability to work well with the machine operators and with the other supervisors.

First step. Stockings, at the end of the production line, are graded into piles--firsts, irregulars, seconds, thirds, and rags. An enterprising man bought the rags and found that some of the rags turned out to be, on scrutiny, salable as third grade or even irregular. He hired menders and raised most of the remaining rags to first grade.

> It is important to note that the cost of production is the
> same for rags as it is for first grade. The profit, however, lies
> in the first grade. The irregulars, seconds, and thirds sell at
> or below cost; the rags fetch nearly zero.

One of the first steps was to institute inspection of the looping, to learn whether the system of looping was under statistical control or if there was evidence of wild variation from special causes. There were two shifts, day and evening. Inspection of 16 stockings per day from each looper commenced the first working day of June. June and July were used as the test period. Forty-seven loopers worked nearly every day through the test period. The overall per cent defective, day by day, for these 47 loopers, is shown in Fig. 27. The overall average turned out to be 4.8 per cent defective, with control limits computed as

$$\begin{matrix} \text{UCL} \\ \text{LCL} \end{matrix} = \bar{p} \pm 3\sqrt{\bar{p}\bar{q}/n} \qquad \begin{aligned} \bar{p} &= .048 \\ \bar{q} &= 1 - \bar{p} \\ n &= 47 \times 16 = 752 \end{aligned}$$

$$= .048 \pm 3\sqrt{.048 \times .952/752}$$

$$= \begin{matrix} .071 \\ .025 \end{matrix}$$

The test period showed pretty good statistical control. Two points (days) were out of control. The explanation of the first point was that there had never before been an inspector in the department, and his presence upset the

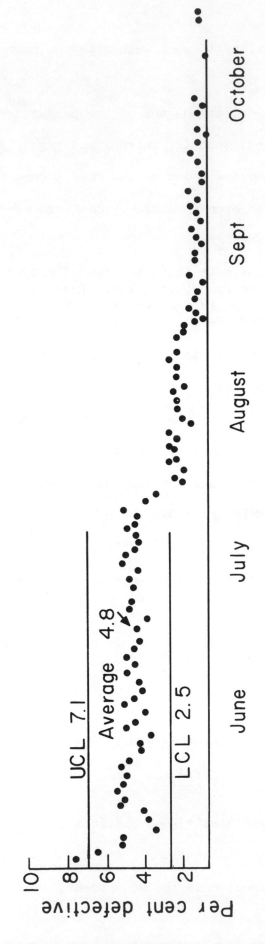

Fig. 27. Chart for per cent defective (per cent down-graded). June and July constituted the test period. Action commenced near the end of July. Improvement commenced at once, as shown by chart for August and September, and continued beyond the range of the chart (see the text for figures on improvement).

MORE EXAMPLES OF IMPROVEMENT OF THE SYSTEM

operators. They eventually grew accustomed to his presence. The reason for the second point out of control was that it was Monday after the week that contained the 4th of July, during which week the plant was shut down--an exaggerated case of problems on a Monday morning.

Shock to management. Incidentally, the vice president of operations almost went into a panic when he saw the figure 4.8 per cent defective. He had never before known how many defective stockings he was producing. He declared that the company could not have been in business making a product that is 4.8 per cent defective in looping: the business would have closed down long ago. He forgot that the plant had been operating for 65 years.

Of course, his problem was that he had never before seen any figures on the proportion defective: the plant had run along without figures. The only record that had been kept was the number of downgraded stockings at the pairing and boxing operation. Causes of trouble could not be traced backward from that point. In other words, the management had no idea where they were.

Charts for each operator. Management provided every looper with her own control chart so that she could perceive week by week how well she was doing. These charts showed that some loopers ran above the upper control limit for the group. Investigation showed that poor eyesight was in a number of cases the source of trouble. On the basis of this discovery, the management provided tests of eyes for each of the 125 loopers, and glasses if needed.

There had previously been no examination for eyesight. The new policy was to examine all operators for eyesight.

Summary of accomplishments. The record was one of continued improvement. Beginning in August, the first month of genuine effort to improve, the level of defectives dropped to 2.4 per cent, then to 1.4, 1.3, 1.2, 1.1, and, finally, by February to 0.8 per cent, a dramatic change in only seven months. Instead

Chapter 8

of making every week 11,500 stockings to be downgraded, the department was by February making less than 2,000. Results:

-- More first grade stockings produced
-- Increase in production of first grade stockings
-- Lower costs; greater profit
-- Increased earnings of employees through increased productivity (incidentally, at less effort)
-- Evidence of maintenance of quality to show customers, an aid to sales
-- Dramatic reduction in complaints from customers

The net cost of the program was close to zero. Some inspectors were added, but some 100 per cent inspection was abandoned, not being needed. One secretary did all the plotting of charts. No positions were added.

All this improvement took place in a short time after a statistician went to work. Statistical theory pointed out how to improve the system, so that people could do better work with less effort.

I remind the reader that the improvements took place without investment in new equipment.

Operator 75. An excellent operator. The supervisor was able to incorporate much of her techniques into general departmental routine to the benefit of all.

Operator 22. This operator did much worse in July than in June. The supervisor, after he studied her work habits in August, referred her to the Personnel Department, with the suggestion that she have her eyes examined. Her previous examination, it turned out, was about 8 years earlier. The physician found her to be blind in the left eye and with vision 6/20 in the right eye. He was able to correct her right eye to 20/20. Her work improved at once. Her earnings increased 19¢ per hour.

This incident with Operator 22 caused management to think about its policy with respect to examination of eyes. They faced the fact that they had no

MORE EXAMPLES OF IMPROVEMENT OF THE SYSTEM

policy, except for new employees, learners in the school for looping, run by the company, a course of six weeks. But if a person with previous experience in looping applied for employment, the procedure was to try her out and let the supervisor decide whether she could do the job. For regular employees, there had been no examination given or required.

The new policy was to examine all loopers for eyesight, and to establish a regular pattern of reexamination.

The initial examination discovered a dozen operators that had difficulty to see what they were doing.

Operator 27. This operator was perhaps the poorest one of all during the test period. All that the supervisor did was to show the chart to her. Her response was, "I have been here for five years, and this is the first time anybody ever told me what looping is. I could do a much better job, if it makes any difference." Her record in August and thereafter showed great improvement.

Concluding remarks. The principles expounded in this chapter, and the examples of application, are all simple, yet the economic gains from corrective action by management are considerable. Some people would call this work operations research. Some would call it systems analysis: others, industrial engineering. To me, it is just a statistician finding problems and trying to be helpful.

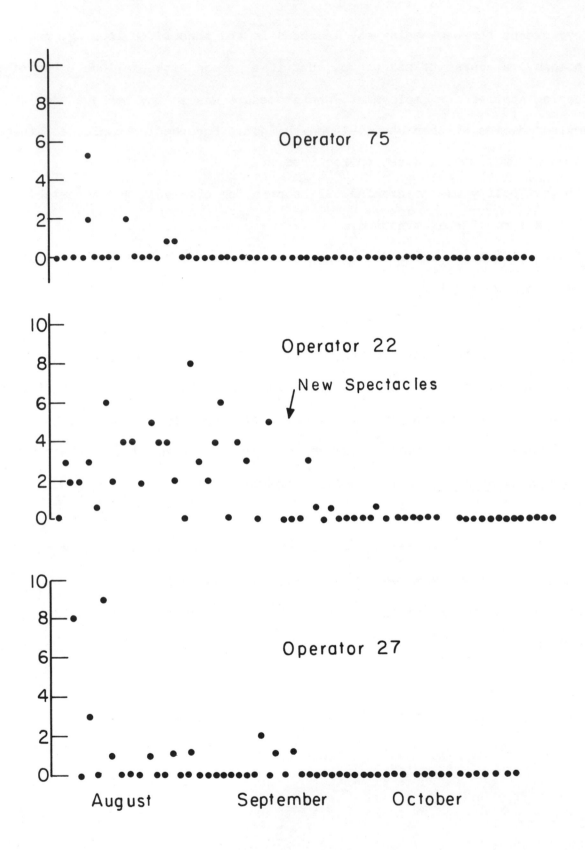

Fig. 28. Charts for three of the loopers.

MORE EXAMPLES OF IMPROVEMENT OF THE SYSTEM

Chapter 9

SOME HAZARDS OF GREAT IDEAS

The aim is admirable, but the method is madness.
--Attributed to the (Republican) minority report of the Joint
Economic Committee, <u>Wall Street Journal</u>, 15 March 1977, page 20.

For every problem there is a solution: simple, neat, and
wrong.--Advertisement of the Mobil Oil Company, 1972. (Perhaps
borrowed from H. L. Mencken, who said, "For every complex
question there is a simple answer, and it is wrong." <u>Business
Week</u>, 21 April 1980, page 25.)

<u>Basic principles to be used here</u>. The examples to be illustrated here
arise from failure to understand four basic axioms:

-- Some points of a group must lie above the average of the group.
-- Not all points will lie on the average (except by rare coincidence).
-- There is in the ideal state of statistical control variation of quality
and quantity, but the ups and downs satisfy criteria of randomness. In
other words, the variation is stable. The quality-characteristic under
control is stable, constant; it reproduces itself hour after hour (Ch. 13).
-- There are not only special causes of variation and loss, but also common
causes of loss arising from the system itself, if there be a system
(Ch. 13).

The two theorems at the top may lead the reader to suppose that I am trying
to write a comic strip. I am not. The sad truth is that the usual practice in
administration and management in America ignores all four axioms.

<u>Example 1. Some people are above average</u>. On a professional engagement,
the president of the company wished to show me his data processing machinery.
In one part of his establishment were about sixty girls punching cards. I
asked him what was the error-rate in punching cards, and to my pleasant surprise, he knew. He was one step ahead of most people. Most people say that

they have no error, or that this is not the place for error. The average error-rate was 3 errors per 100 cards, he told me. He receives every Wednesday a report compiled from the records of verification of punching to show how many errors each girl made during the preceding week.

And here came forth his great idea for supervision. He has a talk with every girl that made more than the average number of errors during the preceding week.

"Well, that means that you talk to about 30 girls every week, week after week." "Yes," he said, "that is about the number. How did you know?"

I thereupon told him about a recent letter to the editor of the London Times. The writer has been studying a report from the Ministry of Health, whence it was obvious that half the children in the United Kingdom were below average weight. A disgrace on the nation. We must do something about the nourishment of our children.

My listener laughed at this joke, but his understanding thereof was not deep enough to see that he was making the same mistake, and causing more errors, not fewer. He was crestfallen when I explained that this kind of supervision would ruin the morale of any organization.

Without knowing it, he was in danger of simply selecting week by week a random selection of girls from the 60. Some simple statistical techniques would have told him which girls need help, if any (e.g., transfer to other work).

How effective have your efforts been? The answer was predictable: he was disappointed: no improvement. Worse, whether he knew it or not, his efforts were creating frustration and difficulties.

Example 2. Stealing second base with the bases full. The end product is refined sugar. The raw materials are mostly raw sugar and sea water. The cost

SOME HAZARDS OF GREAT IDEAS

of water is a factor of importance, because the factory is located on a bay
with no supply of fresh water suitable for use in refining sugar. It is
necessary to make fresh water by removing the salt and other chemicals from sea
water.

Objective: Reduce the consumption of sea water to 3.5 tons per ton of end
product.

Method (wrong): Investigate conditions on any day for which the ratio
falls above 3.5.

What I saw, when I visited the factory at the invitation of the management,
was a bulletin board with a row of slats, some green, some red, one for each
day of the month. The purpose of a green slat was to indicate that the ratio
of sea water to refined sugar was below 3.5. A red slat indicated the opposite.
The production workers were informed day by day about the ratio for the day
before. A red slat sent them into a huddle to try to discover what they did
the day before that was wrong. Naturally, they came up with all sorts of
explanations and with attempts to take corrective action, all wrong. If the
next day went green, they were jubilant over the thought that they had discovered a cause of waste, only to see a red slat turn up in a day or two, or
perhaps two or three red slats in a row.

Was the process in statistical control? The managing engineer did not
know. Had they plotted a chart to show day by day the consumption ratio of sea
water? No. I asked for data and graph paper, and in ten minutes I produced
the run chart shown in Fig. 29.

The process, as it turned out, was in statistical control, NO SPECIAL CAUSE
OF VARIATION. Moreover, the objective 3.5 was very close to the average. Some
points were above the average; some were below. The chart, if they had plotted

Chapter 9

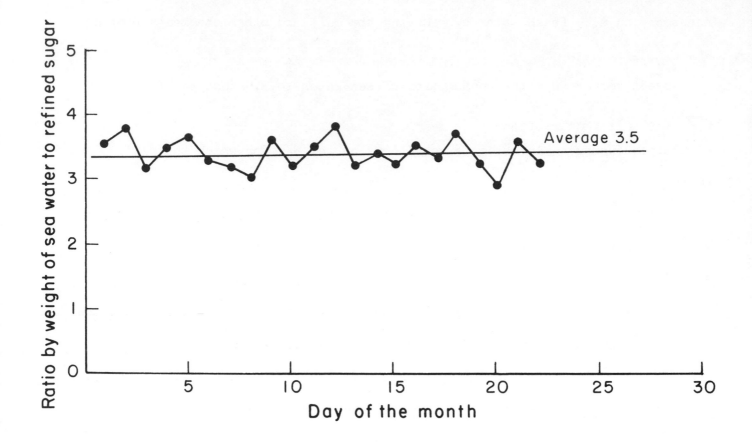

Fig. 29. A run chart to show day by day the tons of sea
water per ton of refined sugar. This chart shows no evidence
of a special cause on any one day. Conclusion: the ratio
of sea water to refined sugar is in statistical control at
an average value of 3.5.

it and understood it, would have told the men that the process was ALREADY
MEETING THE OBJECTIVE.

The nearest parallel that I could think of is the baseball player that
stole second base with the bases full.

Why was management's action wrong? (a) Because it required search for a
special cause when none existed. (b) It failed to point to the need for a

SOME HAZARDS OF GREAT IDEAS

change in the system, the responsibility of management. In short, it confused special causes with common causes.

"Where did the figure 3.5 come from?", I asked.

"We held a meeting and decided that we could meet it."

The joke of it is that they had already been meeting for weeks the objective of 3.5. Here was a great idea that only provided frustration and guaranteed exaggeration of problems.

The management had called their plan quality control, were very happy with it, eager to show it off. It is not easy to tell an artist that the picture that he has just painted is full of flaws.

Lessons learned here. The moral of all this is multifold.

1. Management should have the right kind of goals, but a numerical goal, like a consumption-ratio of 3.5, is outmoded. A better goal would be the greatest possible reduction of use of sea water that is economically feasible with statistical aids and all other aids.

2. The methods that the management were using here would not reduce the use of sea water. The management was confusing special causes with common causes. The chart indicated no special causes. Reduction of sea water must come from changes in the system. Next steps:

a. Discard the bulletin board with the red and green slats. Plot a chart, instead, and study it. Take action when it detects existence of a special cause.

b. Get busy at the engineering level, to work on the process with the aim of reducing the consumption of sea water.

c. What changes in the process might reduce the use of sea water?

d. Observation and experimentation for reduction of sea water should take place on a continuing basis, as a function of engineering and chemistry.

Efforts should not be intensified and then relaxed on the basis of random fluctuations that are in statistical control. Statistical techniques are helpful in understanding complex relationships. Some experimentation might be desirable, for which appropriate statistical design would be required for reliability, economy, and speed.

3. Any hope that the production workers could improve or reduce the ratio, when it is in control, is futile and costly.

4. The company had data, but had for some reason failed to use the data in the form of a chart or other statistical technique to learn whether the process was in statistical control, and to detect the existence of special causes, if any.

5. If the process had not been in statistical control, then there would be no identifiable process. Special causes would be present, manifest by a point out of control or by a trend, the cause to be found by the production workers and eliminated by them.

It should be noted that it is not always necessary to perform experimentation to accumulate data for understanding and improving the process. Temperature will vary, naturally: nothing is constant. There may be a continuing record of the temperatures of a number of solutions and processes and mixing. There may be a continuing record of pressure. There may be a continuing record of speed. Intermittent records will serve the purpose. Engineering judgment to observe the effect of high temperature, low temperature, high pressure, low pressure, etc., on production and on number of defectives, may lead to clues in understanding and improving the process. This is a cheaper and better way than to start out with the express purpose of conducting experiments that will require a plan for varying the temperature, pressure, and speed. My friend, Dr. E. E. Nishibori of Tokyo, first mentioned to me the economy and efficiency of making observations on natural variation, leaving experimentation for problems not solved by simple observation. The same theme has long been voiced by my friend Dr. Hugh Hamaker of Eindhoven.

In other words, as this book pleads in so many places, make use of existing information.

SOME HAZARDS OF GREAT IDEAS

<u>Example 3</u>. Out by automobile near Lancaster, to attend a convention of a client, I discovered possible need of a new fan-belt, and found the agency of the manufacturer. While waiting, I observed a placard on the wall:

TOP TECHNICIAN OF THE MONTH
FOR GREATEST CUSTOMER-SATISFACTION
Tom Jones (fictitious)

"What is greatest customer-satisfaction?" I asked the foreman. "Fewest complaints by customers. Fewest comebacks for the month." Then followed this exchange of question and answer.

Is the number ever zero for some mechanic?

Frequently.

What is the average per month per man? Do you keep any records?

No, but I have a pretty good idea about the average. I have to use a little discretion now and then. For example, those new carburetors. They are difficult to adjust. I don't count a complaint on those new carburetors.

Do the mechanics all have about the same average, month after month?

Yes, they do. It varies, of course, but they all come out about the same. (I ought to have asked him: how do you know?)

Does any one mechanic ride along month after month without ever getting his name on the wall?

Not forever; they take turns pretty well.

What do you do if two men tie over the month?

We put them both on the wall.

How do you know whether they tie, unless you keep records?

I know pretty well how the men do.

Does a man ever get his name on the wall an excessive number of times in the span of a year or two?

No, they take turns, naturally.

Does a man ever achieve zero complaints two months in a row?

Yes, it has happened.

Is this merit system effective, do you think?

Well, it was at first, for a few years. Now it is not exciting.

I thought that the foreman would ask me why I was so interested, but he did not. I would conclude, from his answers, that this honor system is a lottery. His answers fitted neatly a random pattern. Figures would have made possible tests for randomness. Let us look at some of the implications of randomness (state of statistical control).

With an overall average of two complaints per month per man, a man would have a chance of $e^{-2} = 1/7.4$ to have no complaints during any month. With an overall average of three complaints per month per man, on the average, a man would have a chance of $e^{-3} = 1/20$ in one month. These probabilities show that if a man has reached statistical control of his work, with an average of 1 or 2 complaints per month, he need only be patient to make the honor roll. He might in fact find himself man of the month two successive months. If he makes it one month, he has a chance of $1/e$ to make it the next month. On the other hand, he may also have to wait for a long time, purely by chance.

In summary, here we have a system that supposedly improves the quality of service. Actually (on the supposition that the men don't care about it any more), it accomplishes nothing. Or (on the supposition that the men care and try to get on to the honor roll), it actually depresses the morale and quality of service.

Restatement of the moral. A student at New York University, after hearing a lecture on the subject of this chapter, sent to me the following quotation with the resolution: "From now on, I will view differently awards to great generals."

SOME HAZARDS OF GREAT IDEAS

As to the influence and genius of great generals--there is a story that Enrico Fermi once asked Gen. Leslie Groves how many generals might be called "great." Groves said about three out of every 100. Fermi asked how a general qualified for the adjective, and Groves replied that any general who had won five major battles in a row might safely be called great. This was in the middle of World War II. Well, then, said Fermi, considering that the opposing forces in most theaters of operation are roughly equal, the odds are one of two that a general will win a battle, one of four that he will win two battles in a row, one of eight for three, one of sixteen for four, one of thirty-two for five. "So you are right, general, about three out of every 100. Mathematical probability, not genius."

-- John Keegan,
THE FACE OF BATTLE
(Viking, New York, 1977)

Example 4. One may read now and then in a journal of business about a manufacturing concern that has adopted a plan by which, if sales of some product or line of products drop two years in a row, the company will threaten to go to another advertising agency.

Now anyone that has tried by appropriate statistical techniques to measure the effect of advertising is painfully aware of the multitude of forces that can cause a decrease in sales, or a decrease in the share of the market. Advertising, or the failure of advertising, could be one of the forces, but to ascribe hard luck to the advertising agency, in an ocean of possible other causes, is sheer guesswork. Such a system could best be described as a lottery, in which the advertising agency takes a chance: it may win, it may lose.

Again, there is no harm in a lottery, if it be called a lottery. But change of agency carries with it some implication of failure and defeat.

And somebody gets a promotion for thinking up such a great idea. The man's colleagues may be fooled into thinking that his promotion was based on merit. The man himself (the one that gets promoted) can hardly be persuaded otherwise.

Example 5. Fallacies in cost/benefit analysis. Cost/benefit analysis requires $\Delta C/\Delta B$, where ΔC is the additional cost of a plan, in use or proposed, and ΔB is the added benefit. The idea sounds good; catches on. But there are ofttimes serious difficulties.

Problems:

1. Costs are sometimes elusive; difficult to estimate. For example, no one knows the cost of a defective item (e.g., TV-tube) that reaches a customer. A customer dissatisfied with an item of small cost (a toaster, for example) may be influential in the decision on a huge contract, and see to it that some other manufacturer gets it.

2. Same for benefits. Benefits are even more difficult to evaluate in dollars. However, by use of the idea of a trade-off, one benefit against another, a scale of ranks for benefits can sometimes be achieved.*

To some people, cost/benefit analysis means shopping for prices. This is all right, possibly, for soap of definite specifications. It can be a disaster for the professional services of a lawyer, physician, statistician, or engineer.

If you can not estimate satisfactorily the numerator or the denominator of a fraction, it is impossible to calculate the value of a fraction. This is where cost/benefit analysis often leaves us.

I would not participate in any attempt to use cost/benefit analysis for design of product where possible injury or loss of life is at risk.

---

*Jerome Rotherberg, "Cost/benefit analysis," being Chapter 4 in volume 2 of HANDBOOK ON EVALUATION, edited by Elmer L. Struening and Marcia Guttentag (Sage Publications, 1975), pp. 53-68.

SOME HAZARDS OF GREAT IDEAS

Chapter 10

SOME NEW PRINCIPLES OF TRAINING AND OF SUPERVISION

to Leadership +

> Understanding is a wellspring of life unto him that hath it:
> but the instruction of fools is folly.--Proverbs 16:22.
>
> Your views, so far as they have any merit, have already been
> fully considered and rejected.--Dean Rusk, then Secretary of State,
> to John Kenneth Galbraith, then Ambassador to India, as reported in
> Harper's, vol. 235, No. 1410, November 1967, page 54.

Aim of supervision. The aim of supervision should be to improve the performance of man and machine, to increase output, and simultaneously to lighten the load of the production worker, to make his job more interesting as well as more productive. Put in a negative way, the aim of supervision is not merely to find and record failures of men, but to remove the causes of failure: to help people to do a better job with less effort. Actually, most of this book is involved with supervision. Nearly every page heretofore and hereafter states a principle of good supervision of man and machine, or shows an example of good or bad supervision. This chapter summarizes some of the principles already learned, and adds a few more examples, along with suggestions on some simple statistical techniques that are useful in supervision.

First step. The first step in supervision is for the management to relieve foremen of quotas in terms of numbers. A quota in numbers is merely another form of work standard (Point 11, page 40). A concomitant step is to remove the other barriers that rob production workers of the possibility of pride of workmanship (Point 12, page 43).

<u>Tell a worker about a mistake? Why not?</u> How can a man improve his work if we fail to point out to him a defective item that he has made, so that he can see where he went wrong? We wish it to be understood that defectives and mistakes will not be tolerated here. These are the usual responses to the question posed. The answers are in fact spontaneous, as if the answer must be obvious.

<u>Importance of training</u>. Anyone, when he has brought his work to a state of statistical control, whether he was trained well or badly, is in a rut. He has completed his learning of that particular job. It is not economical to try to provide further training of the same kind. He may nevertheless, with good training, learn very well some other kind of job.

It is obviously of the utmost importance to train new people, when they come on to a job, to do the job well. Once the learning curve levels off, a control chart will indicate whether and when a person has reached the state of statistical control. When he reaches it, continuation of training by the same method will accomplish nothing.

Curiously, if a man's work has not yet reached statistical control, further training will help him.

In a state of chaos (poor supervision, bad management, nothing in statistical control), it is impossible for anyone in the organization to develop his potential ability and capacity for uniformity or for quality.

How many production workers ever saw the next operation, their customer? How many ever saw the finished product in the box, ready for purchase? After some study in a plant, I wrote to the management the following:

> Every one in your company knows that the aim is perfection, that you can not tolerate defectives and mistakes. You make every worker responsible for the defectives that he has produced. Yet from the records that you have showed to me, it is obvious that you are tolerating a high proportion of defectives, and have been doing so for years. In fact, the levels of various kinds of mistake have not decreased; they have been pretty constant and predictable over a number of years.

SOME NEW PRINCIPLES OF TRAINING AND OF SUPERVISION

Have you any reason to think that the level of mistakes will decrease in the future? Have you ever thought that the problem could be in the system?

Like so many obvious solutions to a problem, this one is also wrong.

We know now from Chapter 7 that to hold a worker on the job without pay till he has cleaned up the defectives that were detected by inspection of his product, if he is in statistical control, is to charge him with faults of the system.

Another example of bad administration is the management's policy to penalize employees for coming in late in weather that has crippled the transportation system.

It is obviously equally stupid for a customer in a restaurant to blame the waitress for the food, or for delays in the kitchen.

A better way. The correct procedures are contrary to practice and advice in books on administration and management. There are two circumstances to consider.

1. The worker has achieved statistical control of his work.

2. The worker has not yet achieved statistical control of his work.

We first talk about the worker that has achieved statistical control of his work. Under statistical control, the answer to the question posed near the out-set of this chapter is no, do not show to a production worker a defective item nor tell him about it, unless his chart detected the existence of a special cause, in which case he should have already noted it from his control chart, and sought the cause and removed it.

A basic principle presumed here is that no one should be blamed or penalized for performance that he can not govern. Violation of this principle can only lead to frustration and dissatisfaction with the job, and lower production.

Chapter 10

There is a better way: discover which people if any are out of control with respect to the group. If anyone is out of control on the side of poor performance, investigate the circumstances--his eyesight, tools, training, and take any remedial action indicated. Or is he simply in the wrong job? Perhaps the training that you gave him was inept and incomplete. Anyone out of control on the good side is there for reasons that need study. He may use methods or motions that other people could learn and thereby improve their performance.

If a company has a policy to fire people that do not come up to a certain standard level of production, and to retain those that meet it, there is a best way to do it. The standard can be fixed by statistical theory for maximum profit in consideration of:

-- The distribution of abilities in the reservoir of people not yet tried out.
-- The cost of training a man to the point where you decide whether to retain him or let him go.
-- The discounted profit in retention of a man that meets the goal.

My friend Dr. Gerald J. Glasser has worked on this problem in connexion with broadcasting: which programs to retain, which to let go and replace with new programs, some of which will make the grade, and some of which will not.

Example of use of $\bar{x}$- and R-charts in training. Fig. 30 shows average scores ($\bar{x}$) in golf for a beginner. His scores, before the lessons, were obviously not in a state of control: there are points outside the control limits. Then came lessons. His scores thereupon showed a state of statistical control with the desired results, viz., an average score considerably below what his average was before the lessons. Here, lessons changed the system.

SOME NEW PRINCIPLES OF TRAINING AND OF SUPERVISION

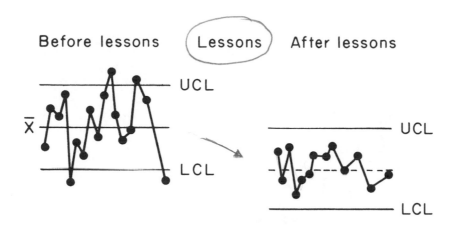

Fig. 30. Average weekly scores in golf for a beginner who took lessons before he reached a state of statistical control. Scores for four successive games constituted a sample of size n = 4 for computation of $\bar{x}$ and R. (The chart for the range is not shown.) Taken from W. Edwards Deming, ELEMENTARY PRINCIPLES OF THE STATISTICAL CONTROL OF QUALITY (Union of Japanese Scientists and Engineers, Tokyo, 1950), p. 22. UCL and LCL mean upper control limit and lower control limit.

Another example comes from Japan.* A patient, after an operation, had to learn again to walk. Lessons in a special training unit in the hospital brought good results. Fig. 31. shows an $\bar{x}$-chart for a characteristic of gait (a complex function of a number of measures, which need not detain us here). Each point comes from 4 successive steps. The patient was wildly out of control before lessons commenced; in better control, with improved characteristics, ten days after lessons commenced; in good control with excellent characteristics three weeks after lessons commenced, showing that his training was finished.

---

*Shunji Hirokawa and Hiroshi Sugiyama, "Quantitative gain analysis," Technology Reports of Osaka University, Faculty of Engineering, vol. 30, No. 1520, 1980.

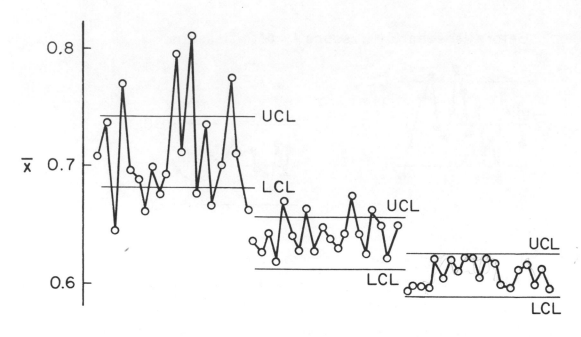

(1) Just before
lessons began.
(2) 10 days after
lessons began.
(3) 3 weeks after
lessons began.

Fig. 31. Average daily scores for a patient learning
to walk after an operation: (1) before lessons began;
(2) 10 days after lessons began; (3) 3 weeks after lessons
began. From Hirokawa and Sugiyama; reference in footnote.
The control limits came from the ~~whole group of patients~~.
this set of steps.

Remark. The R-chart (omitted here) showed good consistency for a few
steps; then good consistency at another level for a few steps. This explains
the narrow limits for $\bar{x}$ in the two left-hand panels.

Statistical control achieved, but output unsatisfactory. The first step
here as well as everywhere else, is to take a hard look at the figures from
inspection.

A worker who is in a state of control but whose work is unsatisfactory
presents a problem. It is usually uneconomical to try to retrain him on the

same job. It is more economical to put him into a new job in which the training may be more expert than it was in his present job.

Fig. 32 provides an illustration. An experienced man in golf hoped to improve his score by taking lessons. The chart shows that the lessons accomplished nothing. His techniques were already engrained: his teacher was unsuccessful in dislodging them and replacing them with better ones.

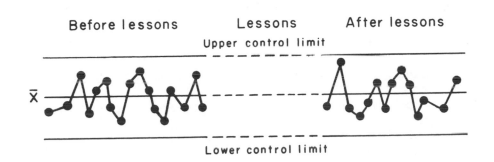

Fig. 32. Average scores in golf for an experienced golfer, before and after lessons. Here the player had already achieved statistical control before he took lessons. The lessons were accordingly ineffective. Scores for four successive games constituted a sample of size n = 4 for computation of $\bar{x}$ and R. (The chart for the range is not shown.) Taken from W. Edwards Deming, ELEMENTARY PRINCIPLES OF THE STATISTICAL CONTROL OF QUALITY (Union of Japanese Scientists and Engineers, Tokyo, 1950), p. 22.

A familiar example is someone who came to the U.S. years ago from a foreign country and learned English by forced draft after arrival. His vocabulary and grammar may be superb, but his accent is beyond repair. Or, perhaps he learned to speak English in his own country, as a faithful, devoted, and admiring pupil of a teacher that himself had been a devoted pupil of a teacher that could not speak good English. The speech therapists that I have consulted tell me that a few rough edges can be smoothed out, but that the benefit is hardly worth the effort of either pupil or teacher. In other words, the man developed long ago a system of speech, and it is too late now to change it.

Another familiar example is the woman that taught herself to sing, without benefit of a teacher, or with benefit of an incompetent teacher, and has been singing for years, in her own way, pleasing some people and possibly herself; reducing others to shudders.

What is the answer, then, for a man that has achieved statistical control of his work, but whose output is not satisfactory, either in quantity or in quality, or both? Transfer him to another job, and be sure to give him good training in the new job. (It may be poor training on the present job that brought on the difficulty.)

Need the new job be completely unrelated to his present job? No. We may return to our familiar example of the man that learned long ago to speak English, but with a bad accent. The same man, under a competent teacher of singing in English, will sing in English without accent. You may be able to place a man, by his speech, a native of Melbourne, Bristol, Edinburgh, Brooklyn, Berlin, Stockholm, or Paris, yet if he has learned under a competent teacher to sing, his singing will give no clue to the language that he spoke in childhood.

A curious example is a man afflicted with stammering in speech, but who sings without trace of it.

A simple principle to observe is that no man can do all things equally well. He may achieve statistical control of his work on one job, only to find that he is not doing well in it; yet, if trained properly in a new job, may do very well in it. Supervision consists in giving people a chance to do their best at whatever they can do.

SOME NEW PRINCIPLES OF TRAINING AND OF SUPERVISION

The following letter from one of my students at the Graduate School of
Business Administration of New York University illustrates the above principles.

> I am a supervisor of a corporate accounting department. Many were
> the times that I would look out on the office and wish that we could
> get rid of one or two mediocre employees and hire two top notch people
> to replace them. In one of your lectures, you showed us that the
> chance of drawing a better replacement out of the labor pool is slim.
> Firing someone, and taking a chance out of the labor pool, was not
> worth the risk of demoralizing the whole department.
>
> When I first started your course, I had a problem in the office.
> One of our graduate accountants was doing consistently poor work on a
> clerical-type assignment, which he had been on for some time. It was
> a rule that an employee could not be promoted until he put in good
> performance on his present job.
>
> After hearing your lecture on new principles in administration, I
> realized that this employee was probably in a state of statistical
> control, even though it was impractical for me to try to prove it with
> statistical methods. I then decided that the right approach would be
> to give to this employee training in another job. I am happy to report
> that this idea has worked out beautifully. The employee has mastered
> the new job and I feel as if I now have an extra member of the staff.

Warnings and exceptions. No problem in administration is simple. We must
be on guard for apparent exceptions and changes that surprise the worker.

1. Even after someone has achieved statistical control of his work, he may
lose it. A point may go out of control, indicating the existence of a special
cause not heretofore encountered. The production worker must run down and
eliminate from future work this special cause. He has lost statistical control
till he does this.

2. Unfortunately, also, people may become careless, relying on momentum of
past performance. It is for this reason that the control chart or other
statistical tests should be reinstituted now and then for short periods of time
to learn whether the work is still under statistical control.

3. New product, or new specifications, possibly on a new contract, may
lead to a new kind of defect to be reckoned with. The production worker may
have to put himself into statistical control with a new set of operations.

4. The inspection department may introduce a new kind of measure for some important quality-characteristic (e.g., viscosity). In effect, this could mean, to the worker, a new product.

Another example: chart shows need of further training. Fig. 33 shows $\bar{x}$- and R-charts for an hourly worker in manufacture of filter nuts. The process had been showing in the past pretty good statistical control, but it suddenly went wild. The cause was attributed to a new operator put into the job without adequate training. The foreman took him off the job for further training, upon which his work showed statistical control at about the level that had been established formerly.

Example in supervision: where are the defects coming from? There are 11 welders on a job. The number of faults produced by one of them is outside the control limits on the high side for the group (Fig. 34). The supervisor has responsibility for action:

a. If the man's work is in statistical control, then further training will not be effective. The company hired the man, and trained him, and has incurred an obligation to him to put him on some other job, with better training, we hope.

b. If the man's work is not in statistical control, then further training of the right kind might bring his work to a satisfactory level.

c. Examine the man's equipment, test his eyes, and look for other possible handicaps. Take any remedial action indicated, and collect new data.

Further improvement (reduction of the average number of faults per 5000 welds) will depend entirely on changes in the system equipment, materials.

The chart shows possible improvement with duration of tenure on this job.

Example of faulty inspection. Faulty inspection brings three types of problems: (1) frustration of production workers; (2) wrong interpretation of points on a control chart; (3) faulty product going out to the consumer.

SOME NEW PRINCIPLES OF TRAINING AND OF SUPERVISION

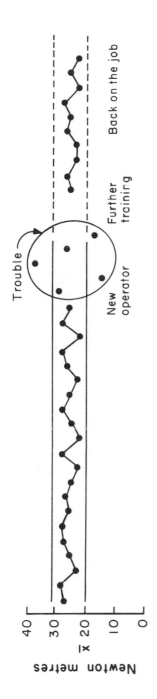

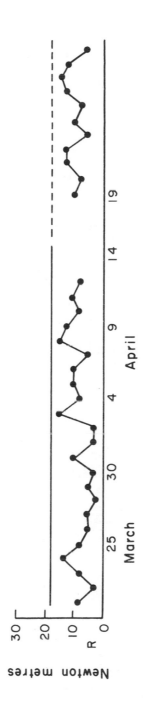

Fig 33. Charts for torque. A seasoned operator worked through the 10th April, when a new operator took on the job, not trained sufficiently. Points out of control on the x̄-chart showed need of further training. Further training accomplished the purpose.

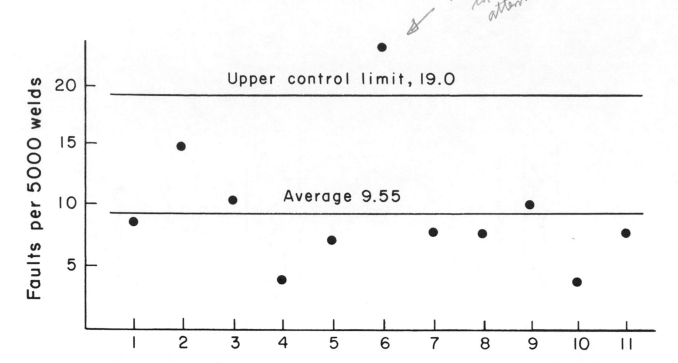

Fig. 34. Eleven welders, faults per 5000 welds. The welders are numbered 1 to 11 in order of duration of tenure on this job. The average is 9.55 faults per 5000 welds. Upper control limits, 19. Lower control limit, 0. No. 6 is outside the upper control limit (see text).

Welder	Number of faults
1	8
2	15
3	10
4	4
5	7
6	24
7	8
8	8
9	10
10	3
11	8
Sum	105

Average $= 105/11$

$\quad\quad\quad = 9.55$

$\begin{matrix} \text{UCL} \\ \text{LCL} \end{matrix} = 9.55 \pm 3\sqrt{9.55}$

$\quad\quad\quad = \begin{matrix} 19.0 \\ 0 \end{matrix}$

The following example illustrates a typical condition of faulty inspection, and a frustration to the production workers. There are 17 operators, 4 inspectors. The work of the 17 operators is allotted to the 4 inspectors by use of random numbers.

The accompanying table shows the results of inspection over a period of three weeks, and Fig. 35 shows in graphic form the results by inspector. There is clearly something wrong: the pattern of differences between inspectors is disturbing. Inspectors 1 and 4 agree well. So do inspectors 2 and 3, but the two pairs lie far apart.

What was needed here is operational definitions of what is acceptable and what is not. We met this problem in Chapter 1. An operational definition consists of a test method, a test, and a criterion by which to judge whether a piece of work may be classified as defective or acceptable (Ch. 15). An operational definition is communicable: it is a language in which people may understand each other.

The accompanying table discloses another condition worth a note. It appears that Operators 11 and 17 are in need of help (see the calculation). They may be making far more than their share of defective items. They are possibly not yet trained to the point of statistical control. If this be so, further training should help them. Or, their machines may be out of order. Maybe they have already reported them a number of times to be so. Transfer to another job, with careful training, might be the answer. On the other hand, it would be wise to bring the inspectors into line with each other through better operational definitions of defective and acceptable workmanship before focusing the spotlight on these two operators.

Record of the number of defective pieces found on inspection over a period of 3 weeks, by operator by inspector. Cases of finished product (5 pieces to a case) are allocated by random numbers to the inspectors. The number of pieces produced is about the same for all operators.

Operator	Inspector				
	1	2	3	4	All
1	1	0	0	3	4
2	2	0	0	3	5
3	0	1	1	4	6
4	3	2	2	2	9
5	7	0	0	0	7
6	0	0	0	1	1
7	1	1	1	4	7
8	3	2	3	6	14
9	2	1	0	0	3
10	1	1	1	0	3
11	9	3	5	10	27
12	3	1	0	1	5
13	4	1	1	2	8
14	4	1	1	2	8
15	0	0	1	3	4
16	1	0	0	4	5
17	11	4	6	15	36
All	52	18	22	60	152
Total number pieces examined, n	400	410	390	390	1590
Proportion defective, $\bar{p}$	.130	.044	.056	.154	.096
Upper control limit	.180	.074	.091	.209	.140
Lower control limit	.080	.014	.021	.099	.052

Formula for control limits for the inspectors:

Upper control limit

Lower control limit

$$= \bar{p} \pm 3\sqrt{\bar{p}\,(1-\bar{p})/n}$$

wherein $\bar{p}$ = .140 and n = 400.

.096

SOME NEW PRINCIPLES OF TRAINING AND OF SUPERVISION

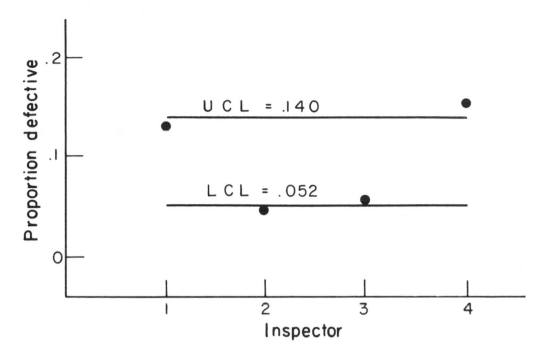

Fig. 35. Summaries in chart form for the 4 inspectors
disclose problems with the inspection.

Revision of definitions of defects, with trial, error, and effort, brought
the inspectors into much better statistical agreement, improved quality,
increased production.

Introduction of the statistical control of quality allocated by random
numbers the work of the operators to inspectors, at no extra cost. The statistical plan not only stopped possible confounding and most of the possible
collusion between inspector and operator; it also gave to the company their
first picture of what was happening in the plant. It answered these questions:

1. Do we have a valid method of inspection? (Answer: no.)

2. Does any operator stand out from the others in respect to a large
number of defects or a small number of defects? (Statistical tests are required
to answer this question; eyeball will not serve the purpose.)

Remark 1. An easy way to see which operators are out of line, if any, is to calculate control limits for the group and observe if any operator falls outside the limits. Control limits for the group could be calculated here as follows. The average number of defective pieces per operator over the period of study was 152/17 = 8.94. Then the limits could be taken as

$$8.94 \pm 3\sqrt{8.94} = \begin{matrix} 18 \\ 0 \end{matrix}$$

Operators 11 and 17 fall beyond 18. However, one can not be sure at this time that these operators are out of line, producing far more than their share of defective items, because of the problems with inspection. Once the problems of inspection are cleared up, then the table of defective items, operator by inspector, together with control limits for inspectors and for operators, will indicate which operators, if any, are in need of help. (Use of random numbers is presumed.)

Note that this simple calculation is possible because the production of pieces over the test period happens to be roughly the same for all operators.

The table, operator by inspector, with randomization, is obviously an important tool for supervision.

Remark 2. The above observations would not be attempted unless allocation of the work of operators to inspectors is governed by random numbers. An inspector cannot pick out work of his favorite operator, nor can an operator take work to her favorite inspector (a condition that did exist before the statistician introduced randomization).

Random numbers reduce another insidious fault of inspection that is sometimes encountered. An inspector may take it into his head that a particular clerk or operator is doing especially poor work, and he is for this reason more critical of her work than that of others. Randomization of the work, and a close watch on the cells of the table will usually discover this condition if it exists.

Remark 3. In one plant that we worked in, the plant manager laid an inspector off without pay for five days for selecting work from good operators instead of simply taking the next lot. No one had reminded her for years to take the next lot. She was only following the crowd. In my judgment, the plant manager is the one that should have been laid off, for failure in administration.

Faulty inspection caused by fear. The control chart in Fig. 36 shows the

daily record for two months of the proportion defective found on final audit of

SOME NEW PRINCIPLES OF TRAINING AND OF SUPERVISION

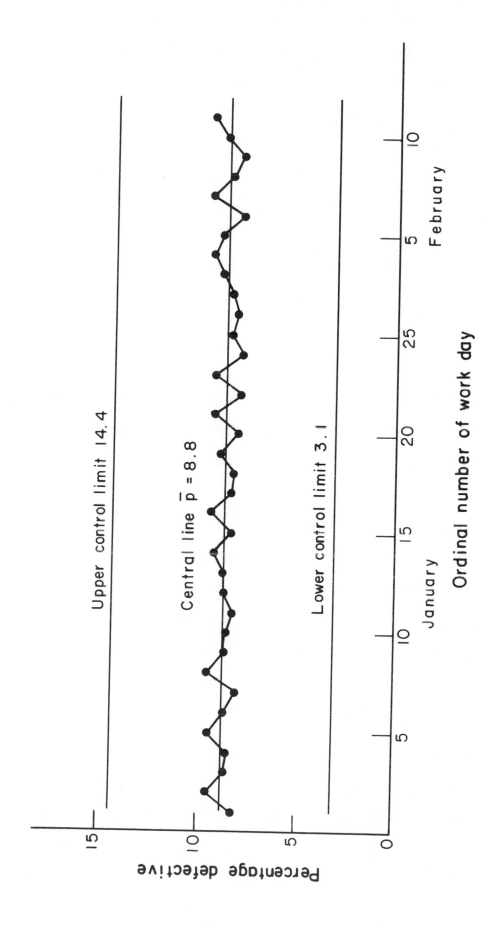

Fig. 36. Daily record of percentage of defective items. 225 items inspected per day.

a product ready to ship out. The average proportion defective over the two months was 8.8 per cent. The control limits are:

Upper limit

$$= \bar{p} \pm 3\sqrt{\bar{p}(1 - \bar{p})/n} \qquad n = 225 \qquad \bar{p} = .088 \text{ or } 8.8\%$$

Lower limit

$$= .088 \pm 3 \times .0189 = \begin{array}{l} .144 \text{ or } 14.4\% \\ .031 \text{ or } 3.1\% \end{array}$$

The chart indicates a curious condition. The points show statistical control with no trend, but their up and down movement is too narrow. They indicate an artifact: the inspector is holding artificially within narrow limits the number of defectives.

Explanation: she is insecure; in fear. She had heard the rumor that the manager would close the place down and sweep it out if the proportion defective on the final audit ever reached 10 per cent. She was trying to keep him tranquil. She may recall from history what sometimes happened to bearers of bad news.

The moral is that it is worse than useless to plot data from inspections that are badly in error. Frustration of workers, and deferred penalties for shipping out defective product, are certain dividends of faulty inspection.

More on fear. The histogram in Fig. 37 shouts a message. It tells us that the inspector distorted the data. One may encounter this histogram almost any day anywhere. Measurements pile up just inside the specification, followed by a gap. Underlying reasons for the distortion are obvious:

1. The inspector is trying to protect the people that make the part.

2. He is afraid of his instrument--afraid that it may reject a part that actually would, with more care in inspection, or with a better instrument, meet the specification.

SOME NEW PRINCIPLES OF TRAINING AND OF SUPERVISION

This is case where distribution helps often a message.

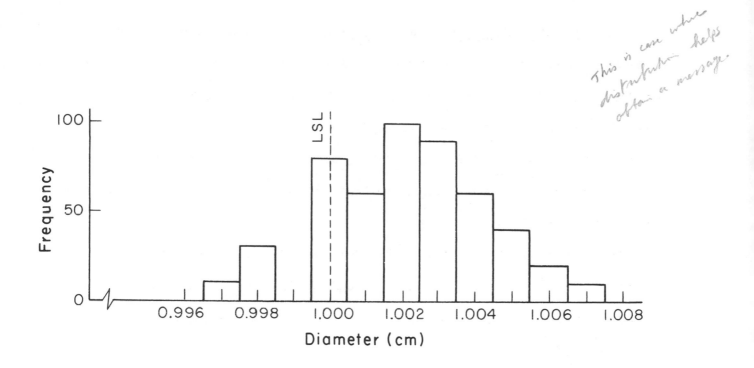

Fig. 37. Distribution of measurements on the diameters
of 500 steel rods. The inspection was obviously faulty.

3. He is afraid of his own use of the instrument, which is of course confounded with No. 2.

Data that produce such a histogram can be misleading for any or all possible
uses. The causes of the distortion are fortunately fairly easy to correct.
Once corrected throughout the organization, the problem will vanish (till it
turns up again).

Chapter 10

Still another example of loss from fear. This actual dialogue reported to me by Miss Kate McKeown. Millwright to his foreman: "That bearing (in a blast machine) is about to go out, and it will ruin the shaft along with it when it goes if we don't take care of it now."

Foreman, thinking to himself, "This load of castings must be on its way today." He is thinking of his production record, and says to the man: "We can't take care of it now."

Before they get the load out, the bearing freezes, as the millwright predicted. In the repair job, the millwright finds, sure enough, that the shaft is badly grooved and must be replaced. The stoppage was costly, as he had to get a new shaft from Baltimore.

The foreman dare not put in his best efforts for the company, as he is judged by numbers only, not for avoiding shutdowns. Can anyone blame him for doing his job? The millwright, after a few experiences like this, not wishing to be a troublemaker, just lets bearings go ahead and freeze and score the shafts. What else can he do?

Requirement of statistical control of a test-method. A recorded measurement, whether visual, manual, or taken and recorded by instruments, is the end-product of a long series of operations on the thing measured, and on the use of the instrument. Repeated measurements of the same item over a period of time must show statistical control in order for the instrument and operator thereof to qualify as a method of measurement. This characteristic alone is of course not sufficient. The level of the $\bar{x}$-chart for repeated measurements for any operator must not be too big, else the precision of the method will not suffice for use. The method must be reproducible within specified limits with different operators (or with other observers, in the case of visual inspection).

SOME NEW PRINCIPLES OF TRAINING AND OF SUPERVISION

No precision, good or bad, can be ascribed to a test-method unless instrument and observer as a combination show statistical control.* This is so regardless of the cost of testing equipment.

Alleged shortages of material from vendors can arise from differences between vendor and purchaser in methods of measurement. What is the area of a hide, for example? What about ragged edges: how would they affect the measurement of the area of the hide, if you were selling the hide? What if you were buying it?

> A vendor, if he feels badly used by the measurements of his customer, can speak up for himself. But a production worker seldom perceives the possibility that he could be right and the figures wrong.

Differences between test instruments. Statistical investigation usually discovers within a few weeks that:

1. Few workers know what the job is.

2. Few inspectors know, either. Production worker and inspector do not agree on what is right and what is wrong. Right yesterday; wrong today.

3. The electronic testing equipment is not doing the job. It passes an item one minute, rejects it the next, and the converse.

---

* Stated by Walter A. Shewhart, THE ECONOMIC CONTROL OF MANUFACTURED PRODUCT (Van Nostrand, 1931), Ch. XXIII: STATISTICAL METHOD FROM THE VIEWPOINT OF QUALITY CONTROL (the Graduate School, Department of Agriculture, Washington, 1939), Ch. IV. An excellent reference is Joseph M. Cameron, Measurement Assurance, NBSIR 77-1240, National Bureau of Standards, Washington, April 1977. See also Charles A. Bicking, "Precision in the routine performance of standard tests," Standardization, January 1979, p. 13. The interested reader may well turn at this point to the masterful work by Churchill Eisenhart, "Realistic evaluation of the precision and accuracy of instrument calibration systems," being a chapter in the book edited by Harry H. Ku, PRECISION MEASUREMENT AND CALIBRATION (National Bureau of Standards Special Publication 300, vol. I, 1969; Superintendent of Documents, Washington 20402).

4. Electronic testing machines do not agree with each other.

5. Vendor and purchaser do not agree: no wonder, the testing equipment used by the purchaser does not agree with itself. The vendor has the same problem. Neither one knows it.

Few people in supervisory positions and in management are aware how important reliable inspection is for morale of production workers.

Example. There are eight testing machines at the end of the line to separate good product from bad in order to protect customers. Around 3000 items run through this inspection every day. The compilation and chart (plotted by machine) shown in Fig. 38 show the results for a week. The rule was to rotate the test-machine with the product as the pieces come off the line. The control limits for each point are too narrow to show in the chart, as the number of pieces tested on each machine is around 2000.

The eight testing machines obviously fall into two groups. The difference between their means is around 11 per cent. A serious problem exists. What the customer gets depends on what machine does the testing--an alarming condition. It is vital to find out the reason for the existence of two groups and for the difference between them.

One can imagine the frustration of the production workers, seeing apparent and unexplainable variation from day to day, unaware that much of the trouble lies in the testing equipment.

One might look first, in such a problem, for confounding of the operator with the machine. A machine does not work by itself. It has no characteristic of its own. The machine and the operator form a team. Change of operator may give different results. In this case, the machines worked three shifts. It would be well to enquire whether the same operators worked all week on any one machine.

SOME NEW PRINCIPLES OF TRAINING AND OF SUPERVISION

scale wrong

Testing Machine	Yield	25%	50%	75%	100%
0	66.1771			X	
7	66.287			X	
8	54.1433		X		
9	56.0381		X		
10	56.8949		X		
11	54.1331		X		
12	66.5099			X	
13	57.3146		X		
TOTAL	60.907				

Fig. 38. Results of 8 testing machines
over the course of a week.

Comparison of two operators on the same machine. The above example is one
in which test instruments (confounded with the operators) disagreed with each
other. One may also expect to find that an instrument disagrees with itself,
and that operators disagree with each other. Good supervision requires achievement of statistical control of the measurement system.

A convenient form of summary of the two sets of results is a 2 x 2 table.
An example of a 2 x 2 table appears on page 291. This table can be readily
adapted to many kinds of comparisons. For this example, we could show Operator
No. 1 on the horizontal and Operator No. 2 on the vertical. Or for testing the
same operator on two instruments, the horizontal label could be one instrument,

the vertical label could be the other instrument. Points on the diagonal indicate agreement. Points off the diagonal indicate disagreement. The scientist in charge of testing should lay down in advance criteria for satisfactory reproducibility of the test; then decide from the table whether the test is satisfactory.

Incidentally, chi-square and tests of significance, taught in some statistical courses, have no application in this decision.

If the inspection is in terms of a scale of centimeters, grams, seconds, millivolts, or other unit, one could plot first test on one axis, and second test on the other axis. Good agreement would appear as points on or close to the 45° line in Fig. 47 on page 293.

<u>Comparison of interviewers to improve performance</u>. A plot of the number yes vs. the number no, by interviewer, on Mosteller-Tukey double square root paper,* for interpenetrating samples of people will indicate whether some interviewer is out of line with the others, or out of line with respect to another but comparable study. An interviewer whose point lies far away from the bulk of the others exhibits a special cause--a cause not common to all the interviewers, but specific to him. He may require retraining; or, if his point indicates extra-high quality (like the points for EM and DFB for no refusals in Fig. 39), the problem is first of all to discover whether his performance is really as good as it looks, and if it is, to try to find out how he does it, and, if possible, to teach the others how to do the same. In this instance, EM and DFB turned out to be extremely good: no refusals.

---

* Frederick Mosteller and John W. Tukey, "The uses and usefulness of probability paper," <u>J. Amer. Stat. Assoc.</u>, vol. 44. 1949: pp. 174-212. The double square-root paper is manufactured by the Codex Book Company of Norwood, Mass.

SOME NEW PRINCIPLES OF TRAINING AND OF SUPERVISION

In another comparison, the bulk of the interviewers differed from some outside result (Fig. 40), and there is indication of a common cause that afflicts all the interviewers. A common cause may lie in the instructions, or in the training, or in the supervision. There is of course the possibility that the outside result may not be trustworthy.

Fig. 40 shows a set of results for 8 interviewers, compared with the results of a recent Census. The initials at a point identify the interviewer. As the legend explains, the disagreement between the present study and the recent Census was a common cause, with weakness in the instructions and in the training, especially for the definition of operatives (bus drivers, trainmen, lift operators, etc.). Retraining brought the interviewers into line with the Census.*

Another example of bringing inspectors into line on a survey. In my own work, I always lay out a study in interpenetrating networks of subsamples to facilitate calculation of estimates of standard errors.** There are other advantages of interpenetrating subsamples. For example, if an investigator stays in the same subsample throughout the job, the variance between subsamples contains and accounts for the variance between investigators. With a little effort, one can allot by random numbers two investigators to units in two subsamples; and thus be able to calculate with ease not only the variance between subsamples for the average of all investigators, but can calculate also the average variance between units within investigators, and the variances between

* These examples and the charts are taken from the author's SAMPLE DESIGN IN BUSINESS RESEARCH (Wiley, 1960), Ch. 13.

** W. Edwards Deming, SAMPLE DESIGN IN BUSINESS RESEARCH (Wiley, 1960). The original idea came from P. C. Mahalanobis.

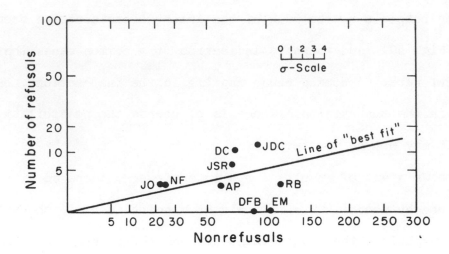

Fig. 39. Refusals and nonrefusals for 9 interviewers at the end of 4 weeks. Interviewers DFB and EM are significantly superior, or else there is something wrong with the records.

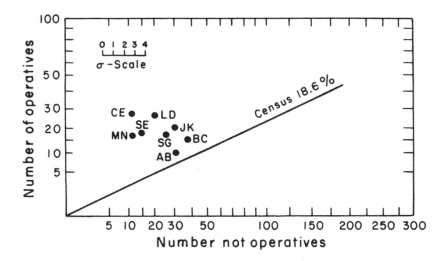

Fig. 40. The number of operatives and the number of not operatives in the occupations recorded by the various interviewers during the first 2 weeks of a survey in Wilmington in 1952, compared with the Census of 1950. The points all fall above the Census, and this fact indicates definitely that the reason for the difference between the sample and the Census arose from causes common to all interviewers. Retraining removed the causes.

SOME NEW PRINCIPLES OF TRAINING AND OF SUPERVISION

investigators. Layouts for other random allocation of investigators are simple, but a description of them would be out of scope here. A reference will suffice.* It is especially simple to lay out such designs for interviewing by telephone.

Results of the field-work can be analyzed two days at a batch, to compare the variance between investigators with the variance within investigators, thus to detect any need of retraining of investigators before it is too late. Sometimes one investigator will go out on a limb. It is necessary to determine the reason why. It may be that his work is superior, and that all the other investigators need retraining.

Example 4. Fallacies of reward for winning in a lottery. A man in the Personnel Department of a large company came forth with an idea, held as brilliant by all people there, viz., to reward the top man of the month on a certain production line (the man that made the lowest proportion defective over the month) with a citation. There would be a small party on the job in his honor, and he would get half a day off. This might be a great idea if he was indeed an unusual performer for the month. There were 50 men on the production line.

What about the whole 50? Does their work form a statistical system like the work of the 20 operators in Fig. 23 on page 160? If the work of the group forms a statistical system, then the prize would be merely a lottery. On the

---

* W. Edwards Deming, SAMPLE DESIGN IN BUSINESS RESEARCH (Wiley, 1960), pages 249-254; also W. Edwards Deming and Morris H. Hansen, "Some theory on the influence of the inspector and of environmental conditions, with an example," Statistica Neerlandica, vol. 26, No. 3, 1972: pp. 101-112. See also Jean Namias, "Use of binomial probability paper for assessing performance of interviewers," Sankhya, Series B, vol. 34, Part I, March 1972, pages 93-96.

Chapter 10

other hand, if the top man is out of control on the side of low proportion defective, then he is indeed outstanding. He would deserve recognition, and he could be a focal point for teaching men how to do the job.

There is no harm in a lottery, so far as I know, provided it is called a lottery. To call it an award of merit when the selection is merely a lottery, however is to demoralize the whole force, prize winners included. Everybody will suppose that there are good reasons for the selection and will be trying to explain and reduce differences between men. This would be a futile exercise when the only differences are random deviations, as is the case when the 50 men form a statistical system.

SOME NEW PRINCIPLES OF TRAINING AND OF SUPERVISION

Chapter 11

QUALITY AND THE CONSUMER

Most of the early problems with this unit (to show
sound-film) were due to an inadequate instruction book,
translated from the German into English by someone illiter-
ate in both languages.--Bulletin of the Washington Society
of Cinematographers, November 1967.

The industry is in continuous development, and so are the
tempers of consumers. Both demand more and better quality...
--Egyptian Cotton Exporting Companies, in the New York Times,
15 January 1971, page 63.

Several faces of quality.

1. Management's decision on specifications for the quality-characteristics
of parts, final product, performance, and service, to offer now. The plant
manager and all the people in production are concerned about the specifications
of today. They have to know what their job is, now.

2. Management's responsibility to plan ahead for product or service of the
future (Ch. 2).

3. The consumer's judgment of your product or service.

For many kinds of product and of service, the consumer's judgment may
require a year or even several years for formation. The purchaser of a new
automobile can give you a year from the date of purchase a more useful
evaluation of the quality of the automobile than he could when it was new.

A man shows off with enthusiasm in the spring his new lawn mower, just
purchased, but future sales depend on how much of the man's enthusiasm remains
at the end of the summer.

What is quality? I have much amusement by enquiring of top management just what quality is, and what quality they wish to produce. They usually confess, after a few questions, that they had not given the matter enough thought. What is quality? What would someone mean by the quality of a shoe? Let us suppose that it is a man's shoe that he is asking about. Does he mean by good quality that it wears a long time? or that it takes a shine well? that it feels comfortable? that it is waterproof? that the price is right in consideration of whatever he considers quality? Put another way, what quality-characteristics are important to the customer? What would one mean by the quality of a woman's shoe? What is a major defect in a shoe? Tack in the insole? Heel that came off straightaway? Smudges? What qualities create dissatisfaction in the customer's mind? How do you know?

The quality of any product or service has many scales. A product may get a high mark, in the judgment of the consumer, on one scale, and a low mark on another. This paper that I am writing on has a number of qualities.

1. It is a sulfite paper, 16 pounds.

2. It is not slick. It takes pencil well; ink likewise.

3. It is heavy enough so that writing on the back does not show through.

4. It is standard size. It fits into my three-ring notebook.

5. Replacement is for sale at any stationery store.

6. The price is right.

7. It does not have the characteristics required for a letterhead. I require rag content for a letterhead.

It rates 100 on all scales except the last one. I nevertheless place an order for 10 reams of this paper, and a separate order for letterheads.

Product put on the market today must do more than attract customers and sales: it must stand up in service. Satisfaction of the customer that buys

QUALITY AND THE CONSUMER

today's output can unfortunately only be assessed some time in the future--too late.

New buses, scores of them, are running around the streets of Washington with windows that obscure the scenery. Nothing seemed wrong when the windows were new. They met the specifications, but once they rattled a few hundred miles on buses, they became translucent. Who would make buses with windows that would change to alabaster in a few days? Somebody did. Who would buy them? The Washington Metropolitan Transit Authority (at lowest bid).

Moving stairs and Farecard machines in Washington's Metro are a constant source of irritation. They worked very well when unveiled after dress rehearsal, but when put into service, problems of design and maintenance painted a new image. The management of the Washington Metro Transit Authority had a goal of 5.7 per cent out of order. Where do you suppose the management's goal of 5.7 per cent came from? Why not 2 per cent? Why not 0 per cent?

Quality of medical care. A suitable definition for quality of medical care is a perennial problem amongst administrators of medical care and people doing research in the subject. It seems simple to anyone that has not tried it. Quality of medical care has been defined in various ways. Each way serves some special type of problem:

1. Comfort of patients under medical care. (How would you measure comfort?)

2. Proportion of people under medical care, male and female, by age in each group.

3. (Applicable to a day care centre for the aged.) The number of people kept out of the hospital or nursing home because of good care at the day care centre.

4. Facilities for tests, such as laboratories, X-ray scan.

5. Public health.

6. Mean life of people discharged from institutions, by age of discharge.

7. Amount of money spent by an institution, per patient.

It is obvious that some of these definitions are antithetical. For example, the number of patients under care, if large, might indicate good medical service--serving many people. On the other hand, it could indicate the opposite. It might be large because of poor measures of public health, or it could be large because day care centres are not doing the job. The rate of patients discharged from nursing homes, if large, could mean that the care that they receive is excellent: patients stay in the institution only a short while, and are soon rehabilitated sufficiently to live at home. It could also mean that the policy of the management is to discharge a patient when he reaches a stage of acute care, and would be a burden in the nursing home. The amount of money spent by an institution is almost no indication of the care offered. Facilities available is one thing: how to use them effectively is another.

I listened to papers on medical care delivered in an international meeting on medical care. One physician measured medical care in terms of physical equipment for medical tests. Another one measured medical care in terms of education of physicians and nurses. Another measure of medical care turned up as men met me on arrival in a city in Europe. They were from the medical service of the country, and had a problem. In spite of the fact that their country has superb medical facilities, and physicians that have studied in the best medical schools in the world, the general population does not make much use of these facilities. A disease left unattended can become serious, as everyone knows, and this was happening. The men had in mind a survey of the general population to learn why people do not make better use of their medical facilities, and how to persuade them to come in for service and for examination.

QUALITY AND THE CONSUMER

The quality of medical care was thus excellent from the standpoint of facilities, physical and professional, but not good, in the judgment of the heads of the service, from the standpoint of service rendered.

This example merely illustrates the difficulty of definition of the quality of medical service.

The consumer, the most important part of the production line. The customer is the most important part of the production line. Without someone to purchase our product, we might as well shut down the whole plant. But what does the customer need? How can we be useful to him? What does he think he needs? Can he pay for it? No one has all the answers. Fortunately, all the answers are not necessary for good management.

Necessity to study the needs of the consumer, and to provide service to product, was one of the main doctrines of quality taught to Japanese management in 1950, and onward.

Foremost is the principle that the purpose of consumer research is to understand the consumer's needs and wishes, thus to design product and service that will provide better living for him in the future.

A second principle is that no one can outguess the future loss of business from a dissatisfied customer. The cost to replace a defective item on the production line is fairly easy to estimate, but the cost of a defective item that goes out to a customer defies measure.

It was Oliver Beckwith who remarked in 1947, in a meeting of Committee E-11 of the American Society for Testing and Materials, that a dissatisfied customer does not complain: he just switches. Or as my friend Robert W. Peach put it:

The goods come back, but not the customer.

Judges of quality are always not the people that will use the product.

Example: Another publishing house was preparing a new edition of its widely used series (elementary readers). One of us, asked to consult, objected in detail to the blandness of the stories proposed. The company's vice president in charge of textbooks confessed that he, too, thought that the stories would bore young readers, but he was obliged to keep in mind that neither children nor teachers buy text-books: school boards and superintendents do.*

Nursing homes furnish another example. A nursing home, to get government funds, must conform to a multitude of government regulations and undergo frequent inspection. The patients have no voice in the requirements and reg-ulations. The physicians and nurses have little voice. A nursing home could conform to all governmental requirements and still render flagrantly bad service to patients.

Triangle of interaction. Neither the building of a product nor tests thereof in the laboratory and on the proving ground are sufficient to describe its quality and how it will perform or be accepted. Quality must be measured by the interaction between three participants, as shown in Fig. 41: (1) the product itself; (2) the user and how he uses the product; how he installs it; how he takes care of it; (example: customer permitted dirt to fall into roller bearing); what he was led (as by advertising) to expect; (3) instructions for use; training of customer, training of repairman; service provided for repairs; availability of parts. The top vertex of the triangle does not by itself determine quality. I am reminded of an old Japanese poem**:

----

* Bruno Bettelheim and Karen Zelan, "Why children don't like to read," Atlantic, November 1981, page 27.

** Quoted by Edward W. Barankin, "Probability and the East," Annals of the Institute of Statistical Mathematics (Tokyo), vol. xvi, 1964: p. 216.

QUALITY AND THE CONSUMER

> Kano ga naru ka ya
> Shumoku ga naru ka
> Kane to shumoku no si ga naru
>
> Is it the bell that rings,
> Is it the hammer that rings,
> Or is it the meeting of the two that rings?

Also, concerning advertising, a clever observation by my friend Dr. Irwin Bross in his book DESIGN FOR DECISION (Macmillan, 1953), page 95:

> The purpose of studies in consumer preference is to adjust the product to the public, rather than, as in studies of advertising, to adjust the public to the product.

The problems inherent in attempts to define the quality of a product, almost any product, were stated by the master, Walter A. Shewhart.* The difficulty in defining quality is to translate future needs of the user into measurable characteristics, so that a product can be designed and turned out to give satisfaction at a price that the user will pay. This is not easy, and as soon as one feels fairly successful in the endeavor, he finds that the needs of the consumer have changed, competitors have moved in, there are new materials to work with, some better than the old ones, some worse; some cheaper than the old ones, some dearer.**

Learning from the consumer. The main use of consumer research should be to feed consumer reactions back into the design of the product, so that management can anticipate changing demands and requirements and set economical production

---

* Walter A. Shewhart, THE ECONOMIC CONTROL OF MANUFACTURED PRODUCT (Van Nostrand, 1931), Ch. IV.

** The reader will at this point enjoy the book by Eugene MacNiece, INDUSTRIAL SPECIFICATIONS (John Wiley, 1953), especially pages 32 and 33 and Chapter 5.

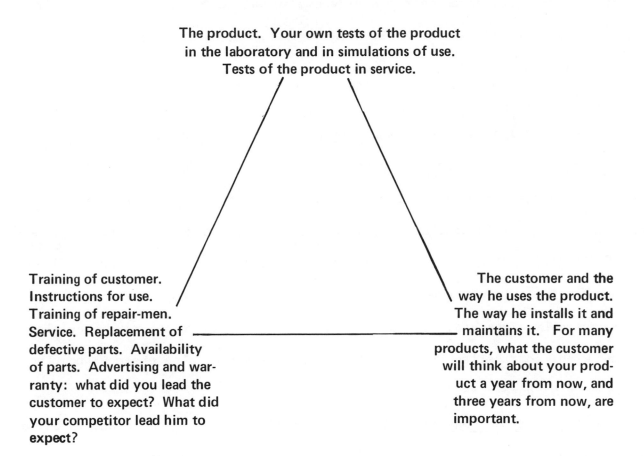

The product. Your own tests of the product
in the laboratory and in simulations of use.
Tests of the product in service.

Training of customer.
Instructions for use.
Training of repair-men.
Service. Replacement of
defective parts. Availability
of parts. Advertising and warranty: what did you lead the
customer to expect? What did
your competitor lead him to
expect?

The customer and the
way he uses the product.
The way he installs it and
maintains it. For many
products, what the customer
will think about your product a year from now, and
three years from now, are
important.

Fig. 41. The three corners of quality.

QUALITY AND THE CONSUMER

levels. Consumer research takes the pulse of the consumer's reactions and demands, and seeks explanations for the findings.

Unfortunately, this ideal working of the organization in industry in America may be hard to find. A student of mine at New York University did her doctoral thesis on a study of uses of consumer research for design of future product and service. The project bore promise of extremely interesting results. The results were indeed interesting: she found little connexion between consumer research and design. The design department did not need consumer research: they were hired because they knew what to do. To depend on consumer research would be admission that they do not have all the answers.

This experience is an example of estrangement between functions, mentioned in Chapter 2, page 35, evidence of poor management, to be corrected by better management.

Consumer research is communication between the manufacturer and users and potential users of his product, like this:

This communication may be carried out reliably and economically today by sampling procedures and tests designed in conformity with appropriate statistical procedures. Through this communication the manufacturer discovers how his product performs in service, what people think of his product, why some people will buy it, why others will not, or will not buy it again, and he is able to redesign his product, to make it better as measured by the quality and uniformity that are best suited to the end-users of the product and to the price that the consumer can pay.

The old way, and the new way.* In the olden days, before the industrial era, the tailor, the carpenter, the shoemaker, the milkman, the blacksmith knew his customers by name. He knew whether they were satisfied, and what he should do to improve appreciation for his product. I quote:

> A grocer used to be very fussy about his cheese. Cheddar was made and sold by hundreds of little factories. Representatives of the factories had particular customers, and cheese was prepared by hand to suit the grocers, who knew precisely what their patrons wanted in rat cheese, pie cheese, American and other cheeses. Some liked them sharper; some like them yellower; some liked anise seeds in cheese, or caraway.--Philip Wylie, The Atlantic, "Science Has Spoiled My Supper" (Boston, April 1954).

With the expansion of industry, this personal touch is easy to lose. The wholesaler, the jobber, and the retailer have now stepped in, and in effect have set up a barrier between the manufacturer and the ultimate consumer. But sampling, a new science, steps in and pierces that barrier.

Manufacturers used to think of manufacturing in three steps, as shown in Fig. 42. Success depended on guess-work--guessing what type and design of product would sell, how much of it to make. In the old way, the three steps of Figure 42 are completely independent.

In the new way, management introduces, usually with aid of consumer research, a 4th step, and runs through the four steps in a cycle, over and over, to generate the helix in Fig. 43, moving ever toward better product and greater economy in producing it.

1. Design the product (with appropriate tests);

2. Make it; test in the production line and in the laboratory;

3. Put it on the market;

---

* Taken largely from Walter A. Shewhart, STATISTICAL METHOD FROM THE VIEWPOINT OF QUALITY CONTROL (Graduate School, Department of Agriculture, 1939), page 45.

QUALITY AND THE CONSUMER

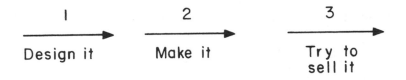

Fig. 42.   The old way

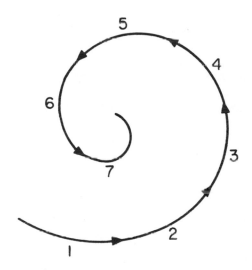

Fig. 43.   The new way

Taken from my book, ELEMENTARY PRINCIPLES
OF THE STATISTICAL CONTROL OF QUALITY (JUSE, 1951), page 10.

4.   Test it in service; find out what the user thinks of it, and why the
non-user has not bought it;

5.   Redesign the product, in the light of consumer reactions to quality and
price.   Steps 6 and 7 will be redesign of the product, new tests, and onward.

Chapter 11

Manufacturers have always been interested in discovering needs and reactions of users and of the potential user, but until recently they had no economical or reliable way to investigate them.

It is not to be supposed that the first three steps are the same in the old and new ways. Consider, for example, the design in Step 1. Proper design today means not only attention to color, shape, size, hardness, strength, and finish, but attention also to a suitable degree of uniformity. Paradoxically, through the statistical control of quality, great uniformity often costs less than non-uniformity without statistical methods.

Communication between the manufacturer and the user and the potential user gives the public a chance. It gives the user a better product, better suited to his needs, and cheaper. Democracy in industry, one might say.

Contact with the customer. In the making of hardware, apparatus, machinery, utensils, automobiles, trucks, railway cars, locomotives, and the like, it is only the salesman and the serviceman that see the customer. These men do not make the items that they sell, repair, and maintain. They are in a service organization, independent, or run by the manufacturer.

Many people work in a bank. The officers and tellers see customers: the rest do not. Some people in a department store, restaurant, hotel, railway, trucking company, bus company, see customers; others do not.

Everyone, whether he sees the customer or not, has a chance to build quality into the product, and into the service offered. The people that see customers have a role that is not usually appreciated by supervisors and other management. Many customers form their opinions about the product or about the service solely by their contacts with the people that they see--contact-men, I will call them. A large trucking company had on a stairway used by their city drivers in their

Baltimore terminal a full length mirror, with the caption: "What you see here is all that our customers know about our company."

Ability to please the customer should be, for good management, a priority for hiring and training of employees that will serve customers directly. My impression is that many people that serve customers in restaurants, hotels, elevators, banks, hospitals, would enjoy the job much more were it not that customers come in and interrupt their conversations. A bus driver in Washington was obviously expert at driving the bus, and knew his route. Customers boarded and descended. His job would have been so much more enjoyable to him were it not for those pesky passengers that need directions and help—such a bother they were.

Actually, the job might be enjoyable to him were he to understand that a sizeable proportion of the people that ask questions for directions and guidance are a potential source of future revenue for the company, and that he can help to build up business to ensure his job in the future. Likewise in hotels, stores, restaurants, banks, trains, and a multitude of other types of shops and services, the people that see customers are the marketing department. Do they know it? Does the management teach drivers that they are not only drivers, but a potential influence to increase patronage? How about screening applicants for their adaptability to this role?

The girl that runs the lift in a department store plays an important role in the customer's opinion about the quality of everything for sale in the store. The Japanese know this. The girl that runs the lift in a department store in Japan receives training over a period of two months on how to direct people, how to answer questions, and how to handle them in a crowded lift—this in spite of the gracious manners that Japanese girls (and boys) grow up in.

Chapter 11

Quality to the plant manager. The plant manager and everyone on the line has the job to produce the quality-characteristics that are prescribed. Plans for product three years from now are not their primary concern. Quality, to the plant management, means the specifications that he must meet today, and we can't blame him for trying to meet them. As the reader of this book must have perceived long ago, the plant manager has also the obligation to achieve ever narrower and narrower distributions of dimensions and other quality-characteristics, to leave the specifications beyond the horizon.

QUALITY AND THE CONSUMER

Chapter 12

QUALITY AND PRODUCTIVITY IN SERVICE ORGANIZATIONS

No English minister to the United States has ever been so popular: and the mediocrity of his talents has been one of the principal causes of his success.--Diary of John Quincy Adams, writing on the departure of the Right Honorable Sir Charles Bagot, Minister from England to the United States, 1819.

A. REMARKS ON SERVICE INDUSTRIES *

<u>Who needs improvement?</u> The answer is that a system of quality control is helpful to anyone that turns out a product or is engaged in service, or in research, and wishes to improve the quality of his work, and at the same time to increase his output, all with less labor and at reduced cost. Everybody knows about quality control in the manufacture of a product that you feel or hear or see or use, such as this pencil, this paper that I am writing on, this desk and the light on it, but service organizations need quality control even more. Anyone that ever registered at a hotel in the United States will endorse this statement I am sure. Inefficiency in a service organization, just as in manufacturing, raises prices to the consumer and lowers his standard of living.

<u>What is a service organization?</u> Service organizations include restaurants, hotels, bars, banks, medical service including hospitals, nursing homes, day

---

* For further reading, three books:
1. Judith Tanur et al., STATISTICS, GUIDE TO THE UNKNOWN (Holden Day, 1972).
2. A. C. Rosander, CASE STUDIES IN SAMPLE DESIGN (Marcel Dekker, 1977).
3. L. H. C. Tippett, STATISTICS (Oxford, 1943); THE METHODS OF STATISTICS (Wiley, 1952).

care centres for children or for old people, education, wholesale and retail establishments, railways, carriers of motor freight, barges, intercity transportation of passengers, local transportation of passengers, insurance companies, sales, printing, news service, software, maintenance of copying machines, computers, typewriters, automobiles, medical equipment, painting and maintenance of buildings, offices, and homes, construction, laundry and dry cleaning, government agencies including the post office.

The Bureau of the Census is a service organization; so is the Census in any other country. It is worthy of note that our own Census in all activities became in 1940 the largest and most successful example of quality improvement seen to date, with world-wide recognition for results (more in Ch. 17).

The purchasing department of a manufacturing concern is a service organization; likewise its payroll department, accounting department, personnel, medical, legal, and service departments.

The proportion of the labor force that is engaged in service is 86:14 or 6 out of 7 if one includes in service the people in manufacturing concerns that work in management, accounting, sales, planning, law, service, transportation, purchase, personnel. * **

It is obvious, however, by simple arithmetic, that because there are so many people engaged in service in the United States, improvement in our standard of living is highly dependent on better quality and productivity in service.

---

* A. C. Rosander, "A general approach to quality control in the service industries," Proceedings of the American Society for Quality Control at Cosa Mesa, California, 2 October 1976.

** Private communication from my friend Dr. Marvin E. Mundel.

QUALITY AND PRODUCTIVITY IN SERVICE ORGANIZATIONS

<u>Some differences and similarities</u>. Perhaps the biggest difference between
service and manufacturing is that the service industries have a captive
market. Service organizations do not lose their markets to foreign invasion.
Our choice of restaurants or of laundries lies within a relatively small area.
In most service industries one finds:

1. Direct transactions with masses of people: customer, householder,
depositor, insured, taxpayer, borrower, consumer, shipper, consignee, passenger, claimant, another bank.

2. Large volume of transactions as in the main business in sales, loans,
premiums, deposits, taxes, charges, interest.

3. Large volume of paper involved in the main business: sales slips,
bills, cheques, credit cards, charge accounts, claims, tax returns, mail.

4. Large amount of processing. Examples: transcription, coding,
calculation of freight charges, calculation of division of revenue, calculation
of interest to pay, punching, tabulation, construction of tables.

5. Many transactions with small amounts of money. However, some
transactions involve huge amounts (as a transfer from one bank to another, or a
huge deposit). A telephone company that I worked with received one day when I
was there a bill for $800,000 which should have gone to another company.

6. An extremely large number of ways to make errors. (A manufacturing
concern also has many chances for error.)

7. Handling and rehandling of huge numbers of small items--e.g., in
communication, mail, federal, state, and city governments, your own payroll
department, your own purchasing department.

> One finds in service organizations, as in manufacturing, absence
> of definite procedures. There is an unstated assumption in most
> service organizations that the procedures are fully defined and
> followed. This appears to be so obvious that authors avoid it. Yet
> in practice this condition is often not met. Few organizations have

up-to-date procedures. Consider a manufacturer who has full specifications for making a product, but whose sales department does not
have guidelines of how to enter an order. A control on errors on
placing orders would require procedures for the sales department. I
have seen numerous service-oriented operations functioning without
them--Contributed by William J. Latzko.

A denominator common to manufacturing and to any service organization is
that mistakes and defects are costly. The further a mistake goes without
correction, the greater the cost to correct it. The cost of a defect that
reaches the consumer or recipient may be the costliest of all, but (to repeat
from other chapters) no one knows what this cost is.

Ask anyone in an airline that knows the figures how much it costs to find
and deliver or hold a piece of luggage that failed to come along with the
passenger. The main cause of failure of luggage to arrive with the passenger
is not sluggish performance of employees, but delays in connexion. Features
built into a large airport on the west coast, newly erected at a cost of many
millions of dollars, impede transfer of luggage from international arrivals to
domestic flights, with great inconvenience to passengers and huge costs to the
airlines--another problem of one of a kind (Ch. 2).

Ask anyone that knows how much it costs to correct a mistake in the
customer's bill sent out by a department store, or the cost of sending the
wrong goods. The direct costs are staggering. The unmeasurable cost of loss
of future business may be much greater.

A remittance sent by a bank to the wrong bank or firm will eventually be
straightened out. One of the costs, piled on top of the cost to try to find
out what happened, is for interest that the bank pays on these remittances till
the mistake is cleared up.

A bank that embarrasses a customer by reporting incorrectly that funds in
the customer's account are insufficient to cover a cheque incurs substantial
cost to set the matter straight, and runs the risk of losing a lot of business.

QUALITY AND PRODUCTIVITY IN SERVICE ORGANIZATIONS

It is amazing to most people to learn how many cheques on payrolls are incorrect, and how many go to the wrong man. The total amount paid out may nevertheless be virtually correct. The cost to clear up these mistakes is not small, and the cost is even greater to explain how it happened.

A debit or a credit posted to the wrong account does not affect the organization's assets nor liabilities. Mistakes in computation of charges that occur in both directions have little effect on the bank's books. A customer, however, seeing an overcharge, or failing to receive a credit sent in, may not be happy about the mistake, and may take it into his head that the bank or department store is careless.

In certain kinds of paper work there will be no disagreement on what constitutes a mistake. Any two people will agree that the figure 67 transcribed as 76 is a mistake: that a cheque for $240 in place of one for $260 is also a mistake. Some mistakes of this kind are of course more serious than others.

In contrast, as we have learned in previous chapters, a defect in manufactured product may be difficult to define operationally. The same kind of problem afflicts some service organizations.

It is not always easy to describe procedures. For example, the correct code, and a mistake in coding, are in many studies as difficult to define operationally as a defect in the production line in the manufacture of shoes. Occupational coding and industrial coding in the Census and in other government bureaus are difficult. Courses of study to the extent of several months are required of people employed for such coding. There are nevertheless disagreements now and then about what code to ascribe on some situations. Disagreement between the verifier and the original coder may be only honest difference of educated opinion.* Calculations of freight charges and divisions of revenue

between railways on interline hauls may lead to honest differences that are

difficult to resolve.

Government service is to be judged on equity as well as on efficiency. I

quote here from an interview with Oscar A. Ornati.**

> A deeply embedded laissez-faire ideology has mistaught this country
> the importance of productivity from a very narrow, very mechanistic
> definition. We have forgotten that the function of government is more
> equity oriented than efficiency oriented. The notion that we must be
> "efficient" in the same way in both sectors is fallacious. For govern-
> ment, efficiency must be subsumed to equity.

> If we do not keep equity in the forefront of the public sector, we
> will destroy our society. It is unfortunate that we tend to lavish so
> much praise on management specialists who laud the techniques of
> private sector management in the public sector. Many such techniques
> are good, but there is a danger in the privatization of public manage-
> ment techniques if we forget about the required orientation to equity
> and the reality of different accountability processes. Actually, we
> need both. The public sector must search for and apply the appropriate
> private management techniques to improve its analyses and evaluations
> of outcomes. On the other hand, some private sector policies such as
> moving to the suburbs, may produce short-run benefits for the company,
> but are counterproductive in the long run for society and the company.

> The public sector can improve its efficiency by utilizing better
> industrial relations and supervision techniques. It can improve pro-
> ductivity by adopting private sector models for position descriptions,
> almost none of which now incorporate the output variables that are
> more frequently embedded in private sector models. It can improve
> productivity by overcoming the unwillingness by line managers and
> supervisors to give commands, which is greater than in the private
> sector.

Adaptation of the 14 points to a service organization. The 14 points of

Chapter 2 apply to a service organization with little modification. For

---

* Dr. Philip M. Hauser: private communication to the author in the Census
of 1940.

** Public Productivity Review, vol. vi, March and June 1982: page 48.
Interview with Dr. Oscar A. Ornati.

example, my friends Dr. Paul B. Batalden and Dr. Loren Vorlicky of the Health Services Research Center, Minneapolis, have rewritten the 14 points for medical service.* They follow.

   1.   Establish constancy of purpose toward service.

     a. Define in operational terms what you mean by service to patients.

     b. Specify standards of service for a year hence and for five years hence.

     c. Define the patients whom you are seeking to serve--those here, those that you seek, those that have been here once and have not been here for some time.

     d. Constancy of purpose brings innovation.

     e. Innovate for better service for a given cost; planning for the future will require the addition of new skills, training, and retraining of personnel, satisfaction of patients, new treatments, new methods.

     f. Put resources into maintenance of equipment, furniture, and fixtures; new aids to production in the office.

     g. Decide whom the administrator and the chairman of the board are responsible to and the means by which they will be held responsible for working for constancy of purpose.

     h. Translate this constancy of purpose to patients and to the community.

     i. The board of directors must hold the purpose constant.

   2.   Adopt the new philosophy. We are in a new economic age. We can no longer live with commonly accepted levels of mistakes, materials not suited to

---

* I am indebted to Drs. Barry Gurland and David Wilder of the Center for Geriatrics and Gerontology of Columbia University, for the privilege to work with them on earlier drafts of these 14 points, with special reference to nursing homes.

the job, people on the job that do not know what the job is and are afraid to ask, failure of management to understand their job, antiquated methods of training on the job, inadequate and ineffective supervision. The board must put resources into this new philosophy, with commitment to in-service training.

3.a. Require statistical evidence of quality of incoming materials, such as pharmaceuticals, serums, and equipment. Inspection is not the answer. Inspection is too late and is unreliable. Inspection does not produce quality. The quality is already built in and paid for.

b. Require statistical evidence of quality, and type of corrective action needed, for all tasks that are performed in the hospital or other facility, ranging all the way from bills that are produced to processes of registration. Institute a rigid program of feedback from patients in regard to their satisfaction with services. This may include performance against one of an established set of quality of performance monitors.

c. Look for evidence of rework or defects and the cost that may accrue as a result--an incorrect bill, an incorrect or incomplete registration.

4. Deal with vendors that can furnish statistical evidence of control. This will require us to examine generic lowest-price buying; it will cause us to ask more penetrating questions about prospective colleagues regarding their interactions and the track record of their interactions with patients and with colleagues.

We must take a clear stand that price of services has no meaning without adequate measure of quality. Without such a stand for rigorous measures of quality, business drifts to the lowest bidder; low quality and high cost being the inevitable result. We see this throughout the United States industry and government by rules that award business to the lowest bidder.

QUALITY AND PRODUCTIVITY IN SERVICE ORGANIZATIONS

Requirement of a statistical measure of quality will, in all likelihood, require us to reduce the number of vendors. The problem is to find one vendor that can furnish statistical evidence of quality. We must work with vendors so that we understand the procedures that they use to achieve reduced numbers of defects.

5.   Similar to Point 5 in Chapter 2, page 30.

6.   Restructure training.

   a. Develop the concept of tutors.

   b. Develop increased in-service education.

   c. Teach employees methods of statistical control on the job.

   d. Provide operational definitions of all jobs.

   e. Provide training until the learner's work reaches the state of statistical control, and focus the training to assist the learner to achieve the status of statistical control.

7.   Improve supervision. Supervision belongs to the system and is the responsibility of the management.

   a. Supervisors need time to help people on the job.

   b. Supervisors need to find ways to translate the constancy of purpose to the individual employee.

   c. Supervisors must be trained in simple statistical methods for aid to employees, with the aim to detect and eliminate special causes of mistakes and rework. Supervisors should find causes of trouble and not just chase anecdotes. They need information that shows when to take action, not just figures that describe the level of production and the level of mistakes in the past.

   d. Focus supervisory time on people that are out of statistical control and not those that are low performers. If the members of a group are in fact

in statistical control, there will be some that are low performers and some
that are high performers.

   e.   Teach supervisors how to use the results of surveys of patients.

   8.   Drive out fear. We must break down the class distinctions between
types of workers within the organization--physicians, non-physicians, clinical
providers versus non-clinical providers, physician to physician. Discontinue
gossip. Cease to blame employees for problems of the system. Management
should be held responsible for faults of the system. People need to feel
secure to make suggestions. Management must follow through on suggestions.
People on the job can not work effectively if they dare not enquire into the
purpose of the work that they do, and dare not offer suggestions for simplification and improvement of the system.

   9.   Break down barriers between departments. Learn about the problems in
the various departments. One way would be to encourage switches of personnel
in related departments.

   10.   Eliminate numerical goals, slogans, and posters imploring people to
do better. Instead, display accomplishments of the management in respect to
assistance to employees to improve their performance. People need information
about what the management is doing on these 14 points.

   11.   Eliminate work standards that set quotas, commonly called also
measured day work. Work standards must produce quality, not mere quantity. It
is better to take aim at rework, error, defects, and to focus on help to people
to do a better job. It is necessary for people to understand the purpose of
the organization, and how their jobs relate to the purpose of the organization.

   12.   Institute a massive training program in statistical techniques.
Bring statistical techniques down to the level of the individual employee's
job, and help him to gather information in a systematic way about the nature of

his job. This kind of in-service training must be a marriage with the management function rather than the personnel function within the organization.

13.   Institute a vigorous training program for retraining people in new skills. People must be secure about their jobs in the future, and must know that their acquisition of new skills in their discipline will be facilitated by the organization.

14.   Create a structure in top management that will push every day on the above 13 points. Top management may organize a task force with the authority and obligation to act. This task force will require guidance from an experienced consultant, but the consultant can not take on obligations that only the management can carry out.

B. EXAMPLES AND SUGGESTIONS

Application in the U.S. Census. One of the earliest and largest and most successful full-scale applications of quality control in all its phases is found in the U.S. Census. It began around 1940 under the leadership of Dr. Morris H. Hansen. The results are reliability of data far beyond dreams of private organizations that are engaged in social and demographic studies, including consumer research. Costs in the Census are far below the costs encountered and charged by private organizations.

Success in improvement of quality and productivity in the Census is largely attributable to effective organization for statistical work, to be described in Chapter 17. Another feature is the total commitment of the top management of the Census for continual improvement of quality and productivity.

Quality and productivity in the Bureau of Customs. The Bureau of Customs weighs a shipload of incoming bales of wool, or of bales of tobacco, or bales of rayon, by weighing only a small sample of the bales and computing the total weight on board by means of the sample, making use of ratio-estimates and other statistical techniques. The Bureau of Customs computes also, in the case of wool, by tests of a sample of cores bored from the sample of bales, the clean content of the wool in order to compute the duty to be paid. Weighing by means of samples of bales reduces greatly the cost of weighing and puts ships out on to the water days before they would be out if every bale were weighed, as was the procedure prior to adoption of statistical methods. The benefit is not only reduction in time and saving of cost to the Bureau of Customs, as well as savings of thousands of dollars for berthing charges to the shipping companies, but improved accuracy of the weights and of the clean content of the incoming wool.

Problem in payroll department. A company had trouble with mistakes on time cards. There were 900 people on the payroll, making 1500 mistakes every day. (Not a bad production record.) The payroll department, because of so many mistakes, succeeded only with great effort to get cheques to the employees four days after the close of the week. Could the burden be lightened? The time card is shown in Fig. 44. Note that two signatures were required, employee and foreman.

Why have two people sign the card? Who is responsible for the accuracy of the card? The requirement of two signatures means that nobody is responsible: trouble guaranteed. Suggestions:

1. Require only the signature of the employee. Make him responsible for the card.

2. Give a cursory daily review to the cards. If there is anything wrong, no matter how slight, send the card back to the employee for correction. Make it clear to him that his pay may be delayed because of his mistake.

3. Do not ask an employee to record nor compute the amount due him for each job, nor to show the total for the day. The payroll department has records and

QUALITY AND PRODUCTIVITY IN SERVICE ORGANIZATIONS

Two signatures — nobody responsible for whole thing

Date _____ _____ 198____
     Day   Month   Year

Identification
number
     _____ _____
                        Signature

Clock		Elapsed time	Job code	Pay code	Amount earned
In	Out				
Total earned this day					

_____
            Foreman

Fig. 44. Payroll card. Too many signatures.
Too much arithmetic for the employee.

machines for this kind of work. An employee should not be asked to do arithmetic at the end of the day.

My prediction was that the problems would evaporate in three weeks. Actually, they evaporated in two weeks. Employees soon learned how to get paid on time--don't turn in a time card with mistakes on it.

Clerical problems in purchase. In another instance, the purchasing department complained that three out of four purchase orders came to them incomplete or incorrect in some way, such as wrong item number, obsolete number, no such vendor, vendor misspelled, no signature of the buyer, and a host of other nuisances. My suggestion was to send the form back immediately to the buyers if anything was amiss. My prediction was that the problem would evaporate in three weeks. Actually, irregularities dropped to three in 100 in two weeks. Most of the remaining problems can be eliminated with care in supervision--e.g., provide buyers with information that is up to date.

Travel vouchers.* Management in the Office of Education in Washington found that several signatures were required on every claim for reimbursement for travel. Every person that signed a claim tried to clean it up before it moved onward for the next review and signature.

A simple change in procedure eliminated most of the problems and hastened reimbursement: (1) revise the instructions, for better clarity; (2) do not correct mistakes nor fill in deficiencies in vouchers. Instead, send it back to the traveler for correction, with an explanation that his error or omission will cause delay in reimbursement. The problem all but disappeared in a short while.

---

* I am indebted to Robert Caccia and to Drs. Emmett Fleming and Joseph Teresa for the privilege to work with them on this illustration.

QUALITY AND PRODUCTIVITY IN SERVICE ORGANIZATIONS

Many companies are equally guilty of piling paper work on paper work. My suggestion is to pay at sight every claim for travel and for petty cash, and to investigate thoroughly a sample of claims, such as one in 50. The sample would include also 100 per cent of any transactions suspected of being shady. Investigation of the sample will tell how the system is working. Some mistakes there will be, but their net effect will be trivial compared with the economy of transfer to useful work of layers of reviewers.

Accounting procedures: present worth of physical plant and inventory. Accounting procedures now require that the auditor's report contain an evaluation of the physical plant, rolling stock, and inventory. For a large company, this evaluation can be carried out only by statistical methods of sampling, to estimate (a) the physical condition of each category of plant, and (b) the reproduction cost new of each category; then by multiplication to estimate the present worth. By use of statistical methods of sampling, it is necessary to inspect only a relatively small number of items, something like (e.g., 4000) for a plant like that of the Illinois Bell Telephone Company, total reproduction cost new minus depreciation, over $2,000,000,000. The work can be done by skilled inspectors in the space of a few weeks. Use of judgment-samples could only be crude guesswork.

Along with the results on evaluation of reproduction cost new minus depreciation, come, free of charge, information by which to forecast the cost of repairs and replacement during the next five years for each type of plant. This forecast is far more objective than the reports of division-managers, all of whom know that he who screams loudest gets the most money for repairs and replacement. Estimates of the proportion of underground duct-space not in use, by size of duct, is an example of another bonus.

Reduction of inventory through study of time of transit.* Parts for automobiles in the United States are made in various cities in the United States
and Canada, and are shipped by rail and by motor freight to the customer.
Study of time of transit of parts from the factory to the customer shows in
some corridors of traffic pretty good statistical control except for special
causes in the nature of delays for repairs of cars that break down en route.
An upper limit of regular time of transit is then a simple calculation.

In an example, the corridor was Buffalo to Kansas City. Inventory en route,
and inventory in Kansas City, constitute investment. The requirement on inventory in Kansas City had been fixed as five days. The upper limit, once the time
of transit was observed to be in statistical control (except for breakdowns)
was calculated as 4.2 days. The difference, .8 day, translates into saving of
$500,000 per year for the parts involved in this calculation.

This and similar calculations for scores of other routes added up to
$25,000,000, interest on which is easily $10,000 per day at present rates.

Time for major repair of a car is hardly ever less than 24 hours, even for
light repairs. Inventory sufficient to cover shortage that arises from breakdowns en route is costly. There is another way to work on this problem. The
whereabouts of every car en route is known at all times at headquarters by
telegraphic communication with the railway. Quick action in the form of rapid
despatch by truck from the car that broke down, or from another plant, of
enough parts to fill in the gap created by a breakdown is a workable solution.

---

* I am indebted to Messrs. Richard Haupt, Charles Richards, and Dr. Edward
Baker of the Ford Motor Company for the privilege to work with them on this
problem.

Tests of foods, drugs, and sundry items. Everyone is much aware these days of safety, liability for accidents from failure of machinery or apparatus, alleged carcinogenous properties of various drugs and chemicals, and even of common food additives, and of materials as common and useful as asbestos. Few people are aware that a decision to ban the sale of goods or drugs, or to restrict their use, is a judgment based on tests, usually of rats.

How many people have seen the statistician's summary of these tests, and his reports on their statistical reliability?

Are such facts made clear in reports given out to the public about safety or hazard in foods and drugs?

I am aware that a statistician's report on tests of a food, drug, or piece of apparatus (some part of your automobile being an example) would be voluminous and costly, as hard to read as it was to write. It would summarize relevant tests carried on anywhere in the world. It would be as difficult for a layman to understand as a report of his medical examination would be. Nevertheless, a taxpayer is entitled to the right to purchase the statistician's report, so that he may engage his own statistician to help him to understand it, just as one may engage a doctor of medicine to decipher and explain the results of a medical examination.

A hotel. The hotel business, like a lot of other businesses, is beset by weekly cycles of heavy demand for rooms Monday through Thursday, and reduced demand Friday, Saturday, and Sunday. Besides, there is strong seasonal variation. Charts of occupancy help the manager to plan ahead, to lighten and balance the loads of employees by adjusting to the ups and downs of demand the type of work that they do, and their hours. Some of the cleaning, decorating, and maintenance can be reserved for slack seasons. Purchases and inventories of food can be partially adjusted to demand, by looking ahead. Mistakes in reservation and in bookkeeping can be reduced. Time required for registration of incoming guests, and for payment of bills on departure is costly both to the hotel and to the guest.

Observations on a statistically planned basis could keep the management informed on characteristics of performance such as these:

-- The proportion of rooms that are put into satisfactory order before registration of new arrivals.
-- The distribution of the time required for putting vacated rooms into order for new arrivals. Do these periods of time form a statistical distribution, or are there outliers?
-- If there are outliers, what is the cause? Would it be economical to remove the cause?
-- The proportion of guests that needed a desk where none was provided.
-- The proportion of rooms without adequate light on the desk.
-- The proportion of rooms without adequate supplies of stationery.
-- The proportion of rooms in which the telephone is not working properly.
-- The proportion of guests that declare that the airconditioning is noisy.
-- Any reader can add other problems found in hotels.*

The bellboy showed to me a beautiful room in a hotel. "At last," said I to myself, "here is a real desk in a hotel room. I can write on it in comfort." On second look, however, I perceived that there was no light on it nor near it, and no electric outlet closer than the opposite wall. It would have cost but

---

* The book by Philip B. Crosby, QUALITY IS FREE (McGraw-Hill, 1979) has on pages 59-63 an interesting story of how easy it is to lose money and fold up in the hotel business.

QUALITY AND PRODUCTIVITY IN SERVICE ORGANIZATIONS

little, when the building was under construction, to put in electrical outlets where they might be needed. Later, makeshift cords are required.

The post office. One may wonder why the mail service in the U.S. is the worst in the industrialized world except for competition offered by Canada. Losses to business from poor mail service in the United States defy calculation. No matter if the employees work hard on their jobs, and if middle management is continually finding ways to cut costs.

Wide variance in time between posting and delivery of mail is costly for business, and annoying to the general public. Messenger service, men carrying envelopes or machine-sheets from one business to another, within the same city or between (e.g.) New York and Philadelphia, has of late become a growth industry in the United States, owing to the collapse of the U.S. mail.

An ordinary postage stamp in England, Germany, Nederland, Denmark, France, buys service equivalent to U.S. Express Mail, at a fraction of the cost.

The problem lies, of course, in the management of the Post Office which has never had the privilege to decide what should be the function of a postal service. Should service be slow and cheap, or speedy at higher cost? Both alternatives would be possible with a priority system of postage.

Over-booking. Any airline that practices over-booking needs statistical guidance to optimize the gains and to minimize the losses that may arise from several sources, including penalties. There are two losses to consider:
(1) seats vacant, representing loss of revenue; (2) seats oversold, with a possible penalty to pay every passenger left behind. The penalty may be a free ride on some other airline, plus a sum of money. (Over-booking in a hotel may not be as serious: the manager can often find a room across the street in another hotel).

The statistical problem is to minimize the net loss from the two possible mistakes (penalty for more passengers than seats, and loss from more seats than passengers). One needs no statistical theory to achieve a clean record on a resolve (a) to never over-book; or (b) to never pay a penalty.

In good management, one has a rational plan dictated by statistical theory to minimize the net loss from both eventualities, including penalty for failure to have a seat for a passenger as booked.

The first step is a historical record of demand for each trip, with a study of weekly and other cycles, on which to base a rational prediction of demand a few days ahead, with confidence limits attached thereto. One can then compute the optimum number of seats to book beyond capacity for greatest profit.

Copying machines. A similar type of statistical plan could be designed for copying machines, as well as for installations of other apparatus and machinery. Records show the time elapsed between (a) the customer's request for service, and (b) the serviceman's call. Analysis of these records, would provide statistical signals that indicate special causes of delay, and would describe in meaningful terms the performance of the service department. It would be profitable to learn from the same records the proportion of trouble that lies in:

-- The machine as a whole; also for any specified component thereof.
-- The customer.
-- The repairman.

It would be useful for a district manager to know which repairmen need further training or should be shifted to other work. It would be useful to learn more about customers. In the case of copying machines, some customers are satisfied with wretched copies. Others are very particular, and call the serviceman at the least blemish. The records kept by servicemen would disclose which category a customer belongs to, and they would indicate where improvements in design might be desirable. They would also indicate whether customers need education on what to expect of a machine, and need of better instruction on how to use it and how to take care of it. Some customers may need a more expensive machine, or one less expensive.*

<u>A restaurant</u>. I have often wondered in a restaurant, seated and helpless waiting for the next course, or equally helpless wondering how to get the bill in order to square up and vacate one seat, seeing a line of people waiting to be seated, how much lost capacity the restaurant suffers from failure of supervision. If people could be served with despatch (not with haste), and the bill delivered when they are ready for it, to give up their places to incoming patrons, productivity, capacity, and profits would all increase substantially, and customers would be better satisfied.

How many patrons, of those seated, are trying in vain to signal a waiter? How many waiters are at this very time standing by, gazing into the heavens? How much food has been ready 10 minutes for waiters to deliver to the table, fit to eat 10 minutes ago, now ready for rejection? What kinds of food are only half consumed? Snap-counts, at random times by Tippett's methods, would provide answers at low cost.**

---

* Two excellent references are these: Nancy R. Mann, Raymond Schafer, Nozer D. Singpurwalla, METHODS FOR STATISTICAL ANALYSIS OF RELIABILITY AND LIFE DATA (John Wiley & Sons, 1974), and Richard E. Barlow and Frank Proschan, STATISTICAL THEORY of RELIABILITY (Holt Rinehart & Winston, 1975).

** Marvin E. Mundel, MOTION AND TIME STUDIES (Prentice-Hall, 1950, 1970), p. 128. L. H. C. Tippett, "Ratio-Delay Study," <u>Journal of Textile Institute Transactions</u>, Vol. XXXVI, No. 2, Feb. 1935; R. L. Morrow, <u>Time Study and Motion Economy</u>, New York, N.Y.: The Ronald Press Company, 1946, pp. 176-199; C. L. Brisky, "How You Can Put Work Sampling to Work," <u>Factory</u>, Vol. 110, No. 7, July 1952, pp. 84-89; J. S. Pairo, "Using Ratio-Delay Studies To Set Allowance," <u>Factory</u>, Vol. 106, No. 10, Oct. 1943, p. 94.

What foods listed on the card outsell others? Which of them hardly ever sell? Which ones cause loss? Could they be eliminated without severe loss of patronage? Which ones could be offered once a week at a profit instead of daily at low profit or downright loss?

Of the various costs, which ones are heaviest? How could they be reduced? Alterations of food and service could be made in anticipation of a heat-wave or a blizzard, predicted by the Weather Bureau.

A city's transit system. Statistical methods help to learn where there is business, and at what time of day, to meet needs of the public. Timetables posted at stops, and rigid adherence thereto, would generate new business. One need only visit any city in Europe to discover what can be done to improve service in the United States.

Transit systems in the United States are hampered by the requirement that, to get federal funds for equipment, they must give business to the lowest bidder (as remarked in Ch. 2).

Carriers of motor freight. Samples of freight bills issued by carriers of general freight in the United States and Canada, selected and processed by procedures that are based on the theory of probability (to get the maximum amount of information per unit cost) furnish information:

> For hearings before the Interstate Commerce Commission, on requests of the carriers for increases or restructuring of rates for hauls of various weights and mileages. The same data furnish also a basis for negotiation with shippers in respect to rates for shipments of various weights and mileages.

> For business purposes. The carriers may observe, from the results of the continuing studies, what routes, weights, mileages, and what classes and commodities, lead to unprofitable business, and which ones to profitable business.

No other industry has information in such detail, accuracy, and timeliness, for use for business purposes or as a rational basis for rates.

These continuing studies of traffic are done by the carriers themselves (not by any government agency), under statistical procedures designed and monitored by this author.

Other types of studies lead to reduction of mistakes in loading, in pickup and delivery, reduction in damage and claims for damage, errors in billing.

Another study shows whether and how effective are various steps aimed at reduction of fuel--heavier loading, idling fans, regular tuning (or irregular, whichever is more cost effective), enforcing economical speed on inter-city routes.

A railway. Statistical methods would help to reduce errors in interline settlements and in local billing as well. They could help to decrease idle time or cars, which would decrease the rent paid out for use of cars, and would improve service to customers, by furnishing empty cars with less delay. These distributions would show:

1. Whether delays form a statistical system. If they are outliers, what are the causes of the outliers? Why not eliminate these causes (if outliers are found)?

2. What can be done to shrink the ranges of the distribution? Shrinkage of the distribution would mean better service to the customer and savings to the railway through more dependable and uniform performance. Customer and railway would both gain more uniform and more dependable performance.

Where is the distribution of time spent by cars in shops for repair, by different types of repair? The railway pays rent for every hour for a car in a shop, no matter who owns the car.

Where, for any important terminal, is the distribution of hours that elapse between the time when a customer informs the railway that he is ready to load a car or several cars, and the time when an empty car or cars are delivered to him? How many of the cars delivered were the right type of car? How many were dirty? Where is the distribution of hours elapsed between the time when the car is ready until it was pulled away?

It would be possible by methods based on probability sampling to make periodic tests of samples of rolling equipment, signalling equipment, equipment in warehouses and docks and on trucks, to determine the proportion and number of items that are depleted and in need of repair or immediate replacement, and to estimate the costs to be incurred next year for maintenance and replacement. Examination of tracks, roadbed, and grading at points selected by statistical methods would furnish information on which to plan repairs. The methods of probability sampling for such studies are a powerful tool of administration.

Do customers care about the service rendered? Even if they don't, improvement in performance would squeeze more profit from existing equipment and tracks, or even permit sale of some existing equipment, and improve service to customers.

A telephone company.*

1. Studies, carried out by appropriate statistical design, to estimate the usage of circuits and carrier equipment: what proportions of the time are circuits and carrier-equipment used for voice, for the press, for transmission of data, private telegrams, public telegrams, etc.? The results are used as a basis for fixing rates for the various services.

---

* I am indebted to friends in telephone companies for help in this section, in particular, to (a) Dr. Robert J. Brousseau of the American Telephone Company; (b) James N. Kennedy of the Illinois Bell Telephone Company; (c) Dr. J. Franklin Sharp, "Managing Statistics and Operations Research for Management," a paper delivered at a meeting of the American Statistical Association held in Boston in August 1976. (d) Last, I am grateful for the privilege to work with a number of telephone companies, from 1949 onward, on numerous types of studies.

QUALITY AND PRODUCTIVITY IN SERVICE ORGANIZATIONS

2. Studies, carried out by appropriate statistical design, are used to estimate the ratio of usage of switches and other central office equipment for local service to toll service. The results are used as a basis for division of revenues between local telephone service and toll service, and ultimately for rates.

3. Studies, carried out by appropriate statistical design, to estimate the physical depreciation of the various kinds of equipment--switches, relays, private branch exchanges, underground exchange cable, underground toll cable, community dial offices, duct, loading coils, poles, aerial cable, terminals on poles and in buildings, telephone apparatus, signalling devices.

4. Reduction of errors in billing, accomplished at reduced cost.

5. Tests of records of physical plant. Are the records satisfactory? What kinds of mistakes need correction, and for what areas?

6. Reconciliation of joint usage of property, such as poles. The telephone company may own a pole, or the electric company may own it, or they may own it jointly 50:50 or otherwise. They pay rent to each other for use of poles. Is one company paying the other too much? Studies by appropriate statistical design provide answers of demonstrable precision. Continuing studies keep the payments in balance. (A complete reconciliation would be impossible because of the sheer size of the job, and if attempted, would introduce a whole new set of errors, and the last state would be worse than at the beginning.)

7. Effectiveness of advertising to boost revenue from long distance calls.

8. Simulation of a telephone office. Certain types of additional involvement of operators were proposed by corporate psychologists with the goal of enrichment of job. As the proposed changes might have drastic effects on productivity, the research group set up a simulated model to study a number of possible changes.

9. Studies to decrease the time for telephone operators by working smarter, not harder, to handle various types of calls. Mechanization of the analysis, with a carefully designed sampling procedure for carrying out ratio-delay studies, provides results on a continuing basis.

10. Optimal routes for messenger service between Bell System locations within a metropolitan area. A telephone company may have one or more central despatch systems for intra-company mail and numerous mail routes for pickup and delivery of company mail in a large number of locations. The Bell Laboratories developed an integer programming algorithm to help to determine the optimal number of routes and the stops to be made on each route.

11. Optimal location of new equipment. Savings in operating costs can be achieved by replacing electromechanical switching equipment by electronic equipment, or by installing electronic equipment rather than additional electro-mechanical equipment. Bell Telephone Laboratories has developed a nonlinear programming algorithm to help determine where and when electronic equipment should be installed. Other research men in the companies have developed some user-oriented software, incorporated some additional procedures for financial analysis.

12. Continuing studies of expenses and usage of common equipment, carried out by all telephone companies, in a joint effort, following statistical procedures designed by Dr. Robert J. Brousseau of the American Telephone and Telegraph Company, in a joint effort with other telephone companies, form the underlying base for interline settlements of revenue and charges for use of joint equipment, mainly toll circuits.

13. Inventory and reconciliation of engineering records and accounting records of underground cable and repeaters, aerial cable and other equipment;

the same for telephone equipment including wiring and installation (station equipment) on the premises of customers.

14. Estimation of unit costs of material and labor in station connexions.

15. Aids for training operators.

16. Estimation of the cost of dental care for employees.

17. Studies by which to reduce the risk of failure of the company to collect the amount due for telephone service rendered to people that move away without settling their bills for telephone service (loss of several million dollars in one year for Illinois Bell alone).

18. Estimation of usage of the Yellow Pages, and how to make them more useful.

19. Study of the problems that customers have to decipher their telephone bills, the aim being to improve the format of bills.

A department store. Observations by department on the length of time that customers wait for service, the number of people that walk away unable to get service, would provide a basis for use of a loss function that would help the management to decide whether, where, and when additional service might pay a dividend.

> There is one big gap in the use of a loss-function for such
> purposes: no one knows the loss that accrues to the store from ill
> will of people that give up and walk away. One unhappy customer can
> influence a lot of other people: so can a happy customer.
> Observations at snap times on:

> --Attitude of clerk toward customer.

> --Attitude of customer toward clerk.

Automobiles and the customer. We pause here for only a brief remark that is easy to expand to wide application. A large manufacturer of automobiles, in recognition of the need to learn about the problems of the purchaser of an automobile sends out to every purchaser, after a year from date of purchase, a questionnaire to learn about his problems and experience.

Half the questionnaires come back; half do not. Now every statistician knows the perils of drawing conclusions from incomplete returns, even if 90 per cent of them come back. Refuge in the argument that the hazards that lurk in incomplete returns may be small if the conclusions are confined to trends is only an expression of hope, with little foundation.

A simple modification, well known,* would be to send out questionnaires to only a sample of 1000 purchasers, appropriately selected; then to follow up by personal interview the nonrespondents. This modification would greatly reduce the cost of the study, and would yield results that could be used with an ascertainable degree of confidence.

The same procedure could be applied to any other product for which a list of purchasers exists. In fact, this suggestion is regular practice with some companies, as anyone engaged in consumer research knows.

C. REDUCTION OF MISTAKES IN A BANK **

A bank. Friends in the banking business acknowledge that the management of banks know less about their customers than the management in any other business. Starts are being made by pulling together the accounts of any one customer--his chequing account, savings accounts, fiduciary accounts, trust accounts, loans. This coordination is greatly simplified by modern data processing machinery.

---

* See any textbook on sampling or survey procedures.
** Part C of this chapter was prepared at my request by Mr. William J. Latzko of the Irving Trust Company, New York. I am indebted to him and to his wife Connie for numerous helpful suggestions in the book.

QUALITY AND PRODUCTIVITY IN SERVICE ORGANIZATIONS

But this is far short of knowing the needs of customers, and to what extent the bank fails to meet these needs. Why does a customer of the bank get a loan elsewhere for the purchase of an automobile or to buy a home, or to remodel his present home? Neither the fact nor the reasons are on the record. Some consumer research might answer this and a host of other questions about customers.

The big mistake. There is, in a bank, as in other businesses, the perennial problem of reduction of mistakes. The search for quality in banking is by no means new; it dates back to the time of the Pharaohs. Traditionally the banker's quest for quality has been the reviewer or signer, with layer upon layer of inspection into the system, under the supposition that the only costly error is the one that leaves the bank to annoy the customer. All work, time, and money spent in forestalling such a disaster has been simply a cost of doing business, absorbed in operational costs and only rarely visible to the management.

There are four kinds of cost:

1. Costs of appraisal, verification and inspection of work. This is the traditional inspection system; the army of people in every bank that are engaged in verifying and verifying again.

2. Cost of internal failure, probably the real villain in banking's story. These are the mistakes that are caught in a bank and reworked, at many times the expense that would have been incurred if the work had been done correctly in the first place.

3. Cost of external failure. These are the errors that get out to the customer and lead to expensive investigations, adjustments, penalties, and lost accounts.

4. Cost of prevention, the analysis and systematic control of quality. The theory is simple. Detection and correction of trouble at the earliest

stage decreases costs all down the line and improves quality at lower total cost.

There are two types of quality in any system, whether it be banking or manufacturing. The first is quality of design. These are the specific programs, procedures, etc., that promise to produce a salable service or product: in other words, what the customer requires. The second type is quality of production, achievement of results with the quality promised.

Quality control works both with the product and with the design of the product. And it is at this point that quality control begins to differ from the traditional system. To find the mistake is not enough. It is necessary to find the cause behind the mistake, and to build a system that minimizes future mistakes.

Improvement of performance. The Quality Improvement Program operates at the level of first-line supervisor. It has brought success (see Fig. 45) and has improved morale, as employees are now confident that they will not be blamed for errors that are not under their governance.

A record, charted on a regular basis by computer, provides the process capability of each individual. The performance of the individual can then be compared with the performance of the group. Help can be given to people that fall outside the tolerances for the group.

Morale of employees. Previously, when rejection rates went up, computer operators began blaming each other. Shift would react against shift and department against department. In the end, everyone would blame "the machine." The results were discord, disharmony, and low morale. With statistical methods, the reason for an abnormal rejection rate can be automatically traced to the department, to the shift, to the machine, to the operator, and finally to the important thing, the problem. For, as stated before, statistical methods

QUALITY AND PRODUCTIVITY IN SERVICE ORGANIZATIONS

require identification of the problem, not the individual. With such a philosophy, everyone works together to point his finger at the real culprit, the problem.

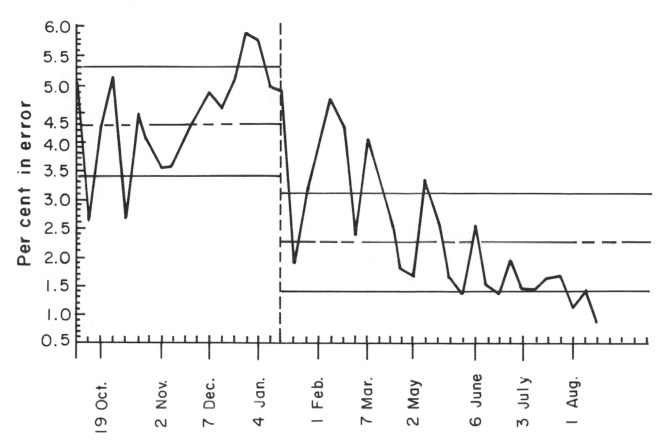

Fig. 45. Results of quality improvement program. It refers specifically to typing in the telegram department. Problems are now detected long before they become critical.

Quality is an economic consideration. Correction of a problem may cost more than its worth. But there is no way for anyone to compute the cost of removal of a cause unless he knows what the cause is.

Some experts on banking declare that between 40 per cent and 60 per cent of any bank's staff is involved in verifying the work of other staff members. Statistical methods help to reduce the frequency of mistakes. They have a far-reaching and dramatic impact on the future of banking. With concentration of inspection on critical items, such as those of high dollar value, and sample verification of other items, greater accuracy can be obtained with decrease in the amount of inspection.

Programs of improvement can be instituted at any bank, regardless of size, for they can be tailored to meet specific needs and designed to grow with the bank, expanding as new areas of application become apparent.

Each unit being studied, whether it be a human operator, a machine or system, is monitored over a period of time to determine its process-capability: what it can predictably do under current conditions (Ch. 7). The process-capability of an operation can usually be determined in about three months.

Should management decide that the process capability is not within the acceptable limits, then management must do something about the process or system. Quality can not exceed the capability of the system. Quality can not be inspected into a product or service; it must be built into it (Harold F. Dodge; Ch. 2).

Chapter 13

PLAN FOR MINIMUM TOTAL COST FOR TEST OF
INCOMING MATERIALS AND FINAL PRODUCT *

I stick fast in the deep mire where
no ground is. I am come into deep waters:
floods run over me.--Psalm 69, v. 2.

A. SOME SIMPLE RULES OF WIDE APPLICATION

Incoming parts, some defective: how much inspection? Even though vendor
and purchaser work together to reduce the proportion of defective parts that he
sends to you, you may not yet be totally successful in your efforts to eliminate
defective parts that come in. We must accordingly prepare ourselves with theory
that will tell us what to do. Should we try to screen out the defective items
in a lot that comes in, if any defectives there be? Or should we send every
lot straight into the production line, defective parts and good ones, just as
they come in?

We shall develop principles that will, in a wide variety of circumstances
met in practice, tell us what to do to minimize the total cost of inspection of
incoming materials plus the cost to repair and test assemblies that fail because of a defective item that went into production. Suppositions:

* It is a pleasure to acknowledge deep gratitude to Dr. Louis K. Kates,
Statistician and Consultant in Software, Toronto, who has helped me on this
chapter with fraternal devotion. I am indebted also to Dr. Gary C. McDonald
of the General Motors Research Laboratories.

— We deal at first only with a single part. We later introduce the problem of multiple parts.

— We shall test every assembly.

— If an incoming part is defective and goes into the assembly, the assembly will fail its test. If the incoming part is not defective, the assembly will not fail.

— Our vendor furnishes to us a supply of parts (call it S), for replacement of any defective part found.

Of course, he adds the cost of these parts to his bill. This cost is an overhead cost. We deal here only with variable costs. There is no point in bringing into the theory overhead costs that would be there anyway, no matter what be our plan of inspection.

A defective part is one that by definition will cause the assembly to fail. If a part declared defective at the start will not cause trouble further down the line, or with the customer, then you have not yet defined what you mean by a defective part. The next step in this circumstance would be to examine the test method that declares a part to be defective or not defective.

There are, of course, examples where a defect in an incoming part can be discovered in the factory only at great expense, and must be left for the customer to discover, often after some months or years. These are commonly called latent defects. Chromium plate is one example. The best solution to this problem is to avoid it by improving the process. This is also the solution to the problem of a destructive test, a test that destroys the item.

Let

p   be the average fraction defective in incoming lots of parts (which could be a day's receipt of material).

k_1 be the cost to inspect one part.

k_2 be the cost to dismantle, repair, reassemble, and test an assembly that fails because a defective part was put into the production line.

k   be the average cost to test one or more parts to find a good one in the supply S. k is evaluated as k_1/q in Exercise 5 at the end of the chapter.

OPTIMUM PLAN FOR INCOMING MATERIALS

<u>All or none</u>. The rules for minimum total cost turn out to be extremely simple under certain conditions, labeled Case 1 and Case 2 in what follows.

<u>Case 1</u>: The worst lot to come in will have fraction defective less than k_1/k_2. In this case,

No inspection

<u>Case 2</u>: The best lot to come in will have fraction defective greater than k_1/k_2. In this case,

100 per cent inspection

The proof of the rules for Case 1 and Case 2 is exceedingly simple: see Exercise 4 at the end of this chapter.

The fraction defective k_1/k_2 is the break-even point. To treat as Case 2 a clean example of Case 1 will maximize the total cost, and the converse is true: see Example 1 further on.

> No inspection is not a directive to proceed in ignorance. One must be sure, for Case 1, on the basis of past performance that the worst lot (or week's receipts) to come in will lie to the left of the break-even point. Control charts that the purchaser keeps for fraction defective, or $\bar{x}$- and R-charts provided by the vendor, preferably a joint venture, will place the product in Case 1 or in Case 2 for the near future. A state of chaos, if it exists, will be no secret; it will be well known. The purchaser will always examine incoming materials to identify them with invoices, and to be sure that this is what he ordered. See the section entitled, "Never be without information."

Cases 1 and 2 achieve minimum total cost for many problems met in practice. Examples appear further on.

We now turn our attention to other possible circumstances.

<u>Binomial straddle</u>. Suppose that the process is in statistical control delivering lots in which the defective items are binomially distributed around the mean p. Then the rules for minimum total cost will be equally simple:

If $p < k_1/k_2$ no inspection

If $p > k_1/k_2$ 100 per cent inspection

Chapter 13

even though the distribution of fraction defective in lots straddles the break-even point k_1/k_2.

Actually, the fact is that in good statistical control, samples provide no information about remainders: see Exercise 1 at the end of this chapter.

<u>Mixture of binomials</u>. One can not expect to meet often in practice a pure (single point) binomial distribution of defective items in incoming lots. More usual, there will be in good control a mixture of binomials, each with its own fraction defective. Let

and
P_L be the least of these means

P_U be the greatest

Then the rules would be:

$P_U < k_1/k_2$ no inspection

$P_L > k_1/k_2$ 100 per cent inspection

Further, if these means lie in a narrow band, so that P_U is not much greater than P_L, then there will be little loss in the rules:

$p < k_1/k_2$ no inspection

$p > k_1/k_2$ 100 per cent inspection

where p is the mean fraction defective of the distribution.

This rule will do well provided the standard deviation of a mixture be less than .3.

If you know the process-average p, but are incorrect in your supposition that the process is in statistical control, or are incorrect in your supposition for Case 1 or Case 2 that the distribution lies entirely to one side of the break-even point, then there may be a scheme that will do better than the all-or-none rule. Yet if you imagine that some evil demon has come along and constructed for us a new distribution with the same process average, so that our all-or-none plan shows up at its worst, the all-or-none plan will do better

OPTIMUM PLAN FOR INCOMING MATERIALS

than any other plan, provided the evil demon also exerts his best efforts to put these other plans under their least favorable distributions.

That is to say, you are protected against Murphy's Law (anything that can go wrong will go wrong). You are protected against worst-case conditions. Unfortunately, this does not imply that you will do well under the best case, or even under likely conditions.

One may in theory improve the rule just given for a binomial mixture by classifying and treating as Case 1 or as Case 2 each lot, one by one, on the basis of a sample drawn at random from the lot. Such gains will be small and not worth the effort if the standard deviation of the mixture be less than .3 (see Exercise 1 at the end of this chapter). If the standard deviation of the means of the binomials that constitute the mixture be wide, let us say .3 or higher, the mixture may be treated as a state of chaos, soon to have our attention.

A better approach is to refuse to accept this state of affairs and to concentrate statistical efforts, not on rules for acceptance, but on work with the vendor, to eliminate the causes of defects. We proceed.

B. OTHER POSSIBLE CONDITIONS

Trend in the fraction defective in the incoming lots. Let us suppose that the trend is upward. Today, we are in Case 1, no inspection, but p is time-dependent, increasing, perhaps with a steady trend, perhaps with irregularities. Two days from now, we shall be in Case 2: we are forewarned. We are never without information about the quality of incoming material, hence we are able to observe the trend. (The best way to keep informed about incoming quality is from the control charts furnished by the vendor.) This problem is simple enough.

State of chaos. Joyce Orsini's rule.* Here, the fraction defective in the incoming material moves in wide unpredictable swings back and forth across the break-even point. In this state, samples taken from lots provide information about the remainders. If the break-even point is greater than .002, there is a simple rule that will in most practice achieve considerable advantage over 100 per cent inspection. The rule is this. Take a random sample of 200 parts from each lot. If there is no defective part in the sample, accept the remainder as it is. If one or more defective parts turn up in the sample, replace the defective parts with good ones, and screen the remainder. This rule originated with Joyce Orsini.

This plan, in a state of chaos, leads to substantial saving over the cost of 100 per cent inspection. The saving will vary, depending on the average quality of incoming parts, the variation of the proportion defective from lot to lot, and the break-even point, k_1/k_2. When $k_1/k_2 = 1/200$ in examples studied, the savings range from about 20 per cent to 50 per cent of the cost of 100 per cent inspection.

The plan is easy to administer. A supervisor with no statistical training can apply the rule with safety and with only a modicum of statistical oversight.

If the break-even point is far below .002, there might be temptation to explore by appropriate statistical theory the possible advantage of 100 per cent inspection. The reader may get a head start on such a project by looking at Joyce Orsini's original work.

In line with advice already offered, statistical knowledge could be put to better use by working with the vendor or by working on previous operations, to improve the quality of incoming production, and to decrease costs.

---

* Joyce Orsini, "Simple rule to reduce total cost of inspection and correction of product in state of chaos," dissertation for the doctorate, Graduate School of Business Administration, New York University, 1982.

OPTIMUM PLAN FOR INCOMING MATERIALS

Another procedure which is easy to describe and which is nearly of minimum total cost, but of powerful practicability in most circumstances is Anscombe's sequential plan.* Anscombe suggests that if the preceding assumptions all fail, we should sequentially sample the lot where the first sample is of size:

$$n = .375 \sqrt{N(k_2/k_1)}$$

(N the size of the lot) and take subsequent samples of size $n = k_2/k_1$. Continue sampling "until either the total number of defectives found is one less than the number of samples inspected, or the whole lot has been inspected."

Joyce Orsini's rule, and Anscombe's, or any other rule by which inspection of the remainder depends on a sample, share a common disadvantage. They all beget grief from a variable workload for inspection. Moreover, the already beleaguered manager of production must now cope with additional woes from an uncertain on- and off-supply of incoming parts. He may need parts, and he may demand them and get them, inspection or no inspection, defective or not, and thus shatter well-laid plans for inspection.

Never be without information. No inspection does not mean to drive in the dark with no lights. One should test small samples from every lot, or possibly on a skip-lot basis, for information and for comparison with your vendor's tests and charts. The best way to keep informed is by use of the control charts furnished by the vendor, with enough of your own inspection or with joint inspection to keep in tune with each other.

If there are two suppliers, keep separate records for each one.

A further point of advice (already offered in a number of lines in the text) is to continue to work with your vendor to improve incoming quality. He could perhaps, with your help, reduce p considerably: why not to 0? This

---

* Francis J. Anscombe, "Rectifying inspection of lots," _Journal of the American Statistical Association_, vol. 56, 1961: pp. 807-823.

effort is especially imperative if your costs of inspection and correction of
the assembly are large.

The same theory and the same rules would apply to repairs and
replacement of parts on a customer's premises (or in a repair-shop),
if we knew the costs. The only hitch is that the out-of-pocket cost
of repairs and replacement, once your product reaches a customer, is
only a small part of the cost of a defective. Loss of future business
from a dissatisfied customer, and from potential customers that learned
about his experience, may be enormous, and is unfortunately impossible
to estimate.

Suggestions in the face of uncertainty. One may be in a quandary when the
first lots come in from a new vendor. A good rule is to start with 100 per cent
inspection, unless you have strong evidence that the average fraction defective
is well below the break-even point.

Mistakes and corrections in a service organization. The above theory
applies to mistakes in processing, in a bank, in a department store, payroll of
any company, and in a host of other situations (see example 3, page 277). Work
moves along in various stages and finally comes out on a customer's bill, or as
figures on a cheque, or on a statement. Work may proceed through several stages
before the mistake is discovered. By the time it has proceeded through several
stages, the cost of correction may be 20, 50, or 100 times the cost to catch it
and correct it in the first place. In Example 3 ahead, furnished by Mr. William
J. Latzko of the Irving Trust Company, k_2 is 2000 times k_1.

Destructive testing. The foregoing theory is based on non-destructive testing: a part is not destroyed by the test. Some tests are destructive; they
destroy the sample that is tested. An example is the length of life of a lamp,
or the number of B.T.U. per cubic foot of gas, or the time to action of a fuse,
or test for the wool-content of a sample of fabric. Screening a rejected lot
would have no meaning, as nothing would be left to put into the production line.

OPTIMUM PLAN FOR INCOMING MATERIALS

Obviously, the only solution in destructive testing is to achieve statistical control in the manufacture of the part, to make it right in the first place. This solution is the best solution, destructive or non-destructive.

Advice. A useful study in any manufacturing plant, bank, department store, accounting department, anywhere, would be to evaluate approximately the costs k_1 and k_2 to discover whether inspection is being carried out where it would be better to do none, or to stop inspection where it is being carried out. Call a halt to any acceptance plan found anywhere in which remainders are being screened on the basis of tests of samples from lots.

C. EXAMPLES OF APPLICATION OF THE ALL-OR-NONE RULES

Example 1. A manufacturer of TV sets was inspecting every incoming integrated circuit.

> Question: How many defective integrated circuits do you find?
> Answer: On the average, 1 or 2 defective circuits out of 10,000 tested.

Thus, we take

$$p = 1/10,000 \text{ or } 2/10,000 = .00015$$

Further questions gave more figures:

$$k_1/k_2 = .01$$
$$k_1 = 30¢$$

As $p < k_1/k_2$, he should do no inspection of the integrated circuits. He was in Case 1, but following the procedure of Case 2. His total cost per integrated circuit was on the average, with his plan,

$$k_1 + kp$$

whereas with no inspection of the incoming integrated circuits, his average

cost would be

$$p \ (k_2 + k)$$

which is less than $k_1 + kp$. The difference is

(1)   Loss $= \left[k_1 + kp \right] - \left[p(k_2 + k) \right] = k_1 - pk_2$

$= 29.6¢$

or about 30¢ on each integrated circuit. There could be as many as 80 inte-

grated circuits in one TV set, or even more. At 80, the loss from the wrong

choice of plan would be 80 x 29.6¢ = 2368¢ or about $24 on each set, easily 15

per cent to 20 per cent of the manufacturer's cost.

> The engineer in charge explained to me at the start that he did
> not need the statistical control of quality because his inspections
> are all 100 per cent. He had been carrying out 100 per cent inspection
> of integrated circuits, he said, because his supplier had not facili-
> ties requisite for conducting the tests under the severity required.
> The manufacturer of the integrated circuits was nevertheless doing a
> pretty good job, it seemed to me--so good that p = .00015.

> As so often happens in the absence of quality control, this man was
> maximizing his cost. The calculations that we have just made, when he
> saw them, marked a turning point in his career.

> Incidentally, the engineer had placed in front of every group of
> production workers on a TV screen a display of the number of faults of
> each type that this group had introduced into their work the day
> before. This display was not only totally useless; it was frustrating
> and counter-productive. It helped nobody to do a better job.

Example 2. A manufacturer of automobiles had under consideration purchase

of testing equipment that would cost $25,000,000. This equipment would perform

tests of a motor before it went further.

Farther along in the assembly line, the average cost is $500 to tear down a

defective motor, replace defective parts, and retest the motor. The company

came up with these figures:

$$k_1 = \$ \ 50$$

$$k_2 = \$500$$

$$p \leqq 1/150$$

OPTIMUM PLAN FOR INCOMING MATERIALS

Thus

$$k_1/k_2 \quad = \quad 50/500 \quad = \quad 1/10$$

As $p < k_1/k_2$, this is Case 1, and the correct procedure for minimum total cost would be to omit entirely the initial test. The company cancelled the order for the testing equipment, but two other manufacturers of automobiles purchased it. In other words, two other companies, without benefit of statistical consultation, are maximizing their cost in this operation. The difference in cost between use of the initial test (maximum cost) and elimination thereof (minimum cost) is

$$k_1 - pk_2 \quad = \quad \$50 - \$500/150 \quad = \quad \$46.67 \text{ per motor}$$

At 4000 motors per day (the level of production at the time), this would translate into a saving of $185,000 per day.

Not bad for an hour's work!

What need one know to come to minimize the total cost in this problem? Answer:

    The appropriate statistical theory, and two figures, the maximum fraction defective expected, and k_1/k_2.

Example 3 (contributed by William J. Latzko, Irving Trust Company). Work moves from one section to another in a bank or in a department store, or payroll department. The cost of review (inspection) in a particular section is 25¢ per transaction processed, and the average cost to correct further down line a mistake made here is $500 = 50,000¢. One error in 1000 transactions is about the limit of accuracy in the section under consideration, so we take

$$p \geq 1/1000$$
$$k_1/k_2 \quad = \quad 25/50,000 \quad = \quad 1/2000$$

As $p > k_1/k_2$, this is Case 2, and the plan for minimum total cost is to do 100 per cent verification here.

Chapter 13

It is difficult to find errors in transactions processed in a service industry, perhaps even more difficult than in manufacturing. A verifier might find only half the errors made, or at best two out of three. It is obviously important to improve the system, which might be to improve legibility of figures, light, hiring, placement, training, and to provide statistical aids to supervision.

A concomitant procedure, frequently used, and mentioned in Chapter 3, is parallel computations by two people, one working from original documents, the other from copies, made before any marks are placed on the documents that would betray the results of a calculation. Punch both sets of computations into a machine, and let the machine detect differences. This is not as simple as it sounds, because the copies must be legible. It runs up costs, because of the cost of copies.

Nevertheless, parallel work and comparison by machine is in my experience the only satisfactory way to verify critical work.

Parallel computations and parallel punching will fail to detect a mistake that was made by both people, as may happen when some figure that they must work on is not clear, and misled both people into the same error. Both people should be encouraged to halt work on any figure that could possibly be misread, no matter how much time be lost to trace the figure to its source for verification. Production of an illegible figure anywhere along the line is as bad as starting off with defective material in manufacturing.

Modification of the rules for value added to substrate.* Work is done on incoming material, the substrate. The finished product will be inspected and

---

* I am indebted to my friends William J. Latzko and Jerome Greene for conversations that led to these rules.

OPTIMUM PLAN FOR INCOMING MATERIALS

will be classed as first grade or second or third grade or scrap. Let k_2 be the net average loss from downgrading the final product or for scrapping finished items. The average cost to inspect one incoming item in the substrate will be

$$k_1 + kp$$

and the average cost to downgrade an assembly will be pk_2 if we do not inspect the substrate in advance. The break-even quality is now the value of p that satisfies

(2) $$k_1 + kp = pk_2$$

With $k = k_1/q$ (Exercise 5, page 304), this gives

(3) $$k_1 + pk_1/q = pk_2$$

The left-hand side is merely k_1/q, so the equation is satisfied if

(4) $$p = k_1/k_2q$$

The rules now become

Case 1. $p < k_1/k_2q$ no inspection

Case 2. $p > k_1/k_2q$ 100 per cent inspection

where k_2 is now the average loss from downgrading or scrapping finished product that fails.

Note that the value of q will nearly always be near 1, so the rules for all-or-none are for practical purposes the same as before.

An example. This example takes the form of a memorandum that I am sending to a company at this date of writing. The memorandum follows.

As I understood it in our meeting yesterday, the coated rods, Part No. 42, are to you an important product, production at present being 20,000 per week, soon to be increased to 40,000. The size of incoming lots of unfinished rods is 2800, though the size of the lot is irrelevant.

The costs that you gave to me, supposedly fully allocated for labor, material, testing, and other burden, are as follows:

$$k_1 = 7¢ \qquad k_2 = 1500¢$$

The average fraction defective, according to your figures, is about 1 per cent. Your break-even point is accordingly

(5) $$p = k_1/k_2 q = 7/1500 \times .99 = .00471$$

or just below 1/200.

I show here the table that I put on the blackboard yesterday. It is obvious that for minimum total cost you ought to carry out 100 per cent inspection of the incoming rods. You are in Case 2.

Costs under the two possible procedures

Costs are in cents per piece

$$k_1 = 7¢, \qquad k_2 = 1500¢, \qquad p = .01$$

Inspection of incoming rods	Total cost per item
None	pk_2 = .01 x 1500¢ = 15¢
100%	k_1/q = 7.07¢

If your incoming quality p were (e.g.) 1/300 or 1/500 on the average, you should do no incoming inspection at all, but rely on inspection at the point where your final product undergoes test.

You raised the question about need for keeping track of the incoming quality. Certainly you must do this. For this purpose, I recommend that you plot a p-chart for all types of defects combined, and one also for the predominant type of defect. You could plot a point for each lot, or possibly, later

OPTIMUM PLAN FOR INCOMING MATERIALS

on, a point every day. As I understood you, your vendor wishes to study with you your methods and your results of inspection. Copies of your p-charts on a current basis, possibly monthly, would be helpful to him. Why are you not receiving charts from him?

D. MULTIPLE PARTS

<u>Probability of defective assembly in the case of multiple parts.</u> There is usually more than one critical part in an assembly. The foregoing paragraphs apply to any one part. It is easy to extend the results to two or more parts. Suppose that there are two critical parts. Let p_1 and p_2 be the respective proportions defective of the two parts. Either part, if defective, will produce a defective assembly. Then, if we put incoming parts into the production line without inspection, the probability that an assembly will be defective is

$$(6) \qquad \text{Pr (def)} \; = \; 1 - \text{Pr (not def)} \; = \; 1 - (1 - p_1)(1 - p_2)$$
$$= \; 1 - \left[1 - p_1 - p_2 + p_1 p_2 \right]$$
$$= \; p_1 + p_2 - p_1 p_2$$

If p_1 and p_2 are both small (and we can tolerate nothing else), this probability will be very near to $p_1 + p_2$. For example, if $p_1 = p_2 = 1/20$, the above equation would say that the probability that an assembly would be defective is $1/20 + 1/20 - 1/20^2 = 1/10 - 1/400$. Clearly, we may neglect, in most practice, the cross-product $p_1 p_2$.

We could go on to three parts and perceive that the probability that an assembly will be defective is approximately $p_1 + p_2 + p_3$. It is easy to extend this calculation to any number of parts.

The probability of failure thus increases as the number of parts increases. A radio may have 300 parts, though the number will depend on how you count them.

An automobile may have 3000 parts, again depending on how you count them. Is the radio in the automobile 1 part or 300? Is a fuel pump 1 part or 7? However you count parts, the number of parts can be enormous in one assembly.

Another problem arises--k_2 (the cost to correct a faulty assembly) increases as the number of parts increases. When an assembly fails, which part is at fault? It is all too easy to make a wrong diagnosis. Moreover, two parts may both be faulty.

The more complicated products become, the more reliable components must be if costs are to be held down. Poor work affects expenses all along the line--in scrappage, repairs, larger inventories to provide a cushion against defective parts, higher warranty costs, and eventually lost reputation and sales.*

Tests of complex apparatus may require time and careful planning, as the various components in the apparatus may require different stresses and different times for failure.**

The problems are not simple. A company may purchase many types of supplies and have many types of problems with them. One problem that appears frequently is where quality and uniformity of some incoming material is vital to the purchaser. Wide swings in quality are a constant problem to him. His purchases, however, may be a by-product of the supplier, and less than one per cent of his business, and he offers little concern and little hope for anything better. If the supplier were to install appropriate equipment for refinement, it might be in running order within a year or two, but the purchaser may by that time find another source of supply. You can hardly expect the supplier to go to this expense and risk.

A possible recommendation is to treat such material like iron ore or other raw materials that come in, variable and impure. Install your own refinery for the material, or send it out for refinement. This plan has turned out, in actual instances, to be a good solution.

---

* Jeremy Main, "The battle for quality begins," <u>Fortune</u>, 29 December 1980: pp. 28-33.

** J. D. Esary and A. W. Marshall, "Families of components and systems," being a chapter in the book RELIABILITY AND BIOMETRY, edited by Frank Proschan and R. J. Serfling (Society for Industrial and Applied Mathematics, Philadelphia, 1974).

OPTIMUM PLAN FOR INCOMING MATERIALS

Multiple exposure to the same defect has the same effect as
multiple parts. A simple example was pointed out to me by Dr. Myron
Tribus of MIT. Suppose that small motors (in the vacuum cleaner,
blender, household space heater) now fail in the hands of a customer
only 1/10th as often as they did 15 years ago. The fact is, however,
that a household may now have, on the average, 10 times as many motors
as it had 15 years ago. Today's household will thus see as many
failures of motors as it had before. Other examples come to mind.

The design of a ceiling light fixture calls for three bulbs of
some specified candle power. A bulb might have an average life of
three months under usage of the household, but with three bulbs in the
fixture, the master of the household has to keep a stepladder handy,
as he will now need it, on the average, once a month.

Take spot welding of seams in the trunk of an automobile. Anyone
that has ever tried to spot weld would agree that one fault in 2000 is
marvelous performance. Automatic machinery does not much better. Yet
such splendid performance leads to expensive testing and rework of
trunks in the factory.

Thus, suppose that there are 70 seams in the trunk of your automobile, and that the welder, whether by hand or by machine, makes one
fault in 2100. Then the chance that a trunk will be found leaky on
test will be 70/2100 = 1/30. In other words, about 3 per cent of the
trunks would leak and require rework. (Fortunately, very few of these
leaks get out of the factory.)

To reduce the frequency of leaks to one per cent per trunk, performance of welding would need improvement to roughly one fault in
7000 welds.

Conclusion: defective material and workmanship not permissible anywhere on
the line. The foregoing theory teaches us how important it is not to tolerate
defective material at any stage of production. The product of one operation is
incoming material for the next one. A defective, once produced, stays until and
unless it is discovered on a later test, to be corrected and replaced at what is
usually great cost.

The costs k_1 and k_2 in the foregoing theory are not the only costs to
consider. Defects beget defects. A production worker suffers a powerful
demoralizing effect to receive a partially finished item or assembly that is
already defective. How can she put forth her best efforts when no matter how
carefully she works, the item will still be defective? If no one cares, why

should she? In contrast, when defects are rare or nonexistent or well explained, she understands that the management is accepting their proper responsibility, and she feels an obligation to put forth her best efforts: they are now effective.

Unfortunately, defects are sometimes created along the line, as by faulty installation of a perfectly good part, criss-crossing a pair of wires, or by handling-damage --i.e., damage suffered by finished or partly finished product as it moves from one location to another. Handling-damage may arise from carelessness or from sheer ignorance. It also happens in packing and shipping, as everyone knows. Simon Collier, when he was with the Johns-Manville Company, showed moving pictures of damage that men do by inadvertent acts, as by bumping a load of finished shingles on a forklift into a steel pillar, ruining the work that men had put forth on the damaged shingles; or by tossing into the gypsum instead of into the waste-barrel the string that had closed the sack. No one had explained to the men how much damage these little acts create. I saw a girl handle a hard disc with forceps, as carefully as a nurse handles surgical instruments in the operating-room, then ruin the disc by putting her thumb on it. Had anyone explained to her that she could so easily spoil the work of all the effort put in on that disc up to that point? I saw a black streak on a white shoe, otherwise perfect, ready to go into the box. Somebody's carelessness caused expensive rework or scrap.

None of these unfortunate incidents makes sense; none should be tolerated, but one must allow for the fact that, in spite of care, defects may appear almost spontaneously along the line.

> We pause to remark that all the excuses for the production of defects along the line, of the kind mentioned above, are faults of the system. The management should eliminate the possibility of faulty installation of a part, such as the possibility to criss-cross wires.

OPTIMUM PLAN FOR INCOMING MATERIALS

A man is not trained on a job until he understands what not to do and why, as well as what to do. Again, how many employees know the cost of introducing a defect along the line, and how easy it is to avoid it?

There will nevertheless be accidents, in spite of care.

Exception. The theory in this chapter does not apply to mixtures that are for practical purposes homogeneous. An example could be a tank car of methanol after agitation with an air hose. A ladle of methanol drawn from almost anywhere in the tank will be closely the same as a ladle of methanol drawn from any other part of the tank. In practice, however, chemical companies draw off ladles of methanol from several levels. A more familiar example might be a jigger of gin or whiskey. We accept the fact that it matters little whether we draw off a jigger from the top of the bottle or from the middle or from the bottom.

A heat from a blast furnace gives problems and is another example that the theory of this chapter does not apply to. The contents of the heat are not homogeneous, but we have to take what we get from a sample. Some companies pour a small sample along with every casting. These samples, if analyzed, would provide data for a run chart that would show variation of quality from the first casting to the last one, and provide clues to improvement.

E. DISPOSAL OF STANDARD ACCEPTANCE PLANS

Standard sampling plans. Inspection of incoming materials is an economic problem, and should be so treated. None of the standard acceptance plans, so popular in courses and in textbooks, minimizes the total cost, the aim of this chapter. Put another way, they minimize the wrong cost.

The theory behind the Dodge-Romig tables is to minimize the cost of inspection, to achieve the level of quality prescribed. It is difficult to understand what the aim of Military Standard 105 D is, except to hit the vendor in the pocketbook if his quality takes a bad turn.*

A company that purchases items on an AOQL of 3 per cent is making it known to the vendor that the purchaser is in the market for 97 good items and 3 bad ones out of 100. The vendor will be pleased to meet these requirements.

One manufacturer told me recently, for example, that he aims to send out to his customers not more than 3 per cent defective items. Some customers will get far more than their share of defective items, while others will get good ones.

Unfortunately, standard acceptance plans occupy a prominent place in text-books on statistical methods of quality control, my own books on sampling being no exception. It is time, as Anscombe says, that "we realize what the problem really is, and solve that problem as well as we can instead of inventing a substitute problem that can be solved exactly but is irrelevant."**

It is time to throw out such plans, and the teaching thereof, and to talk about total cost. Case 1 and Case 2--so simple to apply--cover most of the problems of inspection of incoming materials and assemblies met in practice. Why continue to use plans that solve another problem?

Pro forma application of standard plans. Most applications of the Dodge-Romig plans of acceptance and of Military Standard 105 D are, I fear, pro forma, merely conforming to the requirements of a contract, drawn up by people without

_____

* For a discussion of the economic incentive in sampling plans and its relationship to Military Standard Tables, see I. D. Hill, "The economic incentive provided by sampling inspection," Applied Statistics, vol. 9, 1960: pp. 69-81.

** Francis J. Anscombe, "Rectifying inspection of a continuous output," Journal of the American Statistical Association, vol. 53, 1958: pp. 702-719.

qualifications for drawing up a plan, and carried out by another group of people equally qualified. Everybody does it, so we do too. As Feigenbaum says:*

A major problem...is unwise use of these (acceptance) plans in situations for which they have no application.

The theory displayed in Exercise 1 at the end of the chapter is frightening. We shall see there that it is all too easy to prescribe an acceptance plan that accomplishes little or nothing. In fact, it is easy in many circumstances to prescribe an acceptance plan that will cost considerably more in total than 100 per cent inspection (see Exercise 7 at the end of this chapter).

Example: how to increase costs with Military Standard 105 D.** A subassembly comes from a manufacturer in lots of 1500 assemblies. It takes approximately two hours to test the assembly at an average cost (including burden) of $24 per assembly. The process average of the manufacturer is 2 per cent, and recent quality information confirmed this experience with lots received. The cost to replace defective parts in final inspection is $780, fully distributed. What sampling plan should be used? Here,

$$p = .02 < k_1/k_2 = 24/780 = .031$$

This is clearly Case 1. Hence, for minimum total cost, no inspection. Use of Military Standard 105 D as recommended would run up the total cost to double the cost of 100 per cent inspection.

What could be even worse is that if the process were in good statistical control, tests of samples would provide no more information about lots than tossing coins (Exercise 1, page 298).

---

* A. V. Feigenbaum, QUALITY CONTROL PRINCIPLES, PRACTICE, AND ADMINISTRATION (McGraw-Hill, 1951).

** William J. Latzko, "Minimizing the cost of inspection," Transactions of the American Society for Quality Control, Detroit, May 1982: pp. 485-490.

F. ADDITIONAL PROBLEMS WITH MEASUREMENT AND WITH MATERIALS

Possible economy in intermediate construction of subassemblies. The cost k_2 in the preceding theory usually increases rapidly (perhaps ten-fold) with each stage of work along the production line, and may reach a very high number at the final assembly. It is sometimes possible to avoid extreme cost through construction of subassemblies that flow together to form the final assembly. The several subassemblies, once they pass through inspection and receive attention with whatever replacements and adjustments are found necessary, form a new starting point. The cost k_2 in the foregoing theory will then be the cost to inspect and adjust a subassembly. The theory, along with meaningful records of experience, may show that some subassemblies need not be inspected at all, while others should be subjected to rugged 100 per cent inspection to avoid higher costs further along the line. The theory of this chapter provides the answer.

Our aim in the foregoing paragraphs is merely to show that there are ways to come close to minimum costs and maximum profit if one uses the right theory as a guide.

Meanwhile, we make every effort to eliminate defective items entirely. This we do on a systematic basis, comparing our tests with the vendor's, and by use of appropriate statistical methods, such as $\bar{x}$- and R-charts.

Successful cooperation with suppliers of parts, especially of critical parts, and success in tests and adjustments of subassemblies, reduce to a rarity any major trouble in tests of the final assembly.

Difficulties of finding extremely rare defects. Rare defects are difficult to find. As the fraction defective decreases, there is ever-increasing difficulty to find out just how small it is. Inspection simply does not find all the defectives, especially when they are rare, and this is so whether the inspection be visual or by machine. There would be little reason to put more faith in one manufacturer for his claim that only 1 piece in 10,000 is defective, against another one that claims that only 1 piece in 5000 is defective. The proportion in either circumstance is difficult to estimate.

Thus, if p were 1/5000, one would have to inspect 80,000 parts to find 16 defectives. This number would provide the estimate $\hat{p}$ = 1/5000 for the production process, with standard error $\sqrt{16}$ = 4 or 25 per cent. The estimate of the fraction defective is thus not highly precise, in spite of the load of inspection of 80,000 parts. And one may ask whether the production process stayed stable during the production of the 80,000 parts. Was it the same process at the end of the 80,000 as it was at the beginning? If not, what would be the meaning of 16 defectives? A difficult question.

There are instances of no failure in millions of parts--even of few failures or none in 10^9. No amount of inspection of finished product can provide the required information when the fraction defective is so low. The only possible way to know what is happening under extreme requirements is by use of control charts with actual measurements on the parts in process. One hundred observations, such as on 4 consecutive items 25 times per day, would provide 25 points of samples of 4 for $\bar{x}$- and R-charts. The charts would show that the process is continuing unchanged, or that something had gone wrong, and that a run of product must be held up until the cause of trouble is found. Once the cause of trouble is found, a rational decision can be made on whether to condemn the whole run, or to release some of it. The multiplying power of $\bar{x}$- and R-charts may be seen at once.

Use of redundancy. It may be possible and wise in the design of complex apparatus to put two or more parts in parallel, so that if one fails, another one will jump in automatically to take its place. Two parts in parallel, each with average fraction p_i, are equivalent to one part of average fraction defective equal to p_i^2. If, for example, p_i were 1/1000, p_i^2 would be 1/1,000,000. Restrictions on weight and size may of course not permit redundancy. There are other problems: will the redundant part step in when needed? The best solution may be high reliability of a single part.

The mathematical theory of failure and the theory of redundancy are extremely interesting and are important statistical techniques, but we must drop the subject here with only this glimpse into its importance.

Considerations of cost in use of cheap method of inspection. There will often be an ideal method of inspection of incoming materials, which we may speak of here as the master method, too expensive or too time-consuming to use on a regular basis. In practice we use what we speak of here as the regular method, cheaper and quicker to apply than the master method.*

The regular inspection exhibits two kinds of failure. (1) It allows some parts to slip through and give trouble in the assembly that would be caught and classed as defective by the master method. This failure increases costs. (2) On the other hand, the regular inspection causes another loss by classifying some parts as defective that the master method would class as good.

It is a fairly simple matter to make rough computations of the loss from use of the regular (cheap) method. If the loss would just about cover the extra cost of the master method, it would be wise to adopt it and not take a chance on the cheap method.

---

* W. Edwards Deming, SAMPLE DESIGN IN BUSINESS RESEARCH (Wiley, 1960), Chapters 4 and 5.

OPTIMUM PLAN FOR INCOMING MATERIALS

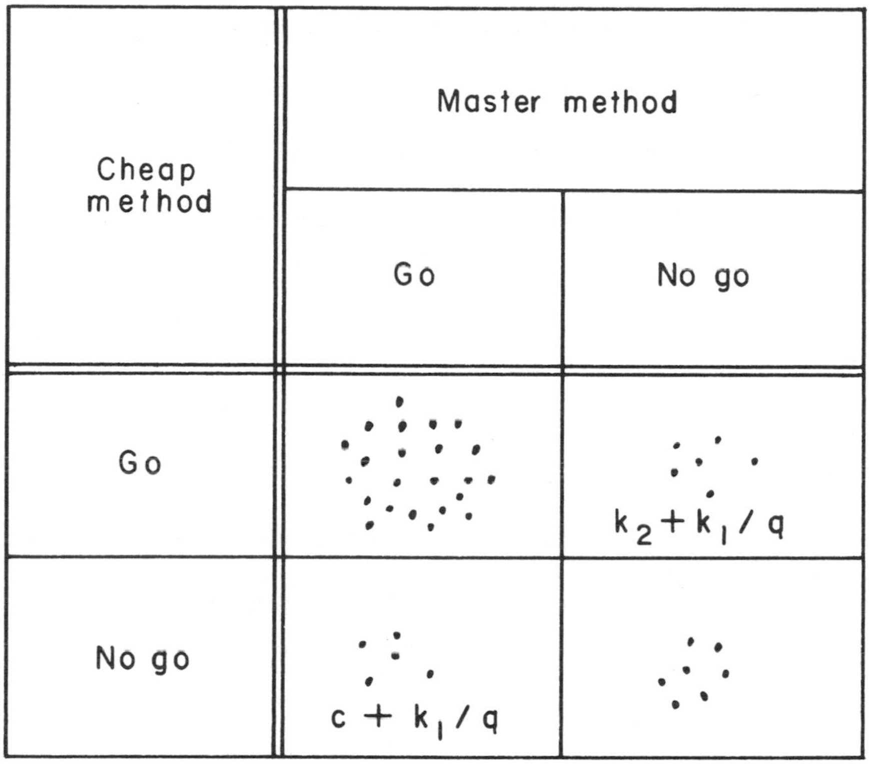

Fig. 46. A 2 x 2 table for tests of a number of pieces by the two methods of test. The two tests produce a point in one of the four cells.

We can spell out in more detail the losses and gains from use of a cheap method of inspection. What one can do on a non-destructive test is to subject 200 items to the two test-methods, and make a 2 x 2 table with the results, illustrated in Fig. 46. Each point is the result of the two tests on one part. A point on the diagonal represents agreement of the two tests. A point off the diagonal represents disagreement. The costs of the two kinds of disagreement may differ greatly. A part that would be rejected by the master method of test, but passed by the cheap method, would cause failure of the assembly at cost $k_2 + k_1/q$. This disagreement could be costly. On the other hand, a part that would be passed by the master method and rejected by the cheap method would incur the cost $c + k_1/q$, where c is the cost of the part.

It would be easy to insert approximate dollar values in the two corners off the diagonal and to calculate the cost of disagreements, then take a hard look at the cheap method: is it really cheap? Is it a wise choice? Tests and figures will provide the answer.

The numbers off the diagonal will usually be small and hence subject to wide statistical fluctuation. The standard error of a number in a cell off the diagonal would with good approximation be the square root of the number itself. Thus, if a number were 16, this figure would be subject to a standard error of 4. If the number were 9, the standard error would be 3.

If it appears to be doubtful that the cheap method is really cheaper than the master method, one could test another 200 parts for more precision, or even another 400. If there still be doubt, my advice would be to adopt the master method of test.

A more efficient method of comparison should be used if the measurements are in units of some sort, such as centimeters, grams, seconds, amperes, psi, or other measure. One may then plot the results of the n measurements on the x, y plane (Fig. 47). A much smaller value of n will suffice than for the 2 x 2 table in Fig. 46. Points on the 45° diagonal line indicate agreement between the two methods. Points off this line indicate disagreement. Study of the chart will quickly indicate where the two methods differ, and how much. Adjustment of the cheap method to bring it into better line with the master

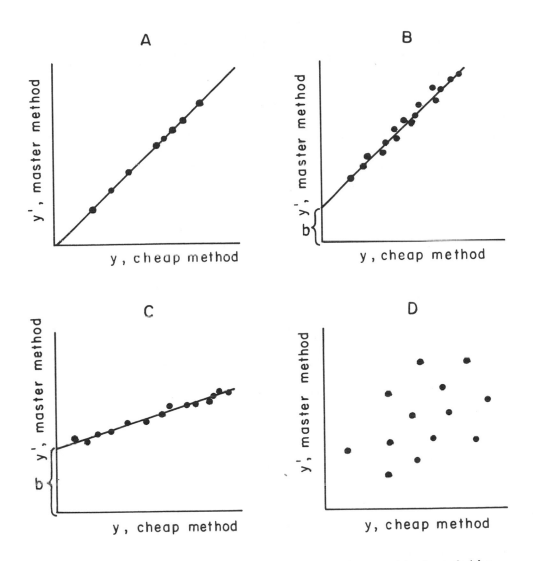

Fig. 47. Comparisons between the master method and the cheap method. Measurement of an item by both methods yields a point on a chart. A point on the 45° line indicates perfect agreement.

A. The points lie on or close to a 45° line. Here the two methods agree well.
B. The slope of the line is close to 45°, but there is an intercept. Some simple adjustment will usually bring the two methods into good agreement.
C. The slope of the line departs far from 45°, and has an intercept. Some simple adjustment might bring the two methods into good agreement. Or, one could use a simple formula for correction of the cheap method.
D. The points are scattered over the chart, indicating serious problems.

method might be obvious to someone with knowledge and skill in use of the two methods.*

Another possibility under the simplicity of Sections B and C of Fig. 47 is to leave the cheap method unadjusted and to convert its readings to the master method. Thus, let

y' be a measurement produced by the master method

y be a measurement produced by the cheap method on the same item

m the slope of the line of best fit in the relationship (assumed to be linear) between the two methods

b the intercept on the y' axis

Then a convenient conversion would be $y' = b + my$ in Section C of Fig. 47, and $y' = y + b$ in Section B. m would be 1 in Section B.

Incidentally, agreement between the two methods does not mean that they are both correct. Agreement merely means that a system of measurement exists.

An excellent treatment of the precision of instruments and errors of measurement is Section B-3 of STATISTICAL QUALITY CONTROL HANDBOOK, produced and printed by the Western Electric Company, 1956.

<u>Hazards of consensus</u>. Consensus that comes forth after everyone has had a chance to present his views and to ask questions, all without fear, secure (page 38), reaps the benefit of the entire team, plus the benefit of interaction from learning from one another.

_____

* John Mandel and T. W. Lashof, "The interlaboratory evaluation of testing methods," a chapter in the book, PRECISION MEASUREMENT AND CALIBRATION, edited by Harry H. Ku, National Bureau of Standards, Special Publication 300 (Washington, Government Printing Office, 1969): pp. 170-178. See also in the same book P. E. Pontius and Joseph M. Cameron, "Realistic uncertainties and the mass measurement process," pp. 1-20, and Churchill Eisenhart, "Realistic evaluation of the precision and accuracy of instrument calibration systems," pp. 21-47.

OPTIMUM PLAN FOR INCOMING MATERIALS

Unfortunately, consensus in inspection or anywhere else may only mean that one head overpowered the other, and the consensus is only one man's opinion.

For example, two physicians may record a consensus in respect to a patient-- improved, unimproved, or worse. This report may only be the older physician's opinion, the younger one glad for the privilege to accompany the older man and to listen to whatever words of wisdom came forth. The cordial relationship between the two men might come to an end if the younger one has too many ideas. Perhaps the younger one is an intern. He dare not run the risk of losing out on reappointment next year, so he agrees to anything, and is careful about questions.

A better plan is for each man to record his judgment on a form, and to keep the form in his pocket till they have made their rounds. Then compare notes, but do not change the record. A simple chart like Fig. 48 will then display agreements and disagreements, which the men can study to advantage. If they disagree wildly, one should enquire whether either man has a useful system.

Notations on the chart could show what kind of patients lead to disagreement, and which to good agreement. Such a chart helps the men to learn from each other.

Incidentally, agreement between independent results of two men would only mean that they have a system. It would not mean that they are both right. There is no right answer. There could be, however, a master standard, the opinion of a third physician, whose judgment is unquestioned, and the judgments of the two men could be calibrated against the master.

Comparison of two inspectors. Two inspectors of leather had for years recorded the consensus of the two on each bundle of leather drawn as a sample for inspection. They readily understood, when we talked it over, the hazards

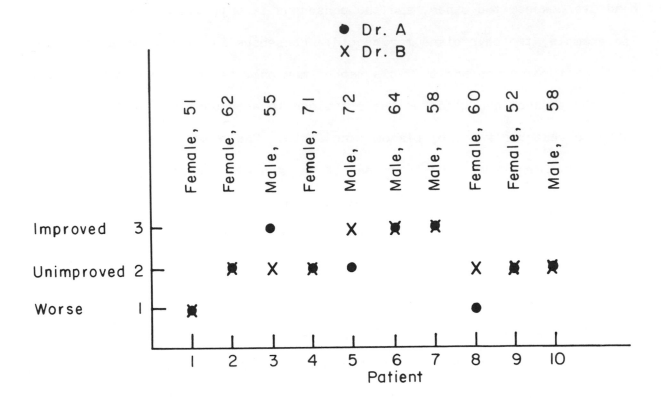

Fig. 48. Record of judgments of two physicians, patient by patient. Study of agreements and of disagreements, by type of patient, may assist both men to understand better what they are doing, and to bring them nearly into full and dependable agreement.

of consensus and the need to have individual data so that they could compare results and learn from each other if their results diverged.

A bundle of leather is graded 1, 2, 3, 4, or 5; No. 1 being the best grade. The plan arrived at is this.

1. Each inspector select from each shipment one bundle of items. Take a bundle from the top, middle, bottom, scattering the selections. (This would be what we have already called mechanical sampling, not use of random numbers.)

2. Examine independently the bundle that you selected, and record the
result.

3. Both men will examine independently every 20th bundle and record their
results. Take turns on the selection.

4. Plot the results on a chart, a simplified section of which is shown in
Fig. 49.

Differences between the two sets of results could arise from two sources:
(a) differences between the two men; (b) differences between the samples. The
results have shown so far (nearly a year) no appreciable difference. One
inspector is not running away from the other one. Disagreement is rare on the
20th bundle that they both inspect. Other applications have showed need of
better definitions.

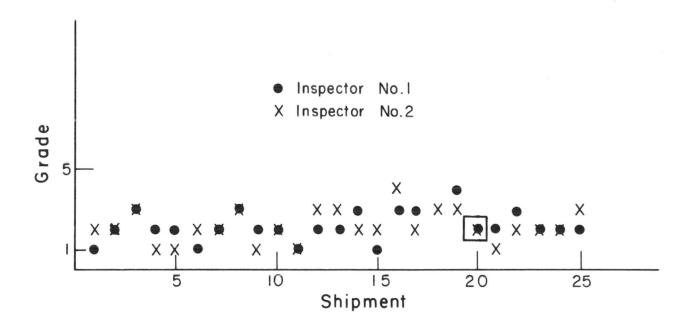

Fig. 49. Scheme for display of the results of two
inspectors working independently. The chart shows no indication of divergence. The box around the 20th point signifies
that, by design, both inspectors examined the same bundle of
hides.

Chapter 13

Again, as has been emphasized elsewhere, their agreement does not mean that they are recording correct values but merely that their sampling and inspection constitute a system of grading.

G. EXERCISES

Exercise 1. Given a bowl of red and white beads, p the proportion red, q the proportion white.

Step 1. Draw from the bowl by random numbers with replacement a lot of size N. Result:

$$
\begin{array}{ll}
N & \text{total} \\
X & \text{red} \\
N-X & \text{white}
\end{array}
$$

Step 2. Draw from the lot by random numbers without replacement a sample of size n. Result:

In the sample	In the remainder
n total	N-n total
s red	r = X-s red
n-s white	N-n-r white

Step 3. Restore to the lot the beads in the sample.

Step 4. Repeat many times Steps 1, 2, 3, holding constant the size of the lot and the size of the sample drawn therefrom. Record the results for r and s.

Show that the theoretical distribution of r and s will be

$$
(7) \qquad P(r,s) = \left[\binom{N-n}{r} q^{(N-n)-r} p^r \right] \left[\binom{n}{s} q^{n-s} p^s \right]
$$

OPTIMUM PLAN FOR INCOMING MATERIALS

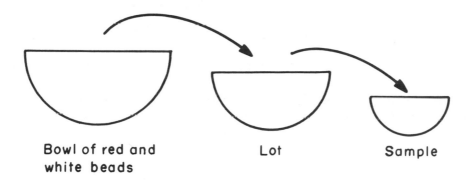

Fig. 50. Lots are drawn from a bowl of red and white beads. A sample is then drawn from the lot. Replacement of each bead drawn into the lot ensures constancy of the proportion p in the lot at every draw.

Conclusions: (a) the number of red beads in the samples of size n, and the number of red beads in the remainders, are both binomially distributed about the same proportion p, and (b) they are independent. That is, the number r of red beads in the remainders that correspond to samples with s = 17 defective items will be distributed exactly the same as in the red beads in the remainders that correspond to samples with s = 0 defective items.

This theorem is frightening. It shows that if the number of defective items in lots is binomially distributed, as will be nearly the case when the process is in fairly good statistical control, any attempt to construct an acceptance plan would accomplish no more than tossing coins for selection of remainders to screen.* (Tossing coins is a lot cheaper than testing samples of items.)

Instead of drawing a sample from a lot, one could merely separate the lot by random numbers into two parts, sample and remainder.

Exercise 2. If the distribution of defectives in lots be tighter than binomial, and if the rule for acceptance of the remainder is based on test of a sample, then the rule should be to accept the remainder as it is when the sample shows many defective parts, and to reject and screen the remainder when the sample shows few defectives, or none, than the reverse.**

An easy way to understand the above results is to consider the circumstance wherein all lots come in with exactly the same number of defective items. Defectives not in the remainder will be in the sample, and the converse. Hence, a large number of defective items in the sample will indicate a small number in the remainder.

I. D. Hill (1960) pointed out a simple way to produce lots of uniform quality. Let there be 20 machines producing the same item, 19 producing no defective items, one of them producing nothing but defective items. Take one item from each of the 20 machines. Then any lot formed as a multiple of 20 items will contain 5 per cent defective items.

Mr. Hill's conjecture on how to form such lots could be more truth than fancy.

----

* Alexander M. Mood, "On the dependence of sampling inspection plans under population distributions," Annals of Mathematical Statistics, vol. 14, 1943, pp. 415-425. The proof of Eq. 7 is also in W. Edwards Deming, SOME THEORY OF SAMPLING, 1950, p. 258.

** I. D. Hill, "The economic incentive provided by sampling inspection," Applied Statistics, vol. 9, 1960: pp. 69-81.

OPTIMUM PLAN FOR INCOMING MATERIALS

Exercise 3. The cost of two plans d_1 and d_2 depend on the incoming fraction defective. Suppose that this relation is given in Fig. 51. The minimax cost plan is the plan whose maximum cost is minimum. Which of the two plans is minimax? (Answer: d_2.)

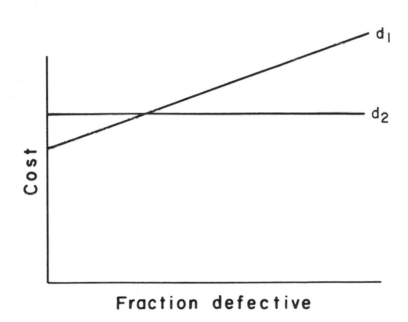

Fig. 51.

Exercise 4. Proof for Case 1 and Case 2. Draw at random (by random numbers) a part from the lot. Call it Part i. It will be defective, or not defective. Should we inspect it, or put it straight into the production line without inspection, defective or not?

Let k be the cost to test a part drawn from the supply S, and to test as many parts as necessary to find a good one for replacement of a defective.

Let

(8) $\qquad x_i = 1 \qquad$ if defective

$\qquad\qquad\qquad\quad = 0 \qquad$ if not defective

(9) $\qquad$ Average $x_i = p \qquad$ the fraction defective in all the lots

Then if the cost of one test be k_1, the cost to inspect Part i will be

(10) $\qquad C_1 = k_1 + kx_i \qquad$ (x_i being 1 if defective, 0 if not)

if we test it, and zero if we do not. The cost to repair the assembly will be

(11) $\qquad C_2 = x_i (k_2 + k)$

if we do not test Part i, and zero if we do. C_1 and C_2 can not co-exist.
If one is not zero, the other is zero. The total cost will be

(12) $\qquad C = C_1 + C_2$

We may now construct the accompanying table of costs.

Costs

Inspect the part?	C_1	C_2	Total cost $C = C_1 + C_2$
For Part i			
Yes	$k_1 + k\,x_i$	0	$k_1 + k\,x_i$
No	0	$x_i (k_2 + k)$	$x_i (k_2 + k)$
Average per part over the lot			
Yes	$k_1 + kp$	0	$k_1 + kp$
No	0	$pk_2 + kp$	$pk_2 + kp$

OPTIMUM PLAN FOR INCOMING MATERIALS

3

03.

We observe that, at the break-even point, where $p = k_1/k_2$, the total cost C is the same for NO as it is for YES. We observe further that if $p < k_1/k_2$, NO will give the lesser total cost, and if $p > k_1/k_2$, YES will give the lesser total cost.

What is more, if the process is in control, Part i is defective or not defective independently of any other part. Thus, regardless of what we know about other parts, we should inspect or not inspect Part i according to whether p is more or less than k_1/k_2. Now, as Part i is any part, the conclusion is the same for all parts. Thus, we inspect every part or none, according to whether p for the lot is more or less than k_1/k_2.

Now, suppose that the observed process is a mixture of processes, each in control and each with its own average fraction defective p. Also, suppose that all these fractions lie to one side of k_1/k_2. Then, each piece comes from one of these processes. Suppose that the current lot comes from a process that is in control at level p'. Then we should accept or reject a random part from this lot according to whether p' is less or greater than k_1/k_2. However, as by supposition all the fractions defective lie to one side of k_1/k_2, regardless of the actual value of p', we should make the same decision for all lots. Thus, we have arrived at the rules for Case 1 and Case 2 for a mixture of processes, every one in control with an average fraction defective to the same side of k_1/k_2.

Exercise 5. Evaluation of k. We make the supposition that the cost to inspect a part drawn from the supply S is the same as the regular cost to inspect a part drawn from the lot of size N. Let $x_i = 1$ if the part is defective; 0 if not. Suppose that $x_i = 1$, Part i turns out to be defective. We must then draw one from the supply S and inspect it, cost k_1. This one may also be defective, in which case we draw and inspect another, and so on until we come to

Chapter 13

a good one. We may show these possibilities in the probability tree of Fig. 52.
The total average cost k will obviously be*

$$(13) \qquad k = k_1 (q + 2pq + 3p^2q + \ldots) = \frac{k_1 q}{(1-p)^2} = \frac{k_1}{q}$$

where

$$(14) \qquad q = 1 - p$$

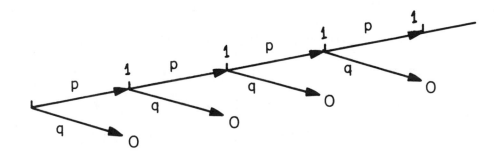

Fig. 52. Inspection of a part leads with probability
p to $x_i = 1$, defective, and with probability q to $x_i = 0$,
not defective.

---

* I am indebted to Joyce Orsini for Eq. 13 and for much other technical
help on this chapter and other parts of the book.

Exercise 6. Lots of constant size N come in with defectives binomially distributed about the mean p. Draw without replacement from each lot a sample of constant size n. Count the defectives in each sample and in each remainder. Let s be the number of defectives in a sample, and r the number in the remainder (as above). Then s and r will be random variables, with the joint distribution shown in Eq. 7. Let

$$\hat{p} = s/n \text{ for a sample}$$

$$\hat{p}' = r/(N-n) \text{ for the remainder}$$

$$E\hat{p} = p$$

$$\text{Var } \hat{p} = pq/n$$

$$E\,\hat{p}' = p$$

$$\text{Var } \hat{p}' = pq/(N-n)$$

$$\text{Cov }(\hat{p}, \hat{p}') = 0$$

Var $\hat{p}$ and Var $\hat{p}'$ decrease as N and n increase. Hence a large sample from a large lot provides information about the number of defectives in the population of remainders; hence also about defectives in lots. This is so, even if the lots be binomially distributed. Thus, it is possible to calculate from a sample that is large enough useful estimates of characteristics of the lot, even if each characteristic of the lots be distributed binomially. Moreover, even for small samples, we may in an enumerative problem (wherein the aim is to learn from a sample characteristics of the lot) disregard the origin of the lot, and apply the theory of sampling for estimates of characteristics of the lot, and for the standard errors of these estimates.*

----

* I am indebted to my friend Dr. Morris H. Hansen for pointing out this feature of samples drawn from large lots for enumerative purposes. See W. Edwards Deming, "On probability as a basis for action," _American Statistician_, vol. 29, No. 4, 1975: pp. 146-152.

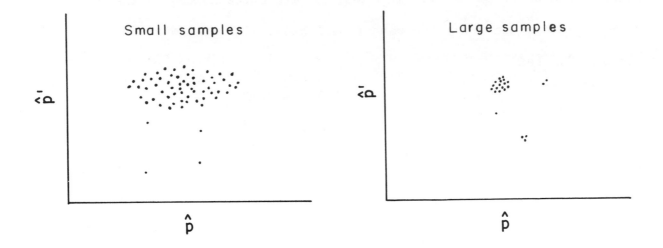

Fig. 53. Schematic plot to show that a sample, if big
enough, provides information with small margin of uncertainty
about all the samples and about all the remainders that would
be drawn in a long series of production of lots. Each point
represents a sample. The symbol $\hat{p}$ = s/n on the horizontal
denotes the proportion of defective items in the sample. The
symbol $\hat{p}'$ = r/(N-n) on the vertical denotes the proportion
of defective items in the remainder. There is no correlation
between the number of defectives in sample and remainder,
whether the samples be large or small, but the results for
large samples converge statistically to a point as the size
of sample increases.

Exercise 7.

Notation

N   the number of pieces in the lot.

n   the number of pieces in the sample (supposedly selected by
       use of random numbers from the lot).

p   the average incoming fraction of pieces. This value of p is
       a rough prediction of an average value over the next few
       weeks.

q = 1 - p

p'   the average fraction defective in lots that are rejected and
       to be screened.

p"   the average fraction defective in lots that are accepted and
       put straight into the production line.

k_1 as before

k_2 as before

P   the average proportion of lots set off for screening at
       initial inspection (rejected).

Q = 1 - P   the proportion of lots accepted at initial inspection.

Whatever be the plan of acceptance, we can be sure that:

P = 0 and Q = 1 if n = 0

P = 1 and Q = 0 if n = N

Now let us see what will happen for the average lot, when we put the plan
into action.

      n   parts will go into the production line with no defectives.

(N - n) Q   parts will go straight into the production line with no testing,
       average quality p.

(N - n) P   parts will be rejected and screened. They then all go into the
       production line with no defectives.

a. Show that the total cost per part will be

(15) $$C = k_1 \left\{ \frac{1}{q} + Q\,(k_2/k_1)\,(p'' - k_1/k_2)\,(1 - n/N) \right\}$$

b. If $p < k_1/k_2$, then $p'' - k_1/k_2$ will be negative, and we shall achieve minimum total cost by setting $n = 0$ (Case 1).

c. If $p > k_1/k_2$, and if we are successful in finding a plan that will render $p'' - k_1/k_2$ negative, then the total cost will be less than the cost of 100 per cent inspection.

d. But if in spite of our best efforts, our plan leaves us with $p'' - k_1/k_2$ positive, then the total cost will be greater than it would have been with 100 per cent inspection of all incoming parts. This would be unfortunate, but it is a trap that is easy to fall into.

OPTIMUM PLAN FOR INCOMING MATERIALS

H. BIBLIOGRAPHY FOR ADVANCED STUDY OF THIS CHAPTER

(Supplied by Dr. Louis K. Kates)

Additional references are found in the books and
papers listed here, notably the book by A. Hald.

F. J. Anscombe, "Rectifying inspection of a continuous output," Journal of the
American Statistical Association, vol. 53, 1958: pp. 702-719.

F. J. Anscombe, "Rectifying inspection of lots," Journal of the American Statistical Association, vol. 56, 1961: pp. 807-823.

G. A. Barnard, "Sampling inspection and statistical decisions," Journal of the
Royal Statistical Society, Series B, vol. 16, 1954: pp. 151-171.
(Discussion of Mood's theorem.)

J. R. Blum and Joan Rosenblatt, "On partial a priori information in statistical
inference," Annals of Mathematical Statistics, vol. 38, 1967,
pp. 1671-1678. (Minimax under partial information.)

Wm. J. Carroll, "Application of an inspection scheme for attributes," Doctoral
Thesis, Graduate School of Business Administration, New York University,
1963.

H. Chernoff and L. E. Moses, ELEMENTARY DECISION THEORY (Wiley, 1959).
(Elementary book on decision theory.)

D. R. Cox and D. V. Hinckley, THEORETICAL STATISTICS (Chapman and Hall, 1974).
(Chapter 11 discusses decision theory.)

J. J. Dahlgaard, Chapter IV in the book KVALITETSOMKOSTNINGER, Studiekredsrapport
No. 9 (Danish Society for Quality Control, 1978).

T. S. Ferguson, MATHEMATICAL STATISTICS--A DECISION THEORETIC APPROACH (Academic Press, 1967). (Decision Theory.)

A. Hald, "The compound hypergeometric distribution and a system of single sampling plans based on prior distributions and costs," Technometrics, vol. 2, 1960: pp. 275-340. (Discussion of prior distributions.)

A. Hald, STATISTICAL THEORY OF SAMPLING INSPECTION BY ATTRIBUTES (Academic Press, 1981).

H. C. Hamaker, "Some basic principles of sampling inspection by attributes," Applied Statistics, vol. 7, 1958: pp. 149-159. (Interesting discussion of various approaches.)

H. C. Hamaker, "Economic principles in industrial planning problems: a general introduction," Proceedings of the International Statistical Conference, India, 1951, vol. xxxiii: Part V, 1951: pp. 106-119.

H. James Harrington, "Quality costs, the whole and its parts," Quality, May and June, 1976.

I. D. Hill, "The economic incentive provided by sampling inspection," Applied Statistics, vol. 9, 1960: pp. 69-81.

I. D. Hill, "Sampling inspection in defense specification DEF-131," Journal of the Royal Statistical Society, Series A, vol. 125, 1962: pp. 31-87.

Alexander M. Mood, "On the dependence of sampling inspection plans upon population distributions," Annals of Mathematical Statistics, vol. 14, 1943: pp. 415-425.

Joyce Orsini, "Simple rule to reduce total cost of inspection and correction of product in state of chaos," dissertation for the doctorate, Graduate School of Business Administration, New York University, 1982.

J. Sittig, "The economic choice of sampling systems in acceptance sampling," Proceedings of the International Statistical Conferences, India, 1951, vol. xxxiii: Part V, pp. 51-84.

B. L. van der Waerden, "Sampling inspection as a minimum loss problem," <u>Annals of Mathematical Statistics</u>, vol. 31, 1960: pp. 369-384.

G. B. Wetherill, SAMPLING INSPECTION AND QUALITY CONTROL (Methuen, 1969). (Gives a concise, excellent summary.)

S. Zacks, THE THEORY OF STATISTICAL INFERENCE (Wiley, 1971). (Discusses in Section 6.7 minimax under partial information.)

Chapter 14

TWO REPORTS TO MANAGEMENT

As Goethe observed, where an idea is wanting, a word
can always be found to take its place.--Quoted from a review
by Ashley Montagu in The Sciences, September 1977, page 29.

A. RECOMMENDATIONS FOR CHANGES IN POLICY AT A FACTORY

This memorandum was written by the author and David S. Chambers
after study of the problems at a factory, owned by a large corporation. The statisticians completed this work and wrote this report in
a space of about three weeks. The management had known for years that
the factory was teetering on the brink between profit and nonprofit
and had supposed that new machinery was the only answer.

The records of the quality-audit (showing $7\frac{1}{2}$ per cent major
defects) had been generated day after day, but they had heretofore
served no purpose.

1.a. Your factory at Nightingale (name fictitious) is running along day

after day sending out items, $7\frac{1}{2}$ per cent of which on the average have one or

more major defects. There are, of course, daily variations above and below the

average. On some days, the average must run up to 11 per cent or even 12 per

cent. These figures are for major defects only: not minor defects.

b. These major defects are going out to customers.

c. This proportion is well documented by your own records that you

collect through your quality-audit.

d. This proportion of major defects in your product may well explain some

of your problems with sales and profits.

2.a. Your factory at Nightingale is a good example of an attempt to build

quality by inspection. The idea never works. The result is always poor quality

and high costs.

b.   There are cheaper ways to produce $7\frac{1}{2}$ per cent defective product, if
that were your aim.

3.   The amount of rework along the production line is stifling your
profits, and is obviously ineffective.

4.a.   The problems start this way. If an inspector at a certain point
declares a defect to be minor, she repairs it herself--i.e., if she sees it and
has time to repair it. The rule is that a major defect should go back to the
operator, provided that the supervisor of production does not intercept it to
avoid getting caught short of material to work on.

b.   Major defects, and minor ones too, once sent into the production line,
cause trouble at nearly every stage of production from that point onward. Once
defective, always defective. Defects beget defects.

c.   An operator turns out work. She looks it over. She may rework a
major defect herself. By a major defect she means one that runs a chance of
coming back to her. The inspector may see it and rework it herself, and not
send it back to the operator. Also, the inspector may not see it. Even if the
inspector sees it, the supervisor may send it on through production. Why not
take a chance? She can't lose, and she may gain a link in her production
record.

d.   As for a minor defect, why bother? The inspector will take care of
it. So on she goes to the next piece.

e.   Supervision that overrides inspection is frustrating to operators and
inspectors.

5.a.   In effect, your inspectors are not inspectors at all. Their job is
rework, as part of the production line. They are unable to keep up with the
rework.

b. In other words, the operator's job is to produce defects. She gets paid for them. This is the system. The operator is not responsible for the system.

6.   Your quality-audit takes place after every finished item is put through 200 per cent final inspection. This final inspection is obviously a joke. Your quality-audit must convince you, we should suppose, that quality by inspection is not working. As we said, it never does. It is in fact working against you.

7.   There are three possible paths for you to consider, as we see it.

   i. Continue with no change.

   ii. Continue to produce items that show $7\frac{1}{2}$ per cent major defects at reduced cost and with greater profit.

   iii. Reduce the proportion of defects, reduce costs, and increase profits. We are only interested in pursuing this course.

8.   A complete overhaul is necessary. Here are some suggestions that we believe would increase production, greatly improve quality, with consequent inescapable greater profit, and more satisfied work force.

9.a. Your factory runs on piece work. There is no better assurance of defective workmanship.

b. Piece work is a sure road to dissatisfaction of employees. Piece work robs the employee of his right to do work that he can be proud of.

c. Our suggestion is to get off piece work. This act will require better training and a new mode of supervision.

10.a. Abolish the distinction between major and minor defects. A defect will be a defect, except possibly in the quality-audit.

b. Construct operational definitions so that the operators may understand what is right and what is wrong. This task was set in the meeting on the 8th

August. As we tried to make clear, this is the responsibility of your company.
It is not a statistical problem, though it is only by statistical methods that
you can learn whether a proposed definition is working to your satisfaction.

c. It is of course our job as statisticians to lay out tests to learn
whether and how well a proposed definition works in practice.

11.a. Meanwhile, cut out rework at inspection. Pieces that need rework
should go (i) back to the operator if she has not yet achieved statistical
control, or (ii) to a special group if her work is in statistical control.

b. Abolish pressure on foremen for production. Make them responsible to
assist their people to produce quality. A control chart for a group may be
helpful, and in some stations individual charts.

12.a. There will be, in the end, fewer inspectors, better inspection,
useful information from inspection by which to improve quality, greater
satisfaction of customers, greater profit.

b. The work load of an inspector would be geared to inspection, not to
production. Her job would be to inspect.

13.a. Randomization of cases of items to inspectors, and random selection
of items from cases would be the rule. (By random, we mean use of random
numbers.)

b. The system of inspection when revised will give to us a picture of
each operator's work, percentage defective by type of defect, by style of
item. It will tell which inspectors are out of line with the others, and which
operators are out of line, perhaps some extra good, some extra poor.

14.a. Our job as statisticians is to provide methods by which you may
discover sources of trouble and reasons for high costs.

b. We do not attempt to tell you whether nor how to go about making the
changes that are necessary.

15.   You must remove barriers that rob your hourly workers of pride of workmanship.

16.   We doubt that new machinery would bring any improvement. In fact, we fear that new machinery would bring on a whole new set of problems until management understands what is wrong under present circumstances and what their responsibilities are for improvement.

B.   EXTRACTS TAKEN FROM ANOTHER REPORT TO MANAGEMENT *

1.   This report is written at your request after study of some of the problems that you are having with production, high costs, and variable quality, which altogether, as I understood you, have been the cause of considerable worry to you about your competitive position.

2.   My opening point is that no permanent impact has ever been accomplished in improvement of quality unless the top management carries out their reponsibilities. These responsibilities never cease: they continue forever. No short-cut has been discovered. Failure of your own management to accept and act on their responsibilities for quality is, in my opinion, the prime cause of your trouble, as further paragraphs will indicate in more detail.

3.   You assured me, when I began this engagement, that you have quality control in your company. I have had a chance to see some of it. What you have in your company, as I see it, is not quality control, but guerrilla sniping--no organized system, no provision nor appreciation for control of quality as a system. You have been running along with a fire department that hopes to arrive in time to keep fires from spreading. Your quality control department

---

* Published in Industrial Quality Control, vol. vi, 1972.

has done their duty, as I understand it, if they discover that a carload of finished product might cause trouble (even legal action) if it went out. This is important, but my advice is to build a system of quality control that will reduce the number of fires in the first place. You spend money on quality control, but ineffectively.

4.a. You have a slogan, posted everywhere, urging everyone to do perfect work, nothing else. I wonder how anyone could live up to it. By every man doing his job better? How can he, when he has no way to know what his job is, nor how to do it better? How can he, when he is handicapped by defective materials, change of supply, machines out of order? Exhortations and platitudes are not very effective instruments of improvement in today's fierce competition, where a company must compete across national boundaries.

b. Something more is required. You must provide road maps to help the hourly worker to improve his work, and to accomplish your exhortation toward perfect work. Meanwhile, the hourly worker sees your exhortations as cruel jokes, management unwilling to take on their responsibilities for quality.

5. A usual stumbling block in most places is management's supposition that quality control is something that you install, like a new Dean or a new carpet. Install it, and you have it. In your case, you handed to someone the job of manager of quality, and paid no further attention to the matter.

6. Another roadblock is management's supposition that the production workers are responsible for all trouble: that there would be no problems in production if only the production workers would do their jobs in the way that they know to be right. Man's natural reaction to trouble of any kind in the production line is to blame the operators. Instead, in my experience, most problems in production have their origin in common causes, which only management can reduce or remove.

Chapter 14

7.a. Fortunately, confusion between the two sources of trouble (common or environmental causes, and special causes) can be eliminated with almost unerring accuracy. Simple statistical charts distinguish between the two types of cause, and thus point the finger at the source and at the level of responsibility for action. These charts tell the operator when to take action to improve the uniformity of his work, and when to leave it alone. Moreover, the same simple statistical tools can be used to tell management how much of the proportion of defective material is chargeable to common (environmental) causes, correctable only by management.

The benefit of this communication with the worker, by which he perceives a genuine attempt on the part of management to show him what his job is, and to hold him responsible for what he himself can govern, and not for the sins of management, is hard to overestimate.

Be it noted, though, that statistical techniques for detection of special causes alone will be ineffective and will fizzle out unless management has taken steps to improve the system. You must remove the common (environmental) causes of trouble that make it impossible for the production worker to turn out good work. You must remove the obstacles that separate the production worker from the possibility to take pride in his work. Failure of management to take this initial step, before teaching the production worker how to detect his own special causes, accounts, in my belief, for some of your troubles.

b. Thus, with simple data, it is possible and usually not difficult to measure the combined effect of common causes on any operation.

8.a. "We rely on our experience," is the answer that came from the manager of quality in a large company recently when I enquired how they distinguish between the two kinds of trouble (special and environmental) and on what principles. Your own people gave me the same answer.

b. This answer is self-incriminating--a guarantee that your company will continue to have about the same amount of trouble. There is a better way, now. Experience can be cataloged and put to use rationally only by application of statistical theory. One function of statistical methods is to design experiments and to make use of relevant experience in a way that is effective. Any claim to use of experience without a plan based on theory is a disguise for rationalization of a decision that has already been made.

9.   In connexion with special causes, I find in your company no provision to feed back to the production worker information in a form that would indicate (a) when action on his part would be effective in helping to meet his specifications, and (b) when he should leave his process as it is. Special causes can be detected only with the aid of proper statistical techniques.

10.a. Statistical aids to the production worker will require a lot of training. You must train hundreds of hourly workers in use of simple control charts. This training will require from six to nine hours initially, and you must provide beyond that point assistance in interpretation and for further training as needed.

b. Who will do the training? My advice is to start with competent advice and assistance for training. For expansion, search in your own ranks for people with a considerable amount of statistical knowledge and talent. Such people, taught and nurtured under competent guidance, may be able to take on training of other people. Leave that to your advisor.

11.   There is no excuse today to hand to a worker specifications that he can not meet economically, nor to put him in a position where he can not tell whether he has met them. Your company fails miserably here.

12.a. When a process has been brought into a state of statistical control (special causes weeded out), it has a definite capability, expressible as the economic level of quality for that process.

b. The only specifications with meaning are those fixed by the capability of the process. The specifications that a process in control can meet are obvious. There is no process, no capability, and no meaningful specifications, except in statistical control.

c. Tighter specifications can be realized economically only by reduction or removal of some of the common causes of trouble, which means action on the part of management. A production worker, when he has reached statistical control, has put into the process all that he has to offer. It is up to management to provide better uniformity in incoming materials, better uniformity in previous operations, better setting of the machine, better maintenance, change in the process, change in sequencing, or to make some other fundamental change.

13. In connexion with the above paragraph, I find that in spite of the profusion of figures that you collect in your company, you are not discovering the main causes of poor quality. Costly computers turning out volumes of records is not quality control.

14. An important step, as I see it, would be for you to take a hard look at your production of figures—your so-called information-system. Under more intelligent guidance, you would have far fewer figures but far better information about your processes and their capabilities, more uniformity, and greater output at reduced cost per unit.

15. I should mention also the costly fallacy held by many people in management that a consultant must know all about a process in order to work on it. All evidence is exactly the contrary. Competent men in every position, from top management to the humblest worker, know all that there is to know about their work EXCEPT HOW TO IMPROVE IT. Help toward improvement can come ONLY FROM OUTSIDE KNOWLEDGE.

16. Management too often supposes that they have solved their problems of quality (by which I mean economic manufacture of product that meets the demands

of the market) by establishing a Quality Control Department, and forgetting about it.

17.a. Most quality control departments work in narrow ranges of knowledge, with little concept or ability to understand the full meaning of improvement of quality and productivity. Unfortunately, management never knows the difference.

b. No good comes from changing the name of a Quality Control Department to the Department of Operations Research, or to Systems Analysis, or to some other fancy name. There is no substitute for brains.

18. Management too often turns over to a plant manager the problems or organization for quality. Your company provides a good example. This man, dedicated to the company, wonders day to day what his job is. Is it production or quality? He gets blamed for both. This is so because he does not understand what quality is nor how to achieve it. He is harassed day by day by problems of sanitation, pollution, health, turnover, grievances. He is suspicious of someone from the outside, especially of a statistician, talking a new language, someone not raised in the manufacturing business. He has no time for foolishness. He expects authoritative pronouncements and quick results. He finds it difficult to accustom himself to the unassuming, deliberate, scholarly approach of the statistician. The thought is horrifying to him, that he, the plant manager, is responsible for a certain amount of the trouble that plagues the plant, and that only he or someone higher up can make the necessary changes in the environment. He should, of course, undergo first of all a course of indoctrination at headquarters, with a chance to understand what quality control is and what his part in it will be.

19. Proper organization and competence do not necessarily increase the budget for improvement of quality and productivity. Management is already, in most instances, paying out enough money or more for proper organization and

competence, but getting tons of machine sheets full of meaningless figures--
getting rooked, I'd say, and blissfully at that. Your company is no exception.

20.a. Your next step will be for your top management, and all other people
in management, engineering, chemistry, accounting, payroll, legal department,
consumer research, to attend a four-day seminar for indoctrination in their
responsibilities.

b. This indoctrination will be followed by a brief course in statistical
techniques and applications under a competent teacher, over a period of five
days, to be supplemented as needed.

21. You must engage a competent consultant to guide your program in the
14 points for the improvement of quality, productivity, and competitive
position. He will guide the teaching that you will require.

Chapter 15

OPERATIONAL DEFINITIONS, CONFORMANCE, PERFORMANCE

I may express the opinion that some of the published
explanations are more remarkable than the phenomenon itself.
--Hugh M. Smith, "On the synchronous flashing of fireflies,"
Science, vol. 82, August 1935: pp. 151-152.

<u>What is an operational definition?</u> An operational definition is one that
people can do business with. In other words, an operational definition of safe,
round, reliable, or of any other quality must be communicable, with the same
meaning to vendor as to purchaser, same meaning yesterday and today to the production worker. An operational definition consists of (1) a criterion to be
applied to an object or to a group, (2) a test of the object or of the group,
(3) decision: yes or no: the object or the group did or did not meet the
criterion.

A specification of an article may refer to measurements of length, diameter,
weight, hardness, concentration, flocculence, color, appearance, pressure,
parallelism, leak, or some other characteristic. A specification may refer to
performance. For example, the average time between failures of a machine must
not be less than eight hours. Or, 95 per cent of the machines bought must run
one hour or more without failure.

We have seen in many places how important it is that buyer and seller
understand each other. They must both use the same kind of centimeter. Use of
their instruments must agree well enough with each other. This requirement has
meaning only if instruments are in statistical control. Without operational
definitions, a specification is meaningless.

There is probably nothing more important to the man in business, whether he be buyer or seller (and he will be one, then the other), and to his lawyer as well, than a healthy appreciation for operational definitions. What is due care, for example (Ch. 18)? Misunderstandings between companies and between departments within a company about alleged defective materials, or alleged malfunctioning of apparatus, often have their roots in failure on both sides to state in advance in meaningful terms the specifications of an item, or the specifications for performance, and failure to understand the problems of measurement.

Operational definitions are vital to lawyers, vital to government regulations, vital to (voluntary) industrial standards. For example, what is care? What is due care? (See Principle 4 in Ch. 18.)

Practice is more exacting than pure science; more exacting than teaching. As Shewhart* said, the standards of knowledge and workmanship required in industry and in public service are more severe than the requirements in pure science.

> Both pure and applied science have gradually pushed further and further the requirements for accuracy and precision.
>
> However, applied science, particularly in the mass production of interchangeable parts, is even more exacting than pure science in certain matters of accuracy and precision. For example, a pure scientist makes a series of measurements and upon the basis of these makes what he considers to be the best estimates of accuracy and precision, regardless of how few measurements he may have. He will readily admit that future studies may prove such estimates to be in error. Perhaps all he will claim for them is that they are as good as any reasonable scientist could make upon the basis of the data available at the time the estimates were made. But now let us look at the applied scientist. He knows that if he were to act upon the meagre evidence sometimes available to the pure scientist, he would make the

---

* Walter A. Shewhart, STATISTICAL METHOD FROM THE VIEWPOINT OF QUALITY CONTROL (The Graduate School, Department of Agriculture, Washington, 1939): pp. 120-121.

same mistakes as the pure scientist makes in estimates of accuracy and precision. He also knows that through his mistakes someone may lose a lot of money or suffer physical injury, or both.

The man in industry has yet another worry. He knows that specifications of quality involving requirements of fixed degrees of accuracy and precision may become the basis of contractual agreement, and he knows that any indefiniteness in the meaning of any of the terms used in such a specification, including those of accuracy and precision, may lead to misunderstandings and even to legal action. Hence the applied scientist finds it desirable to go as far as one can reasonably go towards establishing definite and operationally verifiable meanings for such terms.

No exact value; no true value. The problem in commerce is never whether anything is exactly round, but how far in what way it departs from roundness. The pistons in your automobile are not exactly round. They could not be, because there is no way to define operationally exactly round.

Why not get help from the dictionary? The dictionary says that a figure is round if it is everywhere in Euclidian 2-dimensional space equidistant from a point called the centre. A very useful definition that is, for use in formal logic, such as for a theorem in Euclid. But if we try to use it in practice, we find that the dictionary provides a concept, not a definition for use in industry--i.e., not an operational definition of what is round enough for a given purpose.

The train was not exactly on time.

To understand these truths, one need only try to explain what measurements to make, and what criterion to adopt, to decide whether something is exactly round, or whether the train was exactly on time. He will soon discover that he has driven himself into an Irish bog.

Any physical measurement is the result of applying a given procedure. Likewise with the count of people in an area. No two procedures will give the same count. Neither of two figures is right and the other wrong. The experts in the subject matter may have a preference, however, for Method A over Method B.

Chapter 15

As P. W. Bridgman put it, "The concept is synonymous with the corresponding set of operations."* Or, perhaps easier to understand,

> A preferred procedure is distinguished by the fact that it supposedly gives or would give results nearest to what are needed for a particular end; and also by the fact that it is more expensive or more time consuming, or even impossible to carry out... . As a preferred procedure is always subject to modification or obsolescence, we are forced to conclude that neither the accuracy nor the bias of any procedure can ever be known in a logical sense.**

There is no true value for the number of defective items in a lot. We have already seen that the process average will depend on the method of sampling lots, as well as of the method of test and the criteria imposed. Change the method of sampling or the method of test and you will get a new count of defectives in a lot, and a new process average. There is thus no true value for the number of defective items in a given lot, and no true value for the process average.

It comes as astonishment to most people that there is no true value for the speed of light. The result obtained for the speed of light depends on the method used by the experimenter (microwave, interferometer, geodimeter, molecular spectra). Moreover (as has been stressed before), a method of measurement does not exist unless the results show statistical control. The only test of statistical control on record for results on the speed of light turned out to be negative.***

If two methods for measuring the speed of light, or for measuring anything, were in statistical control, there might well be differences of scientific

___

* P. W. Bridgman, THE LOGIC OF MODERN PHYSICS (Macmillan, 1928), p. 5.

** W. Edwards Deming, SAMPLE DESIGN IN BUSINESS RESEARCH (Wiley, 1960), Chapter 4.

*** Walter A. Shewhart, STATISTICAL METHOD FROM THE VIEWPOINT OF QUALITY CONTROL (Books on Demand, 1939), p. 68.

OPERATIONAL DEFINITIONS, CONFORMANCE, PERFORMANCE

importance. On the other hand, if the methods agreed reasonably well, their agreement could be accepted as a master standard for today.

This master standard would not be a true value, because some other method, yet to be agreed upon, might well give a value substantially different from today's master standard. It is better to regard an unresolvable difference, not as a bias, but as the natural result of a different method.

The speed 3×10^{10} cm per second, as we learned it in school, is still good enough for most purposes for the speed of light, but today's requirements of science and industry need the results of other methods.

Shewhart on page 82 of his book of 1939, already cited, showed a graphical record of all the published determinations of the speed of light, to date (Fig. 54). Every determination shows a lower figure than was ever before obtained. There have been a number of more recent determinations, every one, with two exceptions, still being lower than any ever obtained before.* Both exceptions came from the U.S.S.R.

No true number of inhabitants in a Census count. Some fundamental principle of science seems to have escaped even officials of the Census. I heard one official say that the Census of 1980 was the most accurate ever taken leading himself and other people, I fear, to suppose that an accurate figure exists and could be obtained if only everybody in the Census would work hard enough.

Claims put forth in 1980 by the mayors of various cities in America that the Census of April 1980 failed to count all their people showed dismal failure on the part of the mayors to understand what a count is. Threats by the courts

---

* Halliday and Resnick, FUNDAMENTALS OF PHYSICS (Wiley, 1974), p. 655.

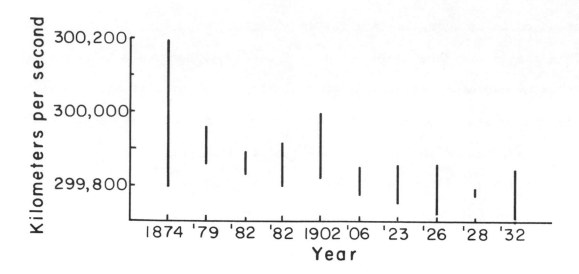

Fig. 54. Graphical record of published determinations of the speed of light, down to 1932. The ranges are the physicist's so-called probable errors, calculation for which is usually not clear.

to award to cities adjustments of recorded counts display equal ignorance. Why not give every area an additional $2\frac{1}{2}$ per cent?

There is no true value for the number of people in Detroit, but there is (was) a figure delivered by the procedures that the Census followed. If the procedures had been different in any way, a different figure would have been obtained.

I submit the thought that a sensible way for a mayor to satisfy himself about the count of people in his city would be to work in advance with the Census. He would:

1. Study and become familiar with the methods that our Census and other Censuses have used to find people in an area, including the definitions of whom to count and whom to omit, plus the rules for allocating people from one area to another.

OPERATIONAL DEFINITIONS, CONFORMANCE, PERFORMANCE

A count of vacant dwelling units in an area presents problems of classification as well as problems of total count. First, what is a dwelling unit? Second, what is a vacant dwelling unit? It seems simple till one enquires into the various kinds of vacant dwelling units. It might seem that a dwelling unit that is not occupied is vacant. But what if the dwelling unit is uninhabitable? Is it vacant? There are dwelling units vacant and for sale; vacant for rent; seasonally vacant (occupied only part of the year); vacant but neither for sale nor for rent; vacant held for occupancy.

Number of vacant dwelling units by type of vacancy is an important economic indicator, and useful for business purposes. Obviously, the Census must put interviewers through a course of training before they can be sent into the field to collect data on vacancies.

2. The best way to learn these procedures would be to apply to the Census for the four-day course of study, and take the examinations.

Anyone familiar with Census methods knows about the well organized attempt on the night of the 8th April of the Census year to find and count all the people in hotels, flop-houses, or other shelter, with no usual place of residence. Many of these people have no information about themselves; some are not sure of their names, still fewer of their ages. An army of enumerators and other Census employees take part in this dragnet, under close supervision and dress rehearsal.

It is notable that further efforts and expense beyond a reasonable level to find more people are singularly unsuccessful, especially for black males 18 to 24 years of age. Intensity of search may easily cost $100 for every addition to the count. Further effort raises the cost to $200 for each addition.

How much is one more name worth?

Again, what do you mean by the number of people in an area?

There would obviously have to be agreement in advance on just what effort is to be expended and who will pay the cost beyond regular authorized Census methods.

Chapter 15

3. Learn the various techniques by which our Census and other Censuses have estimated (a) the number of dwelling units and the number of people missed, (b) the number counted twice, and (c) the number counted in error.

> Incidentally, a roster of people that claim that they were not enumerated in the Census is not worth the paper that it is written on. You do not have to be home to be counted. Only a search of the Census records can answer the question whether some particular person was enumerated, and allocated to his home address.

4. Make suggestions on the procedures until satisfied with them.

5.a. Monitor the Census in action, to provide statistical evidence of exactly what happened, in a sample of small areas, appropriately selected.

> An area in the sample could be a segment that (according to maps) contains housing units, anywhere from 10 to 50 (not rigid). The overriding requirement of an area is that it must have definite, unmistakable boundaries.

AND

b. Accept the results of the Census unless the monitoring shows failure in execution. Failure in execution must be defined in advance.

Without this participation, the mayor must accept what the Census gives him. To complain afterward is to play heads I win, tails new deal. It is hard for me to find partners for a game governed by such a rule, yet this is precisely how the mayors are asking other people to play.

A judge and his staff, to qualify to hear with intelligence a claim for a shortage, would (like the mayor) require a short course in Census methods, and a briefing on the difference between a concept and an operational definition (the contents of this chapter, which ought to be included in education in law, engineering, business, and statistics).

More on an operational definition. An operational definition puts communicable meaning into an adjective. Adjectives like good, reliable, uniform, round, tired, safe, unsafe, unemployed, have no communicable meaning until they are expressed in operational terms of sampling, test, and criterion. Whatever they mean in concept to one person can not be known to another. For commerce and science, both must agree on an operational definition. An operational definition requires a prescribed test, a record of the result, and comparison of the result with the criterion agreed upon.*

Everyone supposes that he knows what pollution means until he begins to try to explain it to somebody. One requires an operational definition of pollution of rivers, pollution of land, pollution of streets. These words have no meaning until defined statistically. For example, it will not suffice to say that air with 100 parts per million of carbon monoxide is a hazard. One must specify (a) that this amount or more is a hazard if it exists at any instant, or (b) that this amount or more is a hazard if it exists throughout working hours. And how is the concentration to be measured?

Even the adjective red has no meaning for business purposes unless it is defined operationally in terms of test and criterion. Clean is one thing for dishes and for knives and forks in a restaurant; something else in the manufacture of hard discs for a computer, or in the manufacture of transistors.

The man in business or in government can not afford to be superficial in his understanding of specifications for performance of product, or medicines, or human efforts. Principles of the theory of knowledge, often regarded as inconsequential or as pastime in pure science, as well as in textbooks on administration and management, become lively and gravely serious to the man that is faced with the problems of industry.

What is the meaning of the law that butter for sale must be 80 per cent butter-fat? Does it mean 80 per cent butter-fat, or more, in every pound that

---

* C. I. Lewis, MIND AND THE WORLD ORDER (Scribners, 1929), Chapters 7,8,9.

Chapter 15

you buy? Or does it mean 80 per cent on the average? What would you mean by 80 per cent butter-fat on the average? The average over your purchases of butter during a year? Or would you mean the average production of all butter for a year, yours and other people's purchases of butter from a particular source? How many pounds would you test, for calculation of the average? How would you select butter for test? Would you be concerned with the variation in butter fat from pound to pound?

Obviously, any attempt to define operationally 80 per cent butter-fat runs headlong into the need for statistical techniques and criteria. Again, the words "80 per cent butter-fat," by themselves, have no meaning.

Does pollution mean (e.g.) carbon monoxide in sufficient concentration to cause sickness in three breaths, or does one mean carbon monoxide in sufficient concentration to produce sickness when breathed continuously over a period of five days? In either case, how is the effect going to be recognized? By what procedure is the presence of carbon monoxide to be detected? What is the diagnosis or criterion for poisoning? Men? Animals? If men, how will they be selected? How many? How many in the sample must satisfy the criteria for poisoning from carbon monoxide in order that we may declare the air to be unsafe for a few breaths, or for a steady diet? Same questions if animals are used.

Operational definitions are necessary for economy and reliability. Without an operational definition of (e.g.) unemployment, pollution, safety of goods and of apparatus, effectiveness (as of a drug), side-effects, duration of dosage before side-effects become apparent, have no meaning unless defined in statistical terms. Without an operational definition, investigations on a problem will be costly and ineffective, almost certain to lead to endless bickering and controversy.

OPERATIONAL DEFINITIONS, CONFORMANCE, PERFORMANCE

An operational definition of pollution in terms of offensiveness to the
nose would be an example. It is not an impossible definition (being close kin
to statistical methods for maintaining constant quality and taste in foods and
beverages), but unless it be statistically defined, it would be meaningless.

The number of samples for test, how to select them, how to calculate
estimates, how to calculate and interpret their margin of uncertainty, tests of
variance between instruments, between operators, between days, between laboratories, the detection and evaluation of the effect of non-sampling errors, are
statistical problems of high order. The difference between two methods of
investigation (questionnaire, test) can be measured reliably and economically
only by statistical design and calculation.

Laws passed by Congress, and rulings by federal regulatory agencies, are
notorious for lack of clarity in definitions, and costly confusion. The
following excerpts taken from the New York Times, 9 April 1980, pages D-1 and
D-3 indicate that the Federal Communications Commission finally gave up on the
distinction between data processing and the transmission and manipulation of
data.

> The distinction between data processing (manipulation of data in
> the form of words and numbers) and telecommunications (the transmis-
> sion of voices, the traditional domain of phone companies) will
> disappear.
>
> It is this last point that ultimately, in the eyes of many
> observers, forced the commission's hand in undertaking what has come
> to be known to the industry as Computer Inquiry II.
>
> For more than a decade the F.C.C. has been trying to resolve the
> basic question of what constitutes data processing and telecommunica-
> tions. For just as long, the two technologies have outraced the
> regulatory environment...
>
> "Every time the commission tried to separate the two fields, they
> got closer together," said one telecommunications industry observer.
> "Now the commission in effect is forcing the issue itself by opening
> up the data processing business to communications carriers."

What means a label, 50 per cent wool? The label on a blanket reads 50 per cent wool. What does it mean? You probably don't care much what it means. You are more interested in color, texture, and price, than on the content. However, some people do care what the label means. The Federal Trade Commission does, but with what operational meaning?

Suppose that you tell me that you wish to purchase a blanket that is 50 per cent wool, and that I sell to you the blanket shown in Fig. 55, one half by area being all wool and the other half all cotton. This blanket is 50 per cent wool, by one definition. But you may, for your purpose, prefer another definition: you may say that 50 per cent wool means something different to you. If so, then what? You may say that you meant for the wool to be dispersed throughout the blanket. You could come through with an operational definition like this:

Cut 10 holes in the blanket, 1 or $1\frac{1}{2}$ cms in diameter, centered by random numbers. Number the holes 1 to 10. Hand these 10 pieces to your chemist for test. Ask him to record x_i, the proportion wool by weight for hole i. Compute $\bar{x}$, the average of 10 proportions.

Criteria:

$$\bar{x} \geq .50$$

$$x_{max} - x_{min} \leq .02$$

If the sample fails on either criterion, the blanket fails to meet your specification.

There is nothing right or wrong about either of the above two definitions of 50 per cent wool. You have a right and a duty to specify a definition that suits your purpose. Later on, you may have another purpose, and a new definition.

There is no true value for the proportion of wool in a blanket. There is, however, a number that you can get by carrying out a prescribed test.

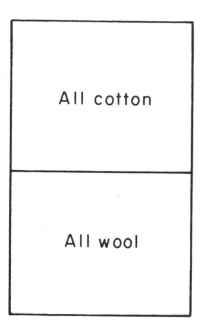

Fig. 55. This blanket is 50 per cent wool by area.

So far, we have been talking about a single blanket. Now comes the problem of a run of blankets. You may be buying blankets for a hospital or for the army. We face here the same fundamental difference that we faced in Chapter 2: a single-time purchase compared with continuing purchases. You could specify that for every 10 kgs of clean wool, the manufacturer will use 10 kgs of cotton; net 10 kgs of wool and 10 kgs of cotton, etc. This would be a possible definition of 50 per cent wool, neither right nor wrong, but satisfying your purpose, if you say so. For another definition, you might insist that nearly equal amounts of wool and of cotton be spun into the fibers that make up the blanket.

Application. The following items appeared in the U.S. News and World Report, 23 Nov. 1981, p. 82.

NEWS - LINES

WHAT YOU CAN AND CAN NOT DO IF YOU RUN A BUSINESS AS
A RESULT OF RECENT COURT AND GOVERNMENT DECISIONS

An importer who relies on labels provided by foreign manufacturers is acting illegally if the labels are not correct, says a consent decree filed in a U.S. district court. A New York-based importer of wool-blend fabrics has agreed to pay a $25,000 fine to settle charges that it sold fabrics with less wool than labels claimed even after being notified by the Federal Trade Commission that to do so was illegal. Under the agreement, the firm will have fabrics tested by an independent laboratory to determine the accuracy of labels.

It would be interesting to learn what operational definition of 25 per cent wool plaintiff and defendant agreed to. It would be still more interesting to learn whether the Federal Trade Commission uses operational definitions as a regular part of their legal procedures, and if so, what is the basis for the definition?

What is a wrinkle?* The product is instrument panels for automobiles. One style of panel was a special source of trouble. The plant manager informed me that the proportion defective was anywhere from 35 per cent to 50 per cent day after day.

Examination of data showed that the inspectors differed markedly. It turned out that each inspector has his own visual perception for the day of what constituted a wrinkle. The manager agreed to devote time to operational definitions. Six men in top management attended the session. The inspectors provided 20 panels for exhibits, some with wrinkles, so they said, some without.

As a first step, I asked everybody present--anyone willing to try--to define a wrinkle. Give us a definition of a wrinkle that everybody can understand. The challenge went unanswered. Let's try again: can any inspector tell me what

---

* Contributed by Byron Doss, Consultant, Nashville.

OPERATIONAL DEFINITIONS, CONFORMANCE, PERFORMANCE

a wrinkle is? No answer. The manager of quality control then pointed to what he called an actual wrinkle. One of the inspectors agreed that that was indeed a wrinkle. Two of the other four inspectors came forth with the question, "What is it that you are looking at?" They could find no trace of a wrinkle.

The solution was to establish operational definitions of what a wrinkle is and what it is not. Definitions of other types of defects followed.

Result: the level of defectives dropped to 10 per cent in the space of one week. Employees on rework had time to do their job. The operational definition provided a basis of communication between the inspectors and operators. They trained themselves and each other. Production went up 50 per cent.

Cost: nothing: same people, same materials, same machinery; nothing new except definitions that people on the job, and inspectors too, understood on a common basis.

Random selection of units. A random procedure for selection of a sample of units from a frame of N units could be defined in this way:

1. Number the units in the frame 1, 2, 3, and onward to N.

2. Read out by an acceptable procedure, to be written out in advance, n unduplicated random numbers between 1 and N. The numbers read out designate by serial number the selection of the sample.

This would be a random procedure. A sample is neither random, nor is it not random. It is the procedure of selection that we must focus on. The procedure that selected the sample satisfies the prescribed definition of a random procedure, or it does not. A random variable is the result of a random operation.*

---

* W. Edwards Deming, SAMPLE DESIGN IN BUSINESS RESEARCH (Wiley, 1960) p. 54.

It is presumed that one uses a standard table of random numbers, or generates random numbers under the guidance of a mathematician who knows the possible fallacies of generation of random numbers.

Exercises

1. Why is it that there can be no operational definition of the true value of anything? (Answer: An observed numerical value of anything depends on the definitions and operations used. The definitions and operations will be constructed differently by different experts in the subject matter.)

2. Explain why the accuracy of any measurement can be defined only as departure from the result of an accepted master standard of measurement. Accuracy varies as the standard is altered.

3. How would you answer the question that a manufacturer of bicycles brought up in Kaoschung?

Your government (U.S.) has a regulation that states that a bicycle must be safe if assembled by a man of average intelligence.

His question was, what means this regulation? How would you explain to him its meaning? What is safe? What is unsafe? What is a man of average intelligence? What kind of intellegence? Could someone of lesser intelligence do better? How would you define lesser intelligence? One could only conclude that the regulation had no meaning.

Comment: A voluntary standard (next chapter) developed by the industry could have forestalled this meaningless and burdensome regulation.

4. Why is it that a careful statistician in practice never speaks of a true value?

5. Why is survey experience desirable in order to understand and use economic and demographic data in business (including marketing research, of course)?

6. Explain why it is that the precision of a result, if valid at the time when an experiment is carried out, or a survey conducted, will always be valid, whereas the accuracy of this result will change from time to time with new definitions and with new preferred procedures.

7. A specification for casting contained this clause:

The castings shall be delivered to us reasonably clean.

What is reasonably clean? Was the specification referring to the flash, or to plain dirt? Obviously, the specification has no meaning.

8. Show that there is no meaning in the content of the following paragraph.

Congress has passed legislation mandating the reconstruction of the northeast corridor, and has gone so far as to specify train speeds of 120 miles an hour, 99 per cent on-time performance, and running times of two hours and forty minutes between New York and Washington, three hours and forty minutes on the New York-Boston leg.

--Tracy Kidder, in The Atlantic,
July 1976, p. 36.

Remarks. Obviously the definition of on-time performance must have an operational definition if we wish to communicate (Ch. 18).

Adjectives like good service, bad service, deplorable service, have no communicable meaning, unless they are defined in statistical terms such as properties of a run-chart of arrivals, or properties of a distribution of arrivals.

It is easy to see that this hope of Congress, 99 per cent on-time performance, without a statistical definition of on-time performance, has no meaning. Anyone could guarantee to put a train into Penn Station day after day, 99 days out of 100, if on-time be defined as arrival any time within four hours of the printed time-table.

This illustration, referring to the performance of a train, is easily adapted to schedules of production.

9.   Show that the following examples, taken from specifications used in industry and in government, have no meaning that can be communicated (i.e., no operational definition).

a. <u>Representative sample</u>. A sample which has the same composition as the material sampled when this is considered as a homogeneous whole. (Quoted from British Standard 69/61888, "Methods of sampling chemical products.")

> How would you determine whether the sample had the same composition as the material sampled? Explain why the words "same composition as the material sampled" have no meaning.

b. <u>Spot sample</u>. A sample of specified size or number taken from a specified place in the material or at a specified place and time in a stream and representative of its immediate or local environment.

What is the meaning of the adjective <u>representative</u>? Answer: The word has no meaning. Statisticians do not use the word. Why not take sampling procedures which are dictated by statistical theory, with the advantage of less cost, and with meaningful, calculable tolerances?

10.   The contractor shall exert his best efforts. Taken from a contract between (a) Tax Division of the Department of Justice and (b) a statistician.

<u>Comment</u>: Who knows his best efforts? How would you decide whether he had exerted his best efforts? Can he deliver his best efforts on every engagement? Will any effort fall below his average?

11.   Show that the following quotation from a famous textbook in experimental design is misleading, because the words <u>exact value</u> have no meaning.

> Obviously, it can not be expected that the solution will provide the exact value of the unknown differences.--Taken from William G. Cochran and Gertrude M. Cox, EXPERIMENTAL DESIGNS (Wiley, 1950), p. 3.

Chapter 16

STANDARDS AND REGULATIONS

    6. Some man holdeth his tongue because he hath not to
answer: and some keepeth silence knowing his time.
    7. A wise man will hold his tongue till he see
opportunity: but a babbler and a fool will regard no time.
    8. He that useth many words shall be abhorred.
--Ecclesiasticus 20

Aim of this chapter. The aim of this chapter will be to show that a government regulation, and likewise an industrial standard,* to be enforced, must have operational meaning. Conformance can be judged only in terms of a test and a criterion (sometimes many tests and many criteria). The criteria and tests must be in statistical terms to have meaning. A regulation or standard that is not so expressed will be devoid of meaning. A regulation without meaning can have no legal force.

Regulations and standards.** There are regulations made by government, voluntary standards made by industry, and unguided choices made by enterprises and individuals. The distinction between a regulation and a voluntary standard lies essentially in the penalties attached to failure to meet it.

A regulation is justifiable if it offers more advantage than the economic waste that it entails. For example, the obligation of a driver to stop at a red traffic light even when it is obvious that there is no vehicle in sight

---

* The word standard in this book means a voluntary standard.

** Adapted from Pierre Ailleret, "The importance and probable evolution of standardization," Standardization News, vol. 5, pp. 8-11. Mr. Ailleret is honorary president of the Union Technique d'Electricité in Paris.

involves a waste of time and fuel, but if no such strict rule were imposed, the number of accidents at crossroads would be considerably higher.

One cannot permit breaches of regulations to take place over any length of time without creating an increasing state of disorder, thereby destroying the public conscience. For this reason it is in the nature of regulations to be strict. In a permanent and well-organized system, checks and penalties are such that in the long run it is in no one's interest to break a regulation. Simultaneously, public authorities must not impose obligations that they are incapable of enforcing.

Ministers are responsible before parliament and public opinion for regulation making and it is for these government officials to decide which activities can be regulated without causing excessive waste or barriers to progress. In particular, the suppression of fraud and protection of citizens against the rashness of others undeniably come within the province of regulations. On the other hand, public authorities may or may not consider themselves obliged to protect individuals against the results of their own imprudence (whether in connexion with safety belts in cars, intoxication, or excessive smoking). They may consider it necessary to make rigid provisions for the packaging of agricultural produce, or unilaterally to select and mandate the technical characteristics of television systems.

Industrial standards. Aside from regulations, there remains a very wide area in which it is desirable for industry to make recommendations (voluntary standards) applicable in the majority of cases, and where enterprises or individuals are perfectly at liberty to disregard such recommendations in particular cases where they would be inappropriate. In this way, economic waste and hindrances to technical advancement are avoided.

STANDARDS AND REGULATIONS

The test of a standard can therefore be simpler, more flexible, and easier to understand than a regulation.

As it does not involve any mandatory prohibitions, such a standard does not require the signature of a minister before it can be put into effect. Instead of passing through the rather rigid filters preliminary to ministerial decisions, it can be prepared by the mutual agreement of all those who have contributed to it by their voluntary work, and who have decided that complete unanimity is not necessary since such a recommendation is not so severely restrictive as a regulation.

The framework of standardization provides greater clarity of expression between all the parties concerned and is much more flexible than the "consultation" process of regulation making, where the number of people that take part is strictly limited. As a general rule, the interested parties are far more at ease in the technical committees of standards organizations than when sitting on the consultative boards of government ministries. For this reason it is often stated when defining standardization that it is based on agreement, although agreements are by no means excluded from the preparation of regulations.

Voluntary standards, if they exist, may avoid government regulation. One of the first advantages of standardization is that it enables public authorities to limit regulations to cases where compulsion is essential. Standardization thus economizes on the making of regulations. Government departments are thereby relieved of a mass of detailed work based on thousands of minor decisions.

For their part, enterprises and individuals benefit from being subjected to fewer restrictive rules and from enjoying greater freedom than if standardization did not exist. This is an important reason why they should contribute time and money to standardization, thus to avoid the useless proliferation of

mandatory regulations to fill the gap left by a lack of voluntary standards.
Many branches of industry have already realized this, but in agriculture, for
example, numerous regulations have had to be imposed due to insufficient
development of voluntary standards.

Advantages of standardization were ably expressed some years ago by Senator
Ralph E. Flanders (deceased):*

> Trains move across the country from one railway to another, with
> no unloading and reloading because of different gauge or different air
> pressure for brakes. A car may in fact move from Halifax through
> Montreal, Toronto, Buffalo, Philadelphia, Mexico, and up to Vancouver,
> over a number of routes, along with other cars, some owned by railways,
> some owned by private investment, as a routine matter. Refrigerator
> cars, when halted, tap into regular city current, anywhere.

Standardization is something that all of us take for granted. We ship an
electric washer across the country with our household goods with never a
conscious thought but that it is sure to meet the same voltage and current
wherever it is plugged in. Our incandescent lamp finds the same socket in
Springfield, Vermont, and Springfield, Illinois. The 15/34 shirt we send as a
present from Iowa will fit the neck and arms that grew up to size in Virginia.
We drive an automobile from coast to coast under uniform traffic signals. In
Chicago we buy a tire that was made in Akron, and it will fit the wheel (made
in Pittsburgh) of the car (built in Detroit) that we bought in New York.

The ratio of focal length to diameter of a lens (e.g., 2.8) is understood
everywhere. We may buy an AA-battery anywhere in the world to replace the one
that just became too weak for service (though the quality may differ markedly
from brand to brand). The convenience of 110 volts and uniform outlets everywhere in the northern hemisphere would be difficult to express in words.

---

* Ralph E. Flanders, "How big is an inch?", The Atlantic, January 1951.

STANDARDS AND REGULATIONS

Competition for price and quality is not stifled by standardization.

On the contrary, as Shewhart often remarked, building codes that differ ever so little from one country to another in Europe, or even from city to city anywhere, by obstructing mass production, raise prices more effectively than tariff walls do.

The fact that we have a high degree of standardization has made life simpler for us in ways so basic and so obvious that we do not even realize they exist. It has given us the free national market which we take so casually. To you as end man, the American consumer, it has given lower prices and better quality, more safety, greater availability, prompter exchange and repair service, and all the other material advantages of mass production. Is this something to be taken for granted?

American mass production, made possible by standardization, was our number one weapon in World War II. And yet we can not possibly estimate the loss we suffered in men and money, in time and resources, because of lack of certain proper standards. Our losses really began in the spring of 1940, when 400,000 Belgian troops might have fought better and longer if British ammunition had fitted their empty rifles. The losses continued at the first battle of El Alamein, where a contributing cause of the British defeat and retreat was the lack of standard interchangeable parts in the radio and other auxiliary equipment of the British tanks. At home we lost the services of thousands of small companies which would have participated in war production if there had been a comprehensive system of national defense standards to which they were accustomed to work. The complicated relationship of prime contractor to sub-contractor would have been simplified.

At one moment early in the war, lack of a standard almost caused disaster on the grand scale. A part broke in one of the radar units protecting the length of the Panama Canal. Those in command were dismayed to discover that no replacement part was in stock. They put through a rush call to Washington to have the part flown from the factory to the Canal. Long before it arrived, however, the officer in charge of stores made a foot-by-foot search of his warehouse. He found eight full bins of the needed part, all marked with a different stock number.

The problem has not been with us for long, for in our industrial beginnings our standards were written by only two men. The maker and the user alone were concerned, and perhaps their only exchange was the oldest of specifications, "Like the last one." Government obviously has the right to set standards for the goods it buys. It is an interested party, and should be an active and watchful one.

There are trends, plans, and proposals currently under way that would make standardization wholly or mainly a function of government, and I am opposed to them. I do not want my talented, capable, and sincere friends in the federal agencies in Washington to write the industrial standards of this country. Too much is at stake.

If you control an industry's standards, you control that industry lock, stock, and ledger. On the day that standards become a governmental function and responsibility, as is now being threatened, the government will take a very long step toward the control of American industry.

In such a setup, government personnel will decide when and what standards should be developed and what the provisions of the standards should be. That method is inflexible. It does not permit the single manufacturer to depart from a standard in order to develop a specialized and useful business.

Standards made under such conditions tend to become limitations, controls, and restrictive procedures. They reduce consumer choice.

STANDARDS AND REGULATIONS

No government planner knows enough to write the standards for the rest of American industry and all other American people.

Nazi Germany practiced standards by decree and paid the price for it, notably when it standardized its military airplanes too much and too soon. Our own experience in World War II demonstrates that we worked best when industry was not only consulted in the development of the standards of the goods it was to manufacture, but also participated in decisions as to what the contents of the standards should be.

If an illustration is needed for an obvious truth, the case of the portable projector for training films may be briefly cited. One branch of the armed forces handed down specifications to the manufacturers that were quite out of line with the rigorous use for which the machine was intended, with the result that it frequently broke down after two or three uses. After the war a number of companies in the photographic equipment industry, working with a technical standards association, drew up specifications that harmonized the requirements of the machine and the ability of the industry to produce it. It is now in full military use.

We must work to achieve a higher degree of harmony and order in our world; to relieve the strain of modern living by simplification; to increase the standard of living through more efficient production of interchangeable parts in a free market. We must use standards as "the liberator that relegates the problems that have already been solved to the field of routine, and leaves the creative faculties free for the problems that are still unsolved."

About 4000 executives and technical experts are now serving on committees that are developing and constantly revising American standards under the clearinghouse machinery of the ASA.

Chapter 16

Those standards range from traffic signals to electric wiring, from specifications for fire hose to recent safety specifications for circus tents. They include standards for gear sizes; for the carat content of articles made of gold; for electric ranges, water heaters, and gas-burning appliances; for refrigeration equipment; and for eliminating variation in the shades of gray on industrial machines. There is an American Standard that fixes the musical note A in the treble clef at 440 cycles, and one that eliminates variation in kitchen measuring cups, pans, and spoons. An ASA committee is now seeking to complete an American Standard which will set minimum standard and informative labeling for rayon fabrics.

In none of these cases did the American Standards Association initiate a standard or hand it down to others as a finished job. It simply provided the machinery by which those who are concerned developed the standard. In drawing up the proposed 160-page rayon fabrics standard, over thirty national organizations participated. Producers, distributors, consumers, service industries, and federal agencies helped in its development.

Links between regulation and standards. Reference in a regulation to an industrial standard provides a link that makes the regulation effective and meaningful. For example, a regulation specifies the maximum content of sulphur in the smoke given off by heating installations. It is left to industrial standards to define how this sulphur content is to be measured in practice by a convenient and effective method not involving excessive costs. Public authorities are always free to withdraw from a regulation, by amendment, a reference to a standard that no longer answers the purpose intended.

Development of techniques and methods. Safety. In the early days of standardization, the main objective was to permit quantity production with the aim of reducing costs.

Today, however, the importance of the product itself is tending to fade into insignificance beside that of the service that it renders. The consumer's choice is nowadays based not only on the quality/purchase price relationship but also on working life, reliability, repairability, ease of replacement, and so forth. Producers have taken stock of this and are concerned not only with after-sales service, but with the subsequent fate of their product and how components can be replaced (such as fittings, leads, and connexions). This is why problems of interchangeability and compatibility are most important in standardization.

Safety remains, of course, an essential preoccupation, but its field is limited by the fact that only a small proportion of products (and the characteristics of each product) are concerned with safety. Here again, changes are taking place. Safety is no longer considered absolute, and the concept of probability is unavoidably introduced since increasing awareness is attached to the uniformity necessary between the degrees of safety in different economic sectors. If in any one of these sectors a great deal more money is spent than in another to save a probable human life, it would be possible to obtain greater safety for the same economic cost by harmonizing the cost/human life compromise between these two sectors. For this reason standards and safety regulations should be increasingly based on probability calculations, and meaningful accident statistics must be developed to provide a sounder basis for such calculations than is the case at present.

The characterization of products and their certification is also of increasing importance in national and international trade. Although the word certification is derived from the word certain, this does not alter the fact that 100 per cent certainty does not exist. Standardizers have understood this quicker in areas other than safety, and some certification is now based on well-developed statistical calculations.

Although world-wide standardization reduces hindrances to trade, on the other hand it does increase the possibility of barriers to technical advancement.

The updating of international standards is a long process that can sometimes constitute a brake on innovation.

Industry lags on standardization. Industry in the U.S. has unfortunately, possibly for lack of sufficient input of funds, possibly also being unwilling to run the risk of collusion, not come forth with suitable industrial standards that would reduce pollution and improve the safety of a host of mechanical and electrical devices. Industry and the public have for this reason had to cope with government regulations, sometimes put together in haste, and sometimes by people that lack the necessary industrial and statistical experience for the job. The mechanism exists for the creation of standards through the American Society for Testing Materials, the American National Standards Institute, and many other organizations.

The problems of difficulties of definition and conflicting results of tests, so often mentioned in previous pages, come to the fore when some government agency must hastily construct a standard. The following headline in the Wall Street Journal for 4 March 1980 is illustrative.

STANDARDS AND REGULATIONS

AUTO CRASH TESTS YIELD BUMPER CROP OF CONFUSING DATA

U.S. Agency Admits Mix-Up In Tests
but Uses Them To Back Its Bumper Rules

How could two collisions together produce less damage than just one of them?

"That's a good question," says the appraiser, Jerry Noel, from his office in Phoenix. After a long pause, he concedes that "It would be physically impossible. I just can't explain it."

Yet the agency is using his figures, along with damage estimates by two other independent appraisers, to support a much-debated federal regulation.

Had the industry gone to work years ago on standards for bumpers, solving in deliberate stride the problems that are now being patched up on a crash basis, the industry would not have to swallow and gag on hastily contrived untested regulations.

Chapter 17

ORGANIZATION FOR STATISTICAL WORK

Research in statistical theory and technique is necessarily mathematical, scholarly, and abstract in character, requiring some degree of leisure and detachment, and access to a good mathematical and statistical library. The importance of continuing such research is very great, although it is not always obvious to those whose interest is entirely in practical applications of already existing theory. Excepting in the presence of active research in a pure science, the applications of the science tend to drop into a deadly rut of unthinking routine, incapable of progress beyond a limited range predetermined by the accomplishments of pure science, and are in constant danger of falling into the hands of people who do not really understand the tools that they are working with and who are out of touch with those that do... It is in fact rather absurd, though quite in line with the precedents of earlier centuries, that scientific men of the highest talents can live only by doing work that could be done by others of lesser special ability, while the real worth of their most important work receives no official recognition.--Harold Hotelling, Memorandum to the Government of India, 24 Feb. 1940 (by permisson of the author).

Knowledge is a scarce national resource. Knowledge in any country is a

national resource. Unlike rare metals, which can not be replaced, the supply

of knowledge in any field can be increased by education. Education may be

formal, as in school. It may be informal, by study at home or on the job.

It may be supplemented and rounded out by work and review under a master. A

company must, for its very existence, make effective use of the store of

knowledge that exists within the company, and learn how to make use of help

from the outside when it can be effective.

Why waste knowledge? Waste of materials, waste of human effort, and waste

of machine-time, have been deplored in earlier chapters. Waste of knowledge,

in the sense of failure of a company to use knowledge that is there and avail-

able for development is even more deplorable, more devastating. No company can

afford to waste knowledge.

Failure of management to break down barriers between activities (production, design, purchase, etc., Point No. 9 of the 14 points in Ch. 2) is one way to waste knowledge. People that are not working together are not contributing their best to the company. People as they work together, feeling secure (p. 33) in the job reenforce their knowledge and efforts. Their combined output, when they work together, is more than the sum of their separate abilities.

<u>Aim of organization of statistical work</u>. No resource in any company is scarcer than statistical knowledge and ability. No source of knowledge can contribute more to quality, productivity, and competitive position. It is therefore very important to make the most effective use possible of existing knowledge of statistical theory and skill in application, and to give this knowledge and skill the best possible chance to improve continually.

The aim of organization of statistical work should be to serve the best interests of the company. The surest way to achieve this aim is to help people that are doing statistical work to improve continually. It is not enough that people should be good in their work. We don't need good people: we need better ones. Good management ensures everyone a chance to learn from a master and to improve month by month. The same statement would apply to any other kind of knowledge, but statistical work will suffice here.

In order for people that are doing statistical work to grow in knowledge and ability, their statistical activities must be guided and reviewed by a master of unquestioned ability, and they must continually acquire further statistical education through self-study, internal seminars, and formal courses in universities.

Statistical work carried out here and there in a company, fragmented, uncoordinated, merely stays at about the same level, or rises only gradually, and too often deteriorates. Good management tolerates no such condition.

Suggested plan. A schematic diagram of organization for statistical work in manufacturing appears in Fig. 56. It is possible here only to sketch principles of statistical organization. No attempt is made here to fit it to any particular company or industry. This type of organization (1) ensures that statistical work done anywhere in the company has the benefit of competent guidance. (2) It ensures that everyone engaged in statistical work shall grow in statistical stature. No one engaged in statistical work can, under this arrangement, simply remain good; he will improve month by month. (3) The teaching of statistics, and guidance in continuing education, are under leadership of unquestioned ability.

There will be in each division a statistician whose job it is to find problems in that division, and to work on them. He has the right and obligation to ask questions about any activity of the division, and he is entitled to responsible answers.

It may be necessary, because of shortage of statistical people, but subject to decision of the statistical leader, to place two or more activities in Fig. 56 under one statistician.

It is clear that no plan will work--not even the one proposed here--without competence and confidence in the statistical leadership, and without people in the divisions that have a burning desire to improve their statistical work.

The statistician in a division must be acceptable to the chief of the division, but his promotion depends also on the excellence of his statistical work and on his ability and desire to advance month by month in knowledge of theory and its effective application as judged by the statistical leader. Under this plan, a man can not be promoted for justifying bad statistical practice proposed by the division. The statistical leader is on hand to assist the statistician in a division and the head of the division, concerning any problem that comes up, or on any difference of opinion. He operates by pedagogy and guidance.

ORGANIZATION FOR STATISTICAL WORK

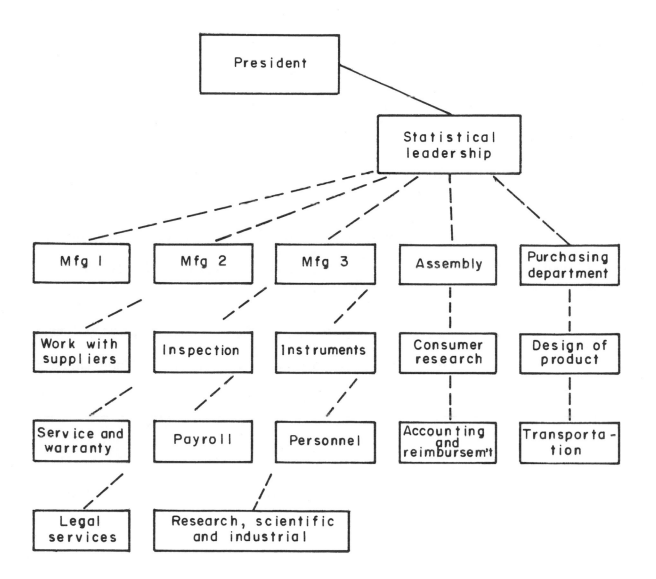

Fig. 56. Schematic plan for statistical organization. No attempt is made here to draw a diagram for any particular company. This type of organization for statistical work originated with Dr. Morris H. Hansen in the Census, about 1940.

It is true that the statistician in a division is responsible to two people, to the head of the division for day-by-day output of procedures and analysis, to the statistical leader for his statistical work and continuing education. The plan nevertheless gives no problems.

The advantages of the plan recommended here can not be questioned. It works. Any other plan that I have seen has failed to serve the best interests of the company, and has brought disappointment. Why? First, under any other plan, the company will lose its statistical power. Some people of ability will move out. The rest will almost certainly deteriorate in statistical ability.

A statistician, coming into a company to assume statistical leadership, can not possibly understand all the problems of the company. Nobody does, or ever will. People that have been for years in a company have a lot to learn about how to do their jobs effectively, as is obvious from an abundance of examples in previous chapters. The statistician will learn by enquiry all over the company where he can make contributions toward improvement in efficiency, and where it would be best to make no change. He must be a participant in any activity that in his judgment is worth his pursuit. The choice of problems for him to pursue must be left to his judgment, not to the judgment of others, though he will, of course, try to be helpful to anyone that asks for advice. The non-statistician can not know when he has a statistical problem.

The statistical leader will coordinate the teaching and dissemination of the 14 points for top management and the teaching of techniques for top management and for everyone else in the company; also for suppliers.

His contribution will be felt in training and supervision throughout the company.

ORGANIZATION FOR STATISTICAL WORK

Part of his job will be to work with universities in an attempt to help them to provide education in statistical theory and methods, and to provide examples of application.

A statistician, coming into a company from outside to assume statistical leadership will need an escort for possibly a year--someone that knows the company inside and out, to introduce him to all the activities of the company and to the heads of these activities. The escort will gradually fade away, as need for his help evaporates.*

The earliest use of quality control in all its phases, and one of the biggest and most successful applications in quality control ever instituted, is found in the U.S. Census. Organization for statistical work in the Census was instituted in 1940 by Dr. Morris H. Hansen along the plan shown in Fig. 56. Preeminence for quality and productivity in the Census was recognized in census offices the world over by 1945. Statistical people in the Census became in time renowned statisticians, in heavy demand today. Incidentally, the Census is a service organization.

Examples of other dotted line relationships.** In fact, a parallel dotted line relationship exists in practically every corporation. A vice president and chief financial officer (VP/CFO), reporting to the president or the chief executive officer, is responsible for the financial condition of the corporation. At each manufacturing facility there is a local comptroller who is responsible for the financial condition (budget, operating expenses) related to

---

* Need for this paragraph was pointed out to me by Mr. Ronald Moen, recalling his own experience coming in for statistical leadership in the Pontiac Division of General Motors.

** I thank Dr. Harold S. Haller for contribution of this paragraph.

that specific location. He reports jointly to the VP/CFO and to the manager of the facility. For example, the budgets are established by the plant, and the degree to which they are met is reported by the plant manager to the local comptroller. But because of the complex nature of the accounting procedures and taxes, the financial direction of the plant is provided by the VP/CFO. The technical aspects of the position are guided by the VP/CFO and the administrative responsibilities are directed by the management of the facility. No one questions the value or necessity of this organization, and no problem arises from the fact that the local comptroller of the plant reports to two men. Other examples of positions requiring dual reporting structures are environmental, medical, legal, and safety.

Achievements at the Census. Papers and books that came out of the U.S. Census have led the whole world of social and demographic studies into better methods of sampling, reduction of nonsampling errors and survey design, as well as the conduct of complete censuses, all with continual improvement in quality of data and with continual reduction in cost.

To appreciate the method of the Census, one needs only the reminder that the results of the Monthly Report on the Labor Force are widely accepted and used. This is a miniature monthly census of about 55,000 households, carried out by the most advanced statistical procedures by the Bureau of the Census. The Census carries out monthly, quarterly, or annually also many other miniature censuses; for example, studies on health and use of medical facilities, housing vacancies, housing starts, retail sales, manufacturing.

Where do you find him? Where do you find a theoretical statistician to take the job of statistical leadership? Enquire of other good statisticians; advertise in statistical journals in the United States, Canada, Bulletin of the Royal Statistical Society, Wall Street Journal, New York Times, etc.

ORGANIZATION FOR STATISTICAL WORK

You may have to be patient. One company advertised for eight months before they found the right man. There are only a pitifully few good statisticians in the world. There is no catalog, no roster.

An alternate plan to think of, in case perseverance and earnest prayer fail to bring forth a competent man to take over the statistical leadership, is to examine your own resources. One may find right within the company people with master's degrees in statistical theory or mathematics or probability that are eager to advance their statistical education and experience under competent leadership, and who enjoy teaching. Some people will be qualified by self-study.

If you find the right man within your company, provide him with counsel of a competent statistical consultant two or three days per month. The consultant will know when he is no longer needed. If you have found the right man, and if the management of the company understand their responsibilities, he will in a few years fulfill your requirements. Expect him to take one course at a time (hardly two at a time) in statistical theory at a university not far away--that is, provided he can qualify for entry.

If you can find two such people, give them both this chance to develop. You can use them both.

Advice to statisticians. Anyone who thinks of going into statistical work in a company should enquire into the organization. He should ask himself, will I have here a chance to advance my education by working with people that are themselves improving their statistical education? Will we have a chance to work together and learn from each other? Is the head a man of unquestioned ability?

Advice to companies in respect to a consultant. The job of a statistician is to find problems that other people could not be expected to perceive. A consultant can not discharge this responsibility unless he is free to work any-where in the company, to learn what is happening. This must be his mandate from the top management. He can not discharge his responsibilities by merely being on call--that is, coming from time to time when somebody calls him, or talking on the telephone when someone has a problem to talk about. The little problems are the ones that walk in: the big ones are the important ones. He will of course try to be helpful to everybody, with big problems and with little ones.

His fee will be an annual fee. He will agree to stay until the company can carry on without him. This might be two years, maybe three. Meanwhile, the company must attract statistical leadership of sufficient caliber to carry on eventually without the consultant.

Three kinds of statisticians: There are (1) mathematical statisticians, (2) theoretical statisticians, (3) practical statisticians. The mathematical statistician engages himself in extension of man's knowledge through new mathematical theory. It is his work that circumscribes the boundaries of knowledge, providing a foundation for more efficient collection and use of statistical information in the future, and for long-range improvement of industrial processes, and of complex equipment, military and civilian. His interest is mathematical. His work is not glamorous, and he receives little recognition outside a close group of specialists.

Second, there is the theoretical statistician. A consulting statistician is a theoretical statistician because he is able to apply the power of theory to his work: he guides his work with the aid of the theory of probability. The theoretical statistician is interested in helping experts in traffic, marketing, medicine, engineering, production, chemistry, accounting, agri-culture, etc., to solve problems. A theoretical statistician develops new theory as required, with help from outside consultants when necessary.

ORGANIZATION FOR STATISTICAL WORK

Third, there is the practical statistician, described years ago by the great Thomas Henry Huxley who said, "The practical man practices the errors of his forefathers." This kind of practical man can be a real hazard in any field.

The theoretical statistician is what any company needs as statistical head-- a man that guides his statistical work with the aid of statistical theory. He will command a high salary, but no company can afford the losses that are ensured by lesser ability. As stated in Chapter 2, it is a mistake to look at price without taking performance and results into consideration. The practical man will be unable to do the job, and will set a company into retrogression.

Additional remark on educational needs of industry. Industry in America (as Shewhart said*) needs thousands of statistically-minded engineers, chemists, physicists, doctors of medicine, purchasing agents, managers. Fortunately, anyone in these fields can learn to use in many problems simple but powerful methods of statistics, and can understand the statistical principles behind them, without becoming a statistician. Guidance from a theoretical statistician is necessary, however. Without such guidance, wrong and costly practices take root, and some problems of production and distribution may be overlooked entirely.

There is a parallel between statisticians and statistical work on the one hand, and medicine and public health on the other. Millions of people have learned useful rules and practices of public health, and understand the basic principles of infection, diet, exercise. Thousands of people have learned how to render first aid without being doctors of medicine. Thousands of people carry out medical and psychological tests, and give innoculations, under the

---

* Walter A. Shewhart, STATISTICAL METHOD FROM THE VIEWPOINT OF QUALITY CONTROL (Books on Demand, Ann Arbor, 1939), Ch. 7.

Chapter 17

direction of doctors of medicine and psychologists. We all live better and longer because of the contributions that these people make.

Almost every large company already has on the payroll people here and there that are studying statistics at a nearby university and whose talents are not being used. I have found such people with master's degrees, wondering if they will ever have a chance to use their knowledge. Companies take inventory of physical property, but they fail in taking inventory of knowledge. Anyone who is getting a statistical education should have a chance to work under a statistician of competence, and to continue his education in statistics.

It is good advice to anyone that is qualified and who is interested in improving his ability to find problems and to help in their solution to take any course that he can get into in theoretical or applied statistics (including, of course, decision theory and theory of failure), provided the teacher is competent in theory. The mature student will recognize and improve inappropriate applications in the classroom and in the text.

ORGANIZATION FOR STATISTICAL WORK

Chapter 18

SOME ADDITIONAL PRINCIPLES FOR LIVING

I speak no more than everyone doth know.--Gardener,
in Shakespeare's Richard II, Act III, Scene iv.

Plan of this chapter. This chapter adds corollaries to principles already

studied.

Principle 1. On-time performance of delivery or product exhibits early

delivery some days and later delivery some days. There is no such thing as

arrival exactly on time. In fact, exactly on time can not be defined.

> This principle came to my mind one day in Japan as I stepped on to
> the platform and observed the time to be 6 seconds before the scheduled
> time of arrival. "Of course," I observed, "it has to be ahead half the
> time, and behind half the time, if its performance is on time."

Principle 2. It is easy to observe and record whether a certain train will

come in late, or will depart late. One need only own or borrow a watch and set

it carefully to the time signal. A train due to arrive today at 3 o'clock may

then be observed to be early or late by so many seconds or minutes.

However, it is not so simple to describe the performance of this train over

a period of time. Performance can be judged only by statistical study of

historical record of arrivals. A run chart of arrivals, day after day, would

be simple and statistically powerful.

A distribution of times of arrival or of delivery conveys a lot of infor-

mation about the performance of a train. Fig. 57 shows a number of possible

distributions. Panel A shows on-time performance but with a spread that indi-

cates uneconomical operation, and uneconomical use of the time of patrons. This

train is on time, on the average, sometimes many minutes early some days, many

Chapter 18

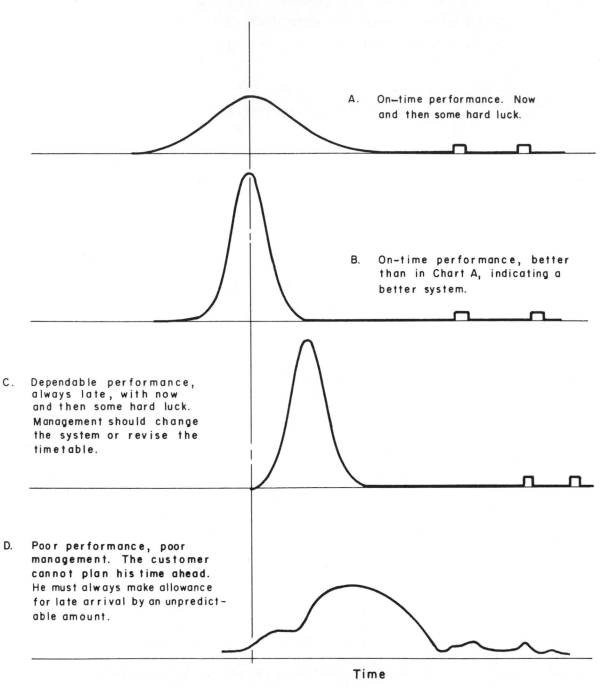

Fig. 57.

SOME ADDITIONAL PRINCIPLES FOR LIVING

minutes late other days, sometimes very nearly on time. Panel B shows on-time
performance with better performance--i.e., less waste of the railway's resources. Patrons can depend on arrival within a few minutes or possibly within
a few seconds, as in Japan. The legend for Panel C is self-explanatory. The
system is working well, but the time table needs to be rewritten. The train
simply can not make the trip in the time shown. This resembles the circumstance
where a production process is in control and is economical, but can not meet the
specifications. Panel D detects a state of chaos.

Principle 3. Tests of components in stages of development can not provide
(a) assurance that they will work together satisfactorily as a system in service; nor (b) the average run between failures of the system; nor (c) the type
and cost of maintenance that will be required in service.

Long continuation of tests in the laboratory and in service leads to
accepted and predictable levels of performance of components and of maintenance
required.

Tests in early stages can of course provide negative results--prediction
that the system will be unsatisfactory.

Principle 4. Due care in manufacture can not be defined operationally,
hence any requirement of due care in manufacture can have no legal force. Care
in manufacture, however, can be defined and measured. Evidence of care in
manufacture and test is provided by records, in the form of meaningful data
(which might take the form of charts and statistical calculations), supplemented by records of corrective action on the process, or action on a particular
machine once designated as a special cause of variation, and the result of this
action. Instructions for use of the product, and warnings on misuse, are part
of the record that measures the care taken on the part of the manufacturer.

Principle 5. No system, whatever be the effort put into it, be it manufacturing, maintenance, operation, or service, will be free of accidents.

Accidents are all around us, like bacteria. Most bacteria are harmless: some cause a lot of suffering. Most accidents are of little consequence. An assistant in a retail store that sells men's clothes put a suit on the rack only to observe that it had no buttons. This suit had slipped through two 100 per cent inspections. It was an accident, to come through without buttons, but it was a harmless accident. No one was hurt. In fact, some of us had a good laugh.

Another example may help the reader to appreciate that accidents are a part of life. The following paragraphs came from the New York Times, 28 February 1980:

CORRECTIONS

Because of a mechanical error, an article about credit controls appeared twice in late editions of Business Day yesterday and one on wage and price controls was missing. The omitted article is printed today on page D13.

A picture in late editions of The Times yesterday, accompanying an article about a nuclear mishap in Florida, was incorrectly captioned. It showed Peter A. Bradford, a member of the Nuclear Regulatory Commission.

I received from the printer 500 copies of an article that I had published, only to discover, after I had distributed a few score of them, that pages 6 and 7 were blank in some of the copies. This was an accident: no harm done. In fact, some readers may have been grateful for the blanks. The supervisor at the printing company nevertheless, when I told him about it, went into a rage about his careless employees. Was it his fault, or theirs?

Figures on accidents do nothing to reduce the frequency of accidents. The first step in reduction of the frequency of accidents is to determine whether the cause of an accident belongs to the system or to some specific person or set of conditions. Statistical methods provide the only method of analysis to serve as a guide to the understanding of accidents and to their reduction.

People naturally suppose that if something happened here and now, there must be something special at the spot where it happened. The usual reaction of almost everyone, when an accident occurs, is to attribute it to somebody's carelessness or to something unusual about the equipment used. It is wise not to jump to this conclusion: it may lead to the wrong answer, wrong solution, continued trouble, more accidents. The system guarantees an average frequency of accidents to occur at unpredictable places and times.

Engineers often predict accidents. Their predictions are uncanny for correctness in detail. They fail in only one way--they can not predict exactly when the accident will happen. The well-publicized trouble at Three Mile Island provides a documented example.*

The trouble was failure of the management to conduct reviews of procedures, and to conduct meaningful tests and observations, routine and emergency, on a statistical basis, of employees, machinery, and apparatus, with statistical criteria for detection of weakness. To look for something special, and to take action on a particular man, or on the particular piece of apparatus that went wrong, or on an installation, when the cause of the accident is a common cause that could have led to an accident at the hands of other men, or with other pieces of apparatus, or with other installations, is doomed to failure. Accidents that arise from common causes will continue to happen with their expected frequency and variations until the system is correct. The split is possibly 99 per cent from the system, one per cent from carelessness. I have

---

* "Three Mile Island," The New Yorker, 6 and 13 April 1981.

no figures on the split, and there will not be any figures till people understand accidents with the aid of statistical thinking.

Unfortunately--incredible to all but statisticians--the proportion of
failures of manufactured apparatus will not decrease as the precision of
manufacture improves, nor will the number of medical disappointments decrease
as medical practice improves. The reason is that as the requirements that
define good quality and good results continually become more severe as precision
and performance improve, the proportion of outliers, by any criterion, remains
constant.

Accidents on the highway: faults of road signs in the United States. What
proportion of accidents on the highways is caused by failure of the driver
(human error, a special cause), or by failure of equipment (another, possibly a
special cause, possibly not), and what proportion is built into and guaranteed
by the system, for example, by road signs whose meaning is misleading or debat-
able? The answer may never be forthcoming because a controlled experiment can
not be carried out. Moreover, it would be hard to find two systems of road
signs that are sufficiently different, all else being equal, to provide numerical data for comparison.

The purpose of a road sign is to teach, to tell a driver what to do, and its
message must do so in a flash. At 60 mph, a vehicle moves 88 feet in one second,
8.8 feet in a tenth of a second. An interval of indecision that extends over a
tenth of a second may land a vehicle against a concrete abutment, or against a
tree, or it may cause a collision from the rear. It is thus of utmost importance that a road sign shall convey instantly its message.

Fig. 58 shows a sign all too common in the United States for an exit. Its
message is exactly opposite to the action needed to go out on Exit 27. It tells
the driver that Exit 27 lies ahead, when actually, he is already upon it

SOME ADDITIONAL PRINCIPLES FOR LIVING

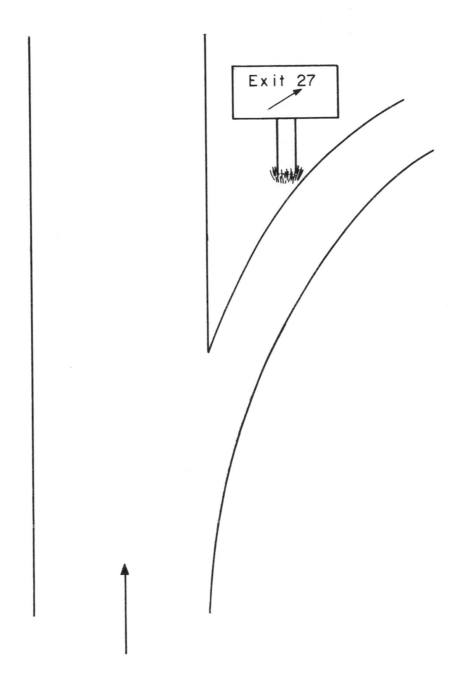

Fig. 58. This road sign is misleading to the driver
that is looking for Exit 27. The first impulse that this
sign conveys to the driver is that Exit 27 lies some distance
ahead, and will lead off to the right. The fact is that the
driver has already arrived at Exit 27. Second thoughts, a
tenth of a second later, may be too late; he is on his way
straight ahead, and must find a way out.

Chapter 18

and may not have time to adjust himself to the fact. In contrast, the sign in Fig. 59 conveys instantly its message to the driver, viz., move into the right lane and go out on Exit 27.

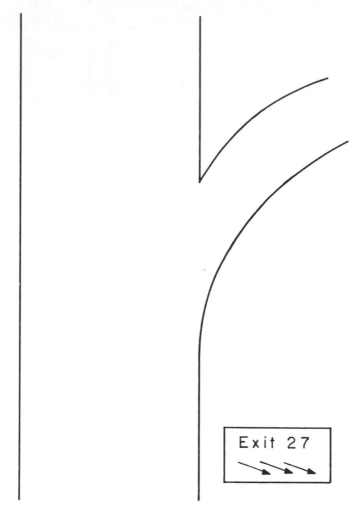

Fig. 59. Good. This sign conveys instantly to the driver the message that to take Exit 27 he must move into the right lane and exit.

Most drivers require no direction, as they are merely moving toward home or toward work, and need no help. Unfortunately, however, one driver in perhaps 100 is new to the route, and requires help. No one will ever know the number of injuries to man and vehicle caused by signs that do not instantly convey their message, or which, unfortunately, convey instantly the wrong message to

SOME ADDITIONAL PRINCIPLES FOR LIVING

drivers that need guidance. No one will ever know the proportion of drivers that fail to make the exit, and the resulting inconvenience and loss of time as they find their way back to the route intended.

Figs. 61 and 62 provide further illustration of confusion.

Malpractice in medicine. This can only be understood with the help of statistical theory. The result of a medical intervention is interaction between physician, treatment, and patient. Two thousand million (10^9) medical interventions take place every year in the U.S. A hundred thousand cases of unfavorable results seem like a large number, yet this number represents reliability of 1 part in 20,000. It would be difficult to find a mechanical or electrical system with greater reliability. Most of the 100,000 unfavorable results (if that be the number) belong to the system. Some small fraction of the 100,000 unfavorable results could possibly be caused by carelessness, including incompetence.

One per cent of 100,000 is 1,000, still a large number. Any number is too big. The problem is to discover whether the cause of an unfavorable outcome (a) lies in the system of medical care, including the patient, or (b) may be ascribed to some special cause such as carelessness on the part of the physician, or carelessness on the part of the patient, who may fail to follow instructions or to get in touch with his physician as directed. An important step would be for medical people to construct operational definitions of special causes of unfortunate results from medical interventions of various kinds. This is a huge task, and a never-ending one, but until it is brought to a usable stage, physicians in the United States, and their insurance companies, will continue to fight off unjustified accusations of carelessness and will live a life liable to legal tangles.

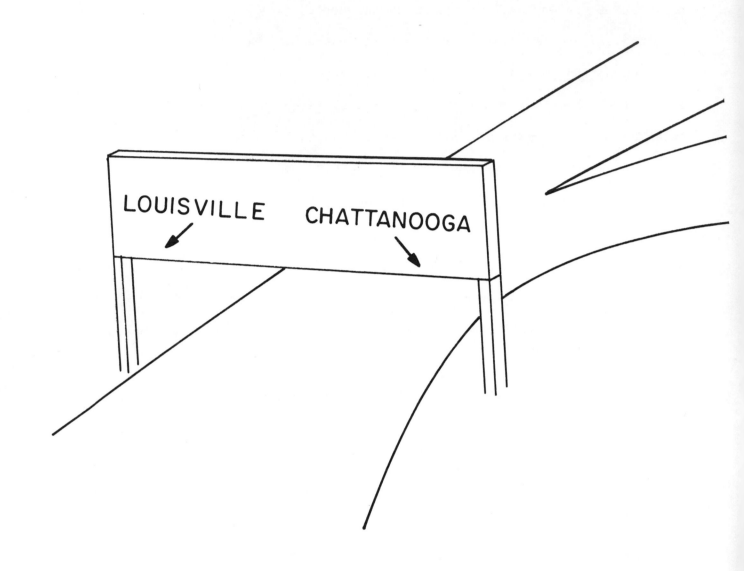

Fig. 60. Overhead sign, very clear. It conveys
instantly its message. It tells the driver to take the left
fork to Louisville, or the right fork to Chattanooga.

SOME ADDITIONAL PRINCIPLES FOR LIVING

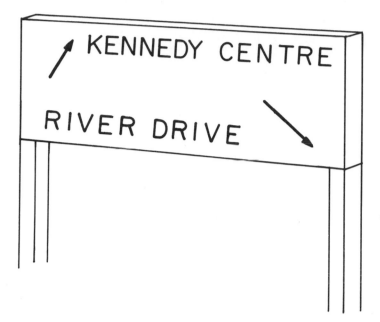

Fig. 61. Which way to Kennedy Centre? Tossing a coin
would be as helpful as this sign.

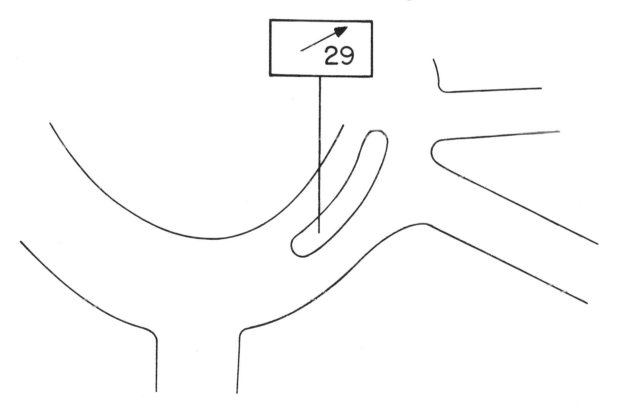

Fig. 62. Which way to Route 29? Taken from Washington
Circle in the City of Washington.

Index